PRAISE FOR *IMPLEME*
KEY ACCOUNT MANAG

CW00518344

'The authors have a proven record of developing and delivering leadership in key account management theory and practice. This book will be really useful to any business leader looking for practical insight into how to grow business relationships and commercial outcomes with their largest, most complex accounts.' **Paul Wilson, Commercial Account Director, Pfizer – KAM Centre of Excellence**

'Incredibly well thought-through, well researched and provides a unique playbook both for newcomers to key account management and for those with decades of experience. Very thought-provoking and a must-read for those serious about building deeper client relationships.' **John MacDonald-Gaunt, Vice President, IBM Global Business Services**

'Professional, practical and pragmatic – an ideal source of information to make key account management work effectively in your organization.' **Richard Daniel, Director of Key Account Coordination and Customer Solutions, Zoetis**

'I like the highly structured approach of this book, combining practical relevance and scientific foundation.' **Hajo Rapp, SVP Global Strategic Account Management and Sales Excellence, TUEV SUED AG**

'Full of practical advice for managers, this book is the product of many years of research and teaching on key account management and sales by the experienced Cranfield team.' **Lynette Ryals, Pro Vice Chancellor and Professor of Strategic Sales and Account Management, Cranfield University**

Implementing Key Account Management

Designing customer-centric processes
for mutual growth

Javier Marcos, Mark Davies,
Rodrigo Guesalaga and Sue Holt

Publisher's note
Every possible effort has been made to ensure that the information contained in this book is accurate at the time of going to press, and the publisher and authors cannot accept responsibility for any errors or omissions, however caused. No responsibility for loss or damage occasioned to any person acting, or refraining from action, as a result of the material in this publication can be accepted by the editor, the publisher or any of the authors.

First published in Great Britain and the United States in 2018 by Kogan Page Limited

2nd Floor, 45 Gee Street	c/o Martin P Hill Consulting	4737/23 Ansari Road
London EC1V 3RS	122 W 27th St, 10th Floor	Daryaganj
United Kingdom	New York NY 10001	New Delhi 110002
www.koganpage.com	USA	India

ISBN   978 0 7494 8275 6
E-ISBN   978 0 7494 8276 3

British Library Cataloguing-in-Publication Data

A CIP record for this book is available from the British Library.

Library of Congress Cataloging-in-Publication Data

CIP data is available.

Library of Congress Control Number: 2018027581

Typeset by Integra Software Services, Pondicherry
Print production managed by Jellyfish
Printed and bound in Great Britain by Ashford Colour Press Ltd.

To Professor Malcolm McDonald

To my family Adrián, Ismael, Julia and Mónica (Javier)

To my wife Carol and our four key accounts: Liberty, Jerome, Quin and Pixie (Mark)

To my wife María and my children Florencia, Diego and Tomás (Rodrigo)

To my family and especially my husband Phill and my mother Jacqui (Sue)

CONTENTS

ABOUT THE AUTHORS

Javier Marcos is the Director of Learning for Performance, a sales and key account management training firm. He has two decades of experience in multinational firms, academia and consulting. He is a Visiting Fellow of Cranfield School of Management and Senior Industrial Fellow at the University of Cambridge IfM. His main areas of expertise and research are Professional Selling and Sales Management, Key Account Management, and Negotiation. Javier emphasizes the blend of leading-edge research with innovative learning methodologies in the delivery of his programmes and in the design of consulting assignments. He has taught programmes and conducted sales coaching interventions globally. He has co-authored *From Selling to Co-creating* (BIS Publishers, 2014), *Sales Management: Strategy, process and practice* (Palgrave, 2016) and numerous academic and practitioner-oriented articles and reports. He is a regular contributor and speaker at conferences, industry events and sales conventions. javier.marcos@learning4performance.net

Mark Davies is the Managing Director of Segment Pulse Limited and a Cranfield University Visiting Fellow, where he has co-directed the KAM Best Practice Club for 10 years and was a member for several years prior to that whilst he was a Customer Management/KAM Centre of Excellence Director for BP. Prior to consulting in the field of strategic selling and KAM, Mark held a number of senior leadership roles in the pharmaceutical, consumer, specialty chemicals and energy industries. He has led both global KAM organizations and centralized customer management functions, developing group value-based selling/KAM best practice. His consultancy helps organizations create, sell and deliver unique customer value propositions, where he typically works at c-level, advising global organizations in the healthcare, technical, professional services, energy and high-value manufacturing sectors. Mark has an MBA, an MSc, is a Chartered Engineer and Chartered Marketer, and is a Fellow of the Institute of Marketing. He is also a Visiting Fellow with Aston University, where he advises the Advanced Services Group.

Rodrigo Guesalaga is a Senior Lecturer at the School of Management at Cranfield University, and leads the Key Account Management and Strategic Sales Forum and the Sales Director's Programme. He is also Visiting Professor at Vlerick Business School (Belgium) and Associate Professor at Pontificia Universidad Católica de Chile. His main area of interest for teaching, research and consulting is strategic marketing, especially in business-to-business markets with a focus on strategic sales and key account management. Rodrigo has published his work in several international journals, including *International Marketing Management, Journal of Personal*

Selling and Sales Management and *Journal of Business and Industrial Marketing*, and he is member of the editorial review board at *Industrial Marketing Management* and other marketing journals. As a consultant, he has worked with companies in a variety of industries, such as forestry, retail, pharmaceutical, advertising, financial, and automotive. He has been invited as a speaker to several practitioner events in Marketing and Sales.

Sue Holt is an independent educator and consultant, a Visiting Fellow at Cranfield School of Management and a Visiting Professor at IESEG School of Management. Her main areas of interest are key and global account management and strategic sales. Sue is the Programme Director of Cranfield's flagship Key Account Management Best Practice (KAMBP) programme and has been the Programme Director for many customized company programmes across a wide range of industries and countries globally, as well as undertaking major consulting assignments on KAM. She has been the author of many academic and practitioner reports and articles and is a leading proponent of fighting for the formal professionalization and recognition of strategic sales and KAM as critical functions in the organizations of the future.

PREFACE

We live in exciting times for key account managers and sales directors, and indeed for marketers, business executives and entrepreneurs. The speed of change and transformation in customer expectations, the degree of globalization and interconnectedness, and the unprecedented opportunities (and threats) brought about by technology make well-founded key customer strategies more important than ever.

Key customers in business markets on one side, and individuals in consumer markets on the other, seek value in a number of different ways, increasingly well beyond the functional attributes of products and services. Thus, businesses must adopt new ways of creating and delivering value to their customers.

Technologies have transformed the information provision role of sales and marketing functions, and have resulted in levels of information and transparency hitherto unknown. Thus, sales organizations must ensure that their product and service 'promise' is consistent with their communication strategies and the perceived experience by the customer at the point of use.

There are well-established approaches to defining a key account management programme. In fact, key account management as a practice or discipline within B2B marketing has been around for more than 20 years. However, we know less about the factors that lead to effective or ineffective implementation of KAM programmes. To our knowledge, there is no single source integrating in a practical and rigorous way the processes and factors that underpin the successful design of customer-centric processes for value creation. We fill this gap with this book.

Implementing Key Account Management is timely because of the shift from traditional models of strategic customer relationship management to technology-enabled and distributed models of customer engagement. It is opportune because the complexity and degree of transformation required to make KAM programmes work often transcend marketing disciplines. This book is relevant because it brings together industry best practice, consulting expertise, and academic research in an integrated, applicable fashion.

We hope you will enjoy the book and look forward to continuing the conversation at www.implementingkam.com.

ACKNOWLEDGEMENTS

The book you have in your hands (or on your screen) is the result of many years of work in programmes and workshops, lengthy research projects, and insightful dialogues with colleagues and clients in a variety of sectors, countries and contexts. We are grateful to all of them, and even taking the risk of forgetting some of them, we hereby gratefully acknowledge their support, help and inspiration.

First, our colleagues at the Centre for Strategic Marketing and Sales (Cranfield School of Management), Malcolm McDonald, Lynette Ryals, Ian Speakman, Daniel Prior, Radu Dimitriu, Paul Baines, Hugh Wilson, Emma MacDonald and Stan Maklan, helped us hone our thinking, arguments and the applicability of analytical tools. Noreen Munnelly, Hayley Brown and Lynne Wall simply made our work so much easier, finding solutions to all sorts of issues in conducting our work over the years. They are a living example of world-class key account management! We would also like to acknowledge the research contribution of some of our MSc students, especially Elisa Campo, Rosario Cutuli and Joao Gonçalves.

The interviewees featured in the book, Jesús Gómez (Mondelēz), Daniel Rodriguez Martin (Unilever), generously contributed with their views and time, and we enjoyed talking to them. The case study organizations also generously gave their views and their time: Jeremy Campbell and Chris Kehoe (EMCOR UK) and Robert Racine (Wipro). Charlotte Owen from Kogan Page motivated us to accomplish each part of the book and Chris Cudmore and the production team at Kogan Page turned a 'loose draft' manuscript into a 'solid book'. Special thanks go to Philippa Fiszzon who put together all the final elements of the book, and to Becky Piper whose design mastery brought our diagrams to life. Thank you all for your help (and patience).

We are also grateful to our students and the delegates to our programmes. They may not be aware, but they also played a part in motivating us to write this book and to integrate into a single source the ideas, frameworks and tools to excel in KAM.

Lastly, we would like to thank the members of the Cranfield Key Account Management Best Practice Club (now the Cranfield Key Account Management and Sales Forum) who shared with us invaluable lessons, possibly so many that we would have needed another book (or two) to capture them. We want to express our gratitude to those that engaged with us over the last couple of years:

Alan Finkelstein, Merck

Alyse Ashton, Eye to Eye
Development Ltd

Andrea Clatworthy, Fujitsu

Andy Hough, Association of
Professional Sales

Anne Blackie, Grant Thornton

Anthony Sacco, Pfizer

Bill Bradshaw, FM Global (FM
Insurance Company Ltd)

Bruce Hall, BP

Carl Lyons

Carlos Arredondo, Repsol

Chris Brown, Allied Mills

Claire Fleming, Pfizer Limited

Dan Robson, International Nuclear
Services Ltd (formerly BNFL)

Dave Recaldin, Kantar Retail

David Epps, Amey

David Floyd, SKF Ltd

Des Evans

Eleanor Musson, ASG

Eric Guinebert, Merck

Gail Hunt, G4S Integrated Services
(UK) Ltd

Geoff Quinn, Pfizer

Grant Jeffrey, BP

Hugo Wahnish

Ian Helps, Consalia

Ian Machan, ASG

James Muir, V-Group (Vouvray
Acquisition Ltd)

Jamie Brannan, Zoetis

Jerid Lydic, Pfizer

Jeroen De Voogd, WD-40

John Baker, Fedex

Jon Snell, Thorn Lighting Ltd

John MacDonald-Gaunt, IBM

Kami Lamakan

Kevin Galliers, SunGard Systems Ltd

Lisa Melling, Office Depot International
(UK) Ltd

Magda Lindeque, Zoetis

Mark Stanton, Trend Control
Systems Ltd

Michael Crean, SKF

Michael Samuels, Grant Thornton

Nandini Basuthakur, Procurement
Leaders

Neil Rackham

Nick de Cent, *The International Journal
of Sales Transformation*

Nick Donovan, Allied Mills

Nieves Olivera, Deusto Business
School

Paul Hassall, Ordnance Survey

Paul Hughes, IE/FT Corporate Learning
Alliance

Paul Wilson, Pfizer

Phil Squire, Consalia

Preston Ley, WD-40

Rafi Habibian, Pfizer

Rajnish Jobanputra, BP plc

Ralph Baillie

Rhona Holland, Zoetis

Richard Vincent, Hewlett Packard
Limited

Richard Brooks, K-International

Richard Daniel, Zoetis

Rob Maguire

Robin Wardle, Merck Animal Health:
Aquaculture, MSD Animal Health

Sarah Holland, BP

Sarah McDonald, Pfizer

Scott Trickett

Simon Harvey

Simona Neil, Pfizer

Steve Brass, WD-40

Steve Fry

Thomas Schmidt, WD-40

Tim Baines, ASG

Todd Snelgrove, ABB

Vince McShane

Overall, we are pleased to give back to our network and the rich community of fellow professionals, something in return for what we have received from them.

If you are reading this and think you should be on the list, please forgive us and tell us. We will include you in the next edition.

Introduction to implementing key account management

01

'You have to think about "big things" while you are doing small things so that all the small things go in the right direction.'

ALVIN TOFFLER

What are the key transformations your organization will need to take into account to sustain differentiation and relevance with key customers?

Overview

Unprecedented levels of change in business markets and customer demands have made managing key customers a crucial process for companies that aspire to remain competitive. In this chapter, we present key challenges faced by senior leaders in business development and customer management functions in the design and implementation of key account management (KAM) programmes. We take a helicopter view outlining the driving forces of change in the marketplace and argue that in the face of those changes KAM is an effective approach to investing in future growth. However, to be effective, KAM needs to balance and integrate a number of approaches. In this chapter we also present the purpose of the book and its structure.

Why this book now?

Managing accounts strategically has become a key requirement for companies that wish to achieve competitive advantage and succeed in business markets. In most sectors key customers make up a significant proportion of revenue, as well as often a large percentage of the companies' profits.

KAM as a practice or discipline within B2B marketing is not new; it has been around for more than 20 years [1],[2],[3]. What is new is the amount of evidence and insight into the factors that lead to effective or ineffective implementation of KAM programmes. To our knowledge, there is no source integrating in a practical and rigorous way the processes and factors that underpin the successful design of customer-centric processes for value creation. This book fills that gap.

A book on KAM implementation is timely due to the shift from traditional models of strategic customer relationship management [4] to technology-enabled and distributed models of customer engagement. Unprecedented levels of change in the sales environment [5] are prompting sales organizations to redefine their customer management strategies and associated structures. One such shift is, on one side, optimizing the management of transactional customers, often using technology, and on the other, deploying dedicated resources to manage strategic customers.

These changes have increased as markets have become more global and the degree of connectedness across different economic areas around the world is growing dramatically [6]. Today, in terms of revenues, about 30 per cent of the firms in the Fortune Global 500 list are enterprises from emerging markets, according to the World Economic Forum [7]. This is in sharp contrast with the 10 per cent of firms 10 years ago. Moreover, a report by McKinsey Global Institute predicts that 45 per cent of Fortune Global 500 companies will come from emerging markets

Figure 1.1   Key transformations in business markets

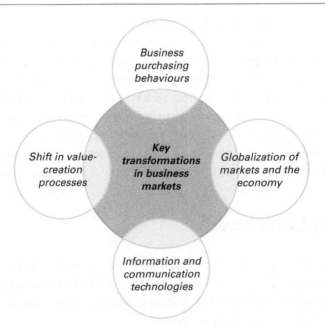

by 2025. These companies will present unprecedented levels of competition to our businesses but also unprecedented levels of opportunity.

These changes in the global market have gradually triggered the evolution of business-to-business and industrial selling from predictable and structured sets of activities [8] to complex and dynamic relationship management roles [9],[10]. This means that the classic activities of selling to customers primarily focused on the product or the service, have evolved towards consultative selling and account management roles focused on the customer business and on adding value beyond the product or service.

We live in a truly global marketplace

Increasing levels of globalization in services and goods markets have resulted in organizations adopting global account management [11]. The business landscape in most sectors and across different economies has dramatically changed as a result of higher degrees of market liberalization in some sectors, and higher levels of regulation in others. For instance, the telecommunication and energy industries have seen increasing degrees of openness with new operators entering the market, creating higher levels of competition and customer choice. A similar trend has been experienced in air transport, where the days of flag carriers' supremacy are long gone. In other sectors such as pharmaceuticals, firms are being required to observe tighter regulations in drug promotion, particularly in Europe and the United States.

Large-scale mergers and acquisitions and renewed efforts towards international expansion have contributed to higher levels of concentration in many sectors, reshaping the competitive arena. Thus, traditional sales territories are losing the relevance that is being gained by regional and global customers, implying more strategic customer management roles are needed. For instance, in mature markets, a small number of retailers make up a large proportion of the fast-moving consumer goods business. Similar trends of consolidation have been seen in banking and financial services, telecoms, pharmaceuticals etc. These large customers have become even more powerful, and thus, suppliers need strategies to deal with them adopting new practices across a number of domains: operational, relational and commercial.

The behaviour of business customers has changed... and will continue changing

In industrial markets, most sectors have experienced a shift in the way customers, and particularly their purchasing organizations, treat their suppliers. Fewer, more sophisticated customers have become more powerful and are seeking to achieve savings and gain additional value by adopting supplier segmentation and other procurement strategies.

This has often resulted in reductions of suppliers by up to 40–90 per cent [12]. Overall, buyers are demanding more value, not just from the product or service but from the relationship, and want to access specialized supplier capabilities with the best possible terms and conditions.

Procurement has become a strategic function, increasingly linked to the customer's business plan with responsibility for realizing higher profit margins, containing costs and contributing to superior shareholder value [13]. Professional purchasing managers are using complex sourcing metrics to select the 'right' suppliers, and are dictating the terms on how they want to be supplied [14]. Selected suppliers are often required to adjust their service and product delivery practices to those required by each customer. In addition, global customers demand global service, giving an advantage to those suppliers who are able to provide their service internationally.

Technologies have redefined the way we do business

Technologies are facilitating new ways of working and opening up new challenges for account management and sales professionals. Business relations are increasingly transcending relational approaches and adopting new ways to co-create value [15].

Over the last few decades, sales organizations have been subject to changes triggered by unprecedented developments in information and communication technologies. Traditionally, the sales function played an important role in informing the customer about the features and advantages of a product or service. However, customers today retrieve readily available information via the internet [16]. As a result, tasks such as gathering information may be better carried out using technology services and platforms; the traditional role of salespeople in providing information is now in question. Information systems are providing new opportunities to store, synthesize and analyse customer information in unprecedented ways. Thus, customer insights are becoming an organizational capability, with Big Data and business information applications having grown significantly in importance [17].

> Four key trends underpin the transformation of selling and customer management: the globalization of markets and the economy, business purchasing behaviours, information and communication technologies, and shifts in the value-creation processes.

Technology has accelerated the evolution of the account management process, which is now much less about making the customer aware of a particular offer, and much more about co-creating value through relationships at the point of use or application.

Table 1.1   Key technological trends

Technological drivers of change – percentage cited
Mobile internet, cloud technology 34%
Processing power, Big Data 26%
New energy supplies and technologies 22%
Internet of Things 14%
Sharing economy, crowdsourcing 12%
Robotics, autonomous transport 9%
Artificial intelligence 7%
Advanced manufacturing, 3D printing 6%
Advanced materials, biotechnology 6%

Thus, essential information for customer management processes is no longer generated only by marketing functions but also by sales, who are increasingly playing a knowledge broker role, gathering customer insights that can be input into market intelligence and the information systems we refer to above.

Advances in technology are not only facilitating customer interactions but also enabling supplier organizations to have a better understanding of their cost structures and calculate the profitability of their customers. Thus, marketing and sales investment in selected customers, segments and channels is increasingly being subject to more scrutiny and requiring more justification [16].

The internet has opened new possibilities to provide services to customers more cheaply, reducing the need for face-to-face sales interactions. Technology has enabled many sales organizations to consider a reduction in the size of their field sales force in some sectors. It has also challenged sales leaders to think about where sales organizations should focus and about alternative mechanisms by which sales can add value. As a result, an increasing polarization between transactional and consultative selling is emerging [18].

The process of value creation has shifted focus

In most sectors customer value is no longer generated fundamentally by the product or service or by the supplier. Value creation, hitherto embedded in the product or service, is now generated 'in-use' [19], that is in the process of embedding the product or service into the customer practices. Likewise, customer value is largely co-created, and this process underpins the achievement of positive customer experiences and long-lasting relationships [20],[21],[22]. In business markets, companies across industries have started to involve customers in a number of ways in order to understand their needs better so they can develop and co-create offerings that generate superior value.

Value co-creation with key customers is about understanding the 'processes, resources and practices which customers use to manage their activities' [23]. Achieving value co-creation requires finding a 'structural fit' between the customer and the suppliers' activities [24] and a great deal of collaboration and interaction. Traditional instrumental relationships, often characterized by conflict and mistrust, have evolved, particularly in complex service delivery, to trusted collaboration amongst different players within the value ecosystem.

Thus, value is co-created in interactions between customers, sellers and other actors in complex B2B systems. Specifically, customers interact with the seller to access the resources needed for their own value-creation process, with the final value realization happening in the customer organization, thereby also giving rise to the notion of 'customer-dominant logic' [25].

Airbus, as a leading integrator of complex systems, relies on its suppliers to deliver superior products and services to airlines and defence organizations. It adopts the approach called 'two companies, one team' with a number of its strategic suppliers.

In a number of industries, the delivery of superior offerings requires tight collaboration between suppliers and customers. Very often supplier and customer teams come together to tackle the design and delivery of complex systems. When these individuals are observed working together, one cannot differentiate between who works for the supplier and who for the customer. Their relationships have evolved from clearly delineated roles and boundaries to highly interdependent and blurred partnerships.

The migration of value generation, hitherto embedded in the product or service, towards a situation where value is created 'in-use' poses significant challenges to both customer and supplier organizations. The latter need to think about how account managers can add value beyond the core offering; the former, how to establish relationships that will enable the customer to extract maximum value from the product–service solution. Account managers today are required to both meet the expectations of more demanding customers and at the same time contribute to the sustainable growth of their business.

Figure 1.2 Shifts in focus in value creation

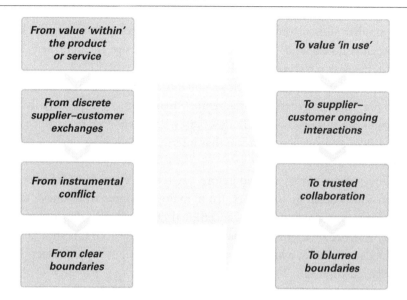

From value 'within' the product or service	To value 'in use'
From discrete supplier–customer exchanges	To supplier–customer ongoing interactions
From instrumental conflict	To trusted collaboration
From clear boundaries	To blurred boundaries

Why should your company consider implementing KAM (or not)?

This book focuses on implementing KAM, and thus assumes that KAM as a strategic approach and organizing principle focused around the most important customers is a decision already taken by your company. But before describing the reasons in support of the implementation of KAM we should perhaps discuss 'why your company should consider *not* implementing KAM'.

KAM is a resource-intensive and significant endeavour for any business. It will be rarely justified in contexts where the value-creation process is simplistic and where there is very low complexity in the offering. In markets characterized by undifferentiation and over-commoditization the substitution of suppliers is often easy for customers. Transactional behaviours in the customer may emerge, often driven by short-term gains, possibly resulting in the decision to switch to alternative, cheaper suppliers.

Investments in KAM become onerous and unjustified when the product lifecycle is short, such as in some fashionable consumer goods sectors. When innovation and investment in R&D are not required to develop offerings that meet customer requirements, price is likely to be the driving factor in supplier selection.

The appropriateness of KAM and the levels of investment in key customers need to be considered carefully when dealing with dominant customers. Commentators claim that 'powerful customers will ultimately exploit that power to their own advantage' [26]. KAM programmes will pay off when there is alignment of expectations between supplier and customer; that is, when there is commitment to a relationship that transcends quick gains and advantage, and a desire to build new long-term capabilities through a partnership relationship.

In some regulated industries, close collaboration between a supplier and a customer may be construed as 'preferential treatment', thus potentially violating competition laws and regulations. In these cases, suppliers need to enhance the transparency of their approaches to ensure that interdependent relationships do not turn into monopolistic ones.

KAM investments, as we argued before, are responses adopted to meet the escalating demands faced by suppliers from major business-to-business customers. However, these investments and organizational efforts should not increase the risk of over-dependence on a small number of customers. Key accounts should be seen as part of a wider portfolio, where clear difference is made between transactional, large and *strategic* customers.

Figure 1.3   Risk factors in KAM

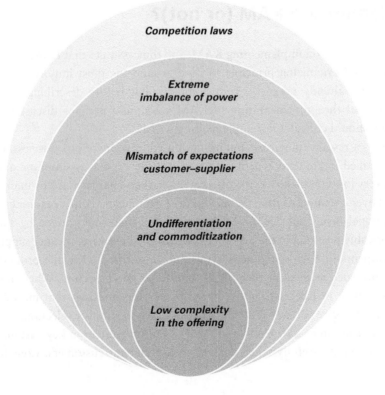

Competition laws

Extreme
imbalance of power

Mismatch of expectations
customer–supplier

Undifferentiation
and commoditization

Low complexity
in the offering

Figure 1.4   Process outcomes and benefits of implementing KAM

Your company should consider implementing KAM if managing accounts strategically has become a key requirement to achieve competitive advantage and to succeed in your markets. KAM is appropriate when establishing a consistent long-term relationship with key customers is crucial to facilitate a context conducive to innovation, and when that innovation lies at the core of the long-term sustainability of the business [27].

KAM is often an effective response to the need to adapt to changing customer demands, for instance, when these demands result from modifications in purchasing strategies, pressures to optimize costs, or after the creation of a new organization after a merger or a major acquisition [28].

When organizations, typically mature companies, have grown in structure to the point where people work in silos and departments that are no longer connected, and when this separation impacts on the significance and value delivered to the customer, KAM will help in restoring coordination efforts and getting the voice of the customer into the organization. KAM will help create a critical mass to legitimize renewed customer focus and thus, prioritization of efforts and investment of management time and resources.

This book addresses a crucial question for business leaders – how to develop some of the firm's most strategic assets: its key customers. We claim that KAM provides a powerful framework with which to generate the capabilities to achieve, amongst other things:

- increased information sharing and transparency between customers and suppliers [29];
- reduction of conflict within and across organizations working in partnerships [30];
- higher levels of customer commitment and satisfaction [31],[32];
- customer loyalty and retention [33] and customer share [34],[35].

Organizations implementing and sustaining KAM will achieve profitable growth as a result of some of the above process outcomes. However, not all KAM programmes achieve their initial intended benefits due to flaws in their conception, and not all KAM programmes are rolled out adhering to best practice. We address these two issues now, before presenting the overall structure and key features of the book.

Effective KAM programmes

KAM programmes are often expensive interventions and as such, need to be measured against goals and expectations. KAM is not the sort of intervention an organization would adopt if the primary aim is to achieve financial outcomes in the short run. Though we have argued that profitable relations are at the core of KAM, key measures of account management effectiveness go beyond the financial [36] and should take into account a wider range of aspects such as measures of collaboration, coordination, value created for the end customer and nature of the evolved relationships.

> The purpose of measuring KAM performance is to ascertain the value created in the relationship and to gain insights into how the value has been created.

Frameworks to evaluate key account performance are available [37] and include relational outcomes as well as financial outcomes. A model to measure key account performance should consider the impact of strategic decisions made in the key account programme, and thus it must capture their impact on both the quality of the relationship and the level of financial performance [37]. Holistic KAM frameworks contemplate three types of customer equity: value equity, brand equity and relationship equity, which, together with trust and commitment, often affect the performance of the key account.

Value equity refers to an objective and rational judgement of a firm's product or service offering, and typically is found to centre around price, quality, and convenience. Brand equity denotes the customer's subjective appraisal of the brand. This evaluation is often intangible and represents the value involved in a product or service beyond the physical product itself. Relationship equity includes the customer's willingness to remain in the relationship and the intangible benefits it generates such as knowledge and insight generation.

> If you were a major aircraft manufacturer and one of your key customers was a commercial airline seeking to increase their fleet for short-haul routes, how do you think they would go about framing and assessing *value equity*, *brand equity* and *relationship equity* from a supplier like you?

Despite the phenomenal development of the field of KAM over the last three decades, there is still a lack of a consolidated model for KAM effectiveness. Our colleagues Davies and Ryals [38] addressed this gap by building a framework of the measures that constitute the effectiveness or perceived success of a KAM programme. These include relationship improvement, greater customer satisfaction, increased revenues, improved customer retention, increased advocacy, increased share of spend, reduced cost to serve, increased profit margins, and shared investment.

Figure 1.5   KAM effectiveness measures

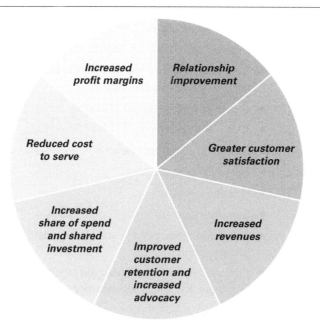

Thus, an effective KAM programme is one that creates value beyond financial measures. In fact, the test of a KAM programme is whether it creates value in ways that otherwise would not have been created. The measurement of value creation in buyer–seller relationships needs to acknowledge that value co-creation occurs during three cyclical and interrelated phases through which customers and suppliers inter-act: (1) joint crafting of value propositions, (2) value actualization, and (3) value determination [39]. Thus, the measurement approach could consider outcomes as well as input processes. Representatives from the dyad supplier–key account can qualify (rather than quantitatively measure) the extent to which joint efforts are enabling innovation, creative problem solving and value co-creation.

Table 1.2   Performance areas in KAM [40]

What is the performance KAMgrs are tasked with delivering?	
Financial	• Agreed return on investment
	• Revenue growth
	• Secure profit margins
	• Market share and share of wallet
Customer-related	• Increased customer satisfaction
	• Manageable customer risk
	• Customer selection and engagement aligned with business strategy
	• Provision of appropriate levels of service and innovation
	• Fostering customer loyalty, retention and trust
	• Enhanced reputation
	• Development and maintenance of long-term relationships
	• Understanding customer: its organization, value chain, its performance goals and metrics
	• Create and deliver an account plan
	• Cross- and up-selling
	• Designing customer solutions
Internal organization	• Effective communication
	• Process innovation
	• Stimulate cross-functional collaboration
	• Champion action plans to realize the (customer) critical success factors
	• Embedding KAM throughout the organization, fostering alignment and customer-centricity
	• Leading internal (virtual) teams

Overall, a holistic approach to measuring account performance should not trade off between objective and subjective, financial and relational outcomes. A well-designed KAM system will measure retrospective (lagging) and also prospective (leading) indicators.

A good proxy for relevant indicators of KAM effectiveness and performance is the expectations placed upon an account manager. The following example describes the tasks inherent to the role of key account manager (KAMgr) that were derived from a session at the Cranfield Key Account Management Best Practice Club.[1]

Other frameworks have been produced that include quantitative as well as qualitative indicators, such as the one issued recently by the Strategic Account Management Association [41].

We have argued that KAM should avoid an overemphasis on financial outcomes, although profitable customer relations are at the core of strategic account management [36]. Experts typically propose frameworks to evaluate key account performance that include relational outcomes as well as financial performance outcomes [37] and argue that a model of key account performance should consider the impact of strategic decisions made in the key account programme, and thus, must capture their impact on both the quality of the relationship and the level of financial performance.

Figure 1.6 Examples of KPIs for the key account manager

Company KPIs	Customer KPIs
Gross revenue Gross profit Activity-based sales costs Customer P and L Market share % customer spend Year-over-year account growth Environmental/sustainability metrics	Customer engagement in account planning process Product innovations linked to solutions Customer metrics/dashboard Joint customer–supplier scorecard Business reviews SAM's performance evaluation Customer satisfaction

Team KPIs	SAM process KPIs

Team sales
Team profit
Team account plan execution/milestones
Account penetration
Executive sponsorship
Operational performance
  (ie project completions on time/on budget)
CRM dashboard updating
	Gross sales
	Gross profit
	Customer loyalty (retention/contract renewal)
	Strategic account plan completion
	Participation in customer planning meetings
	Account penetration
	  (executive decision makers and influencers;
	  other business units, divisions)
	Executive sponsors' events/meetings
	Innovative/scaleable solutions
	Monetization of solutions
	# or size of opportunities/pipeline
	Competitive win rate
	Delivering the ROI

Personal KPIs
Training and development Coaching (for self/coaching others) MBOs Business reviews

Key guiding principles for quality KAM implementation

Throughout the book we will provide you with detailed tools and techniques to guide the implementation of KAM. We argue that KAM implementation is a holistic and integrated endeavour and in this introduction we present some well-established guiding principles that underpin effectively implemented KAM initiatives.

Systematic processes for selecting key customers

One of the critical practices of KAM is the selection of the key accounts. Since these customers will require significant investments from the supplier, only a small number of accounts will typically be viable. The number may vary from sector to sector but typically, a given organization will have between five and twenty key customers [42].

What we find in the process of KAM implementation is that once the strategic accounts are selected, there is often a time lag (that can be up to several years) between the initiation of the KAM programme and the selection of the strategic accounts, and the realization and achievement of additional financial value. KAM is a future-oriented strategy that depends fundamentally on achieving coherence between the supplier and customer expectations. We term it 'supplier delusion': the phenomenon when a supplier selects a customer as key, but for that particular customer the supplier is just a commodity or transactional vendor.

In the next chapter we will argue that the factors that influence the appointment of accounts may be diverse and vary from industry to industry. However, a key criterion for selecting a key account should be the potential for profitable growth in the future. Another important element is organizational fitness, in other words, the degree of compatibility of policies, processes and practices between the supplier and the customer. The creation of superior value for the key customer and its resulting financial returns for the supplier will require both organizations to work in a highly collaborative and coordinated fashion.

The account portfolio needs to be regularly reviewed. Most industries these days experience significant change and transformation, meaning that the strategic importance of customers will change on a continuous basis. Some customers that are no longer aligned or whose future potential has been extinguished may need to be de-selected as key accounts. This is likely to trigger conflict, particularly from account managers and teams dedicated to 'former' strategic accounts.

Organizations need to resource and plan the process of both selection and de-selection and be aware of some of the pitfalls and errors in strategic account selection such as:

- overemphasis on short-term results versus longer-term outcomes, potentially sending the wrong message to the account about the genuine interest in the relationship;

- not enough prioritization between accounts in a way that gives guidance to the appropriate allocation of resources and definition of organizational structures;

- lists of strategic accounts that are too long and unmanageable, resulting in potential failure to deliver the agreed distinctive offerings;

- unclear criteria for assessing potential new key accounts and poorly defined key account onboarding or development processes;

- internal pressure to keep unsuitable accounts in the key customer portfolio, often current customers that may be large but with limited prospects for future growth.

A study of KAM implementation (Part 1)

In November 2016, Elisa Campo at Cranfield School of Management conducted a study with the objective, amongst other things (see later boxes) of measuring the general satisfaction level of organizations regarding their KAM programmes.

The study asked participants to identify the length of their KAM capability across the four stages identified by Davies and Ryals [43]: *Introducing KAM, Embedding, Optimizing* and *Continuous Improvement*.

The research surveyed 57 organizations, predominantly with mature KAM programmes (those in place for more than six years).

Figure 1.7   Years of KAM implementation experience within the sample

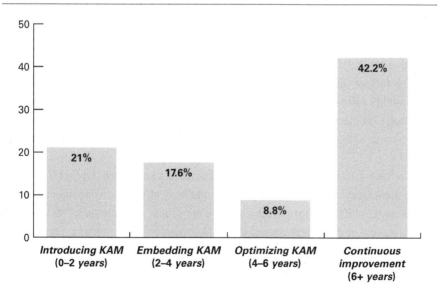

Respondents were asked to rate their perception of the quality of implementation of KAM in their companies. An almost even split of respondents emerged. On one side, 52.7 per cent of respondents rated the implementation of their KAM programmes positively (ratings 5–7). Conversely, 43.6 per cent of respondents indicated the implementation of KAM programmes in their organizations could be improved (ratings 1–3). These percentages do not take into consideration the respondents that were unsure of how to rate the quality of the KAM programme in their companies.

Figure 1.8   Degree of perceived quality of implementation of KAM

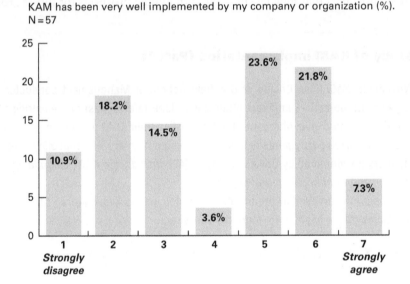

KAM has been very well implemented by my company or organization (%).
N = 57

The perceived quality of KAM implementation shows interesting differences between the organizations depending on whether they were at the beginning of their journey or were further ahead, having reached a more mature stage of implementation. Respondents whose organizations were at a more advanced stage of KAM implementation were far more likely to have an overall better perception of the quality and the effectiveness of their KAM programmes than those in companies at the initial stages of KAM.

Some further statistical tests were carried out and supported the fact that during the *Introduction* phase of KAM, organizations often fail to consider the time requirements of KAM programmes and have unrealistic expectations that may lead them to have a more critical view of the KAM implementation process. This could result in either abandoning the entire programme or restructuring it. Organizations that have reached a more mature stage of the programme are more aware of its benefits and show a more positive and enthusiastic attitude towards KAM.

Adopting KAM implementation as an ongoing process

The conception and planning of strategic account initiatives have generated much interest and literature over the years. Much of what we know about KAM is located within the foundation domain, particularly focused on the planning and formulation of KAM. Less is known about the implementation of KAM [44],[45] and the evolution from sales to KAM approaches.

There is growing evidence that KAM requires investments throughout the lifecycle of strategic account management [46] and that KAMgrs and senior executives need to devise comprehensive frameworks to enable the continuous development of account management programmes. These frameworks often include the following dimensions [44]:

- *Strategy*: refers to the purpose of the supplier–customer relationship and how KAM fits within the overall corporate strategy.

- *Structures and processes*: includes current and future ways of working and processes with the key account, and processes such as the way in which performance targets will be defined. The location of the KAM function within the overall organization is also a key element to consider and review. In some companies, KAM sits alongside the sales structures; in others, it becomes a separate entity altogether.

- *Product/service solutions*: includes the bundles of products and services that will be offered to the strategic account in order to co-create the expected value, deliver against the account plan and build a profitable long-term relationship.

- *People*: includes the definition of roles, competency profiles, reward systems and succession planning. A key aspect is the leadership approach adopted for the people involved in the supplier–key customer relationship, which may need to be different to the approach taken for leading the sales organization.

- *Knowledge capabilities*: refers to activities, systems and information to generate insights, measure process and monitor account activities. Organizational learning and knowledge sharing are also included in this category.

A study of KAM implementation (Part 2)

The study mentioned in the previous box also sought to identify which of the elements identified by Davies and Ryals [43] as conforming KAM are implemented to a greater extent in organizations.

The table overleaf shows the descriptive statistics (mean and standard deviation) of the responses of the 57 organizations with regards to the extent to which they had implemented each of the 31 elements of KAM programmes.

Table 1.3   Degree of implementation of KAM elements

Elements	N	Min.	Max.	Mean	Std. deviation
We have appointed key account managers	57	1	7	5.67	1.629
We have clearly identified our key accounts	57	1	7	5.30	1.700
Our key accounts enjoy higher service levels than non-key accounts	53	1	7	5.04	1.544
We have defined clear criteria for how to select key accounts	56	1	7	4.71	1.765
Our senior managers have really bought into KAM	56	1	7	4.66	1.861
We have made the business case for KAM	54	1	7	4.57	1.879
We have clear goals and targets for each of our key accounts	56	1	7	4.38	1.864
We have individual key account plans for all key accounts	56	1	7	4.38	1.922
We have someone who is the KAM champion within our company	54	1	7	4.35	2.340
Our KAM managers have good access to internal resources	56	1	7	4.32	1.664
Our organization has well-defined key account teams	57	1	7	4.28	2.094
The top management in the company have an active involvement in KAM	56	1	7	4.21	1.856
Our company's key account managers are fully trained	56	1	7	4.16	1.776
We have joint activities with key accounts (eg process improvements)	54	1	7	4.11	1.501
We have changed our organization structure to accommodate KAM	55	1	7	4.05	2.164
Our company has good overall knowledge of KAM	56	1	7	4.00	1.849
We have joint workshops with key accounts to plan our future relationship and joint expectations	52	1	7	3.98	2.005

Statement					
We have joint investments in the relationships between ourselves and our key accounts	55	1	7	3.96	1.721
We have developed an organizational culture that supports KAM	56	1	7	3.95	1.793
We measure the performance of our KAM programme	54	1	7	3.93	1.902
We became more selective (eg reduced number of key accounts) at a mature stage of the programme	41	1	7	3.80	1.750
We have well-developed feedback processes with our key accounts	56	1	7	3.75	1.841
We have established clear policies and procedures for handling key accounts	55	1	7	3.67	1.925
We have IT support systems for KAM	55	1	7	3.55	2.026
We have developed specific motivation and reward schemes for key account managers	55	1	7	3.51	1.999
We scaled up to a larger set of key accounts after the piloting/trial phase	36	1	7	3.42	2.103
We initially did a pilot with a few selected accounts in order to test that it could be applied	47	1	7	3.38	1.783
We rejuvenated our KAM programme in order to have continuous improvements at an mature stage of the programme	41	1	7	3.34	1.783
We have created an internal KAM manual (eg with key account information, planning details, etc)	53	1	7	3.04	1.675
Everyone in our organization understands KAM	56	1	7	2.80	1.458
We benchmark against other organizations about KAM	54	1	7	2.74	1.592

The first 16 elements listed in Table 1.3 are those with a mean of 4 or above. This means that we can consider that 16 of the 31 elements are being regularly implemented within current companies' KAM programmes. Some of the elements with the highest mean can be viewed as vital to every KAM programme and are generally given priority. One could therefore argue that *having clearly identified the key accounts*, the *appointment of specialist key account managers*, and *having clearly defined criteria to select the key accounts* are 'must have' elements in KAM. These elements may not represent a real competitive advantage or significantly affect KAM performance. These are *necessary* but possibly not *sufficient* elements for a high-performing KAM programme.

It is interesting to notice that at the bottom of the table, the element that is least implemented by the respondents is *we benchmark against other organizations about KAM*. This suggests that organizations may not be involved in benchmarking, most probably due to a lack of proper benchmarking tools in KAM.

Creation and revision of strategic account plans

KAM is an *integrated* process for the profitable management of customer relationships [47]. The integration is in fact a complex, multifaceted endeavour that requires enhanced awareness of the strategic customer's intent, the gathering and transfer of specific customer knowledge, and ultimately the functional alignment to realize joint business opportunities. The role of the strategic account plan is precisely to serve as the platform for integrating these elements of effective strategic customer management.

Account plans should be live documents that are regularly updated to capture the opportunities and risks for the business with the strategic account. If the plans are based on insights supplied by the customer, and the relationship enjoys a high level of trust, the plans should be shared with the customer and used as a compass to direct and guide the allocation of resources and capabilities and the efforts for the value creation endeavour.

Strategic account plans may be lengthy documents or succinct sets of tools depending on the complexity of the account and on the thoroughness of the planning process. Generally speaking, key account plans [46],[47] capture:

- a description of strategic account: political, economic, social, technological, environmental context;
- current offerings and value propositions: product and services sold to the customer and sales records;

- customer business: customer's value-creating process, opportunities and threats, future business potential and opportunities;
- customer management team: allocation of resources and responsibilities between account manager and team;
- financial information including details of revenues and profits;
- analysis of the relationship, including contact matrixes describing the contact points between firm team members and customer representatives;
- action planning: goals and objectives, action plans with timelines and allocation of resources.

A key feature of powerful account plans is the degree to which the plans are actionable, thus the importance of translating strategic analysis into specific courses of action. Overall, a solid strategic account plan is linked to the overall business strategy.

A study of KAM implementation (Part 3)

The KAM implementation study also aimed to address the research question: '*Which of the elements that companies have applied have led to the successful and satisfying performance of their KAM programme?*'

This box presents the results of the third research objective: to benchmark best practices in companies' KAM programmes by understanding which of the implemented elements have led to a perceived successful implementation.

The quantitative analysis focuses on the correlation between the implementation of each KAM element and the respondents' perceptions of how well their organizations had implemented KAM. These are detailed in Table 1.4.

As we can see in Table 1.4, most elements present a strong correlation with the perceived success of KAM. Only six elements (see the darker grey shaded cells) were not statistically significant. All other elements presented a significant correlation at the 0.05 (*) or the 0.01 (**) level of significance, meaning there is a significant association between the KAM element and the perceived performance of the KAM programme. The top 10 elements of KAM presented correlation coefficients above 0.5.

Table 1.4 Correlation results between element implementation and perceived overall KAM performance/satisfaction

Spearman's rho		My company or organization is very good at key account management	Our senior managers have really bought into KAM	Our company has a good overall knowledge of KAM	We have defined clear criteria for how to select key accounts	Our organization has well-defined key account teams	We have developed specific motivation and reward schemes for key account managers	We have well-developed feedback processes with our key accounts	The top management in the company have an active involvement in KAM	We have changed our organization structure to accommodate KAM	We benchmark against other organizations about KAM	We have established clear policies and procedures for handling key accounts
My company or organization is very good at key account management	Correlation coefficient	1.000	.328*	.368**	.271*	.668**	.490**	.590**	.267	.477**	.458**	.680**
	Sig. (2-tailed)		.017	.007	.050	.000	.000	.000	.053	.000	.001	.000
	N	54	53	53	53	54	53	54	53	52	52	53
We have clearly identified our key accounts	Correlation coefficient	.493**	.372**	.570**	.555**	.534**	.588**	.261	.375**	.445**	.539**	.434**
	Sig. (2-tailed)	.000	.007	.000	.000	.000	.000	.062	.006	.001	.000	.001
	N	54	51	54	54	54	54	52	53	54	53	53
Our organization has well-defined key account teams	Correlation coefficient	.668**	.322*									
	Sig. (2-tailed)	.000	.017									
	N	54	54									
We have well-developed feedback processes with our key accounts	Correlation coefficient	.590**										
	Sig. (2-tailed)	.000										
	N	54										
Our organization has well-defined key account teams	Correlation coefficient	.668**	.477**	.458**	.680**	.446**	.586**	.391*	.243	.302	.624**	.378**
	Sig. (2-tailed)	.000	.000	.001	.000	.001	.000	.012	.108	.074	.000	.006
	N	54	52	52	53	53	41	41	45	36	52	52

Statement elements appearing in the matrix:

- My company or organization is very good at key account management
- We have made the business case for KAM
- We have individual key account plans for all key accounts
- We have someone who is the KAM champion within our company
- We have appointed key account managers
- Our company's key account managers are fully trained
- We have clear goals and targets for each of our key accounts
- Our KAM managers have good access to internal resources
- We have developed an organizational culture that supports KAM
- Our key accounts receive higher service levels than non-key accounts
- We have joint activities with key accounts (eg process improvements)
- We have joint investments in the relationships between ourselves and our key accounts
- We manage the performance of our KAM programme
- We have joint workshops with key accounts to plan our future relationship and joint expectations
- We have created an internal KAM manual (eg with key account information, planning details, etc)
- We have IT support systems for KAM
- The top management in the company have an active involvement in KAM
- We have changed our organization structure to accommodate KAM
- We benchmark against other organizations about KAM
- We have established clear policies and procedures for handling key accounts
- We have established clear policies and procedures for handling key accounts
- Everyone in my organization understands KAM
- We initially did a pilot with a few selected accounts in order to test that it could be applied
- We scaled up to a larger set of key accounts after the piloting/trial phase
- We became more selective (eg reduced number of key accounts) at a mature stage of the programme
- We rejuvenated our KAM programme in order to have continuous improvements at a mature stage of the programme

NOTE: * 0.05 level of significance, ** 0.01 level of significance

Purpose and structure of the book

We, the authors, have been practising, researching, providing training and consulting on KAM for more than 25 years. As we indicated in the preface, we felt there was a need to consolidate the collective insight deriving from practice and from scholarly work into a practical but also academically grounded book on the implementation of KAM.

In writing the book our sole purpose is to help you, the reader, become more effective at implementing KAM in your organization or helping others do so. We believe most benefit from the book will be derived when you:

- *Think* from multiple angles about your KAM programme, both in the short term and the long term; from the financial outcomes as well as the structural inputs. In order to help you, we have compiled questions for managers and/or summary points at the end of each chapter.

- *Evaluate* and critically analyse your current investments in KAM by applying the analytical tools and frameworks contained in the book. Some will surely reinforce your current practice and the results of other tools may compel you to change your current approach.

- *Drive the development of the role* of KAMgr towards a more rounded, strategic and influential role within your organization.

This book contains a combination of existing research, which you can find referenced at the end of each chapter, case studies, interviews and vignettes of real-life cases. We have aimed to intertwine and seamlessly combine them throughout the book. However, we are mindful that some of the topics are more conceptual than others.

Implementing KAM programmes will require redefining business unit or product line success for corporate and company-wide success. This is, for most companies, a change in processes, structures and very often a change in culture. The book provides an integrated approach to achieve it, divided into four key parts:

Part 1. Re-engaging strategic customers.

Part 2. Developing winning offerings.

Part 3. Designing customer-centric approaches and processes.

Part 4. Assessing your KAM programme: a framework.

Structure of the book

Each chapter focuses on a key element of KAM implementation as follows.

Chapter 2, *Adopting key account management (KAM)*, describes the drivers of KAM. It also presents an implementation model together with the risks and challenges that companies face at each major stage of implementation.

Figure 1.9 Structure of this book

PART ONE

Re-engaging strategic customers

Chapter 2
Adopting key account management

Chapter 3
Building customer understanding and value planning

Chapter 4
Developing customer relationships

PART TWO

Developing winning offerings

Chapter 5
Creating compelling customer value propositions

Chapter 6
Co-creating value with key customers

PART THREE

Designing customer-centric approaches and processes

Chapter 7
The role of the key account manager and the KAM team

Chapter 8
Measuring KAM performance

Chapter 9
Motivating, incentivizing and rewarding for KAM

Chapter 10
KAM and procurement: the buyer's perspective and value-based negotiation

Chapter 11
International key account management

PART FOUR

Assessing your KAM programme: a framework

Chapter 12
The KAM Framework

Chapter 3, *Building customer understanding and value planning*, focuses on presenting approaches to develop an in-depth understanding of the customer leading to the definition of specific relationship development strategies. Amongst other things, it presents research-based tools such as the 'wheel of customer understanding' which informs the strategic enquiry of the customer.

Chapter 4, *Developing customer relationships*, provides powerful sets of tools to map the relevant players within the customer organization, across functions and levels. This chapter is essential reading to help produce a sophisticated map of the customer, drawing amongst other things on social network approaches to understand relational processes that are crucial for delivering value beyond the product or service.

Chapter 5, *Creating compelling customer value propositions*, presents a structured approach to implement what is possibly the most critical component of the strategic KAM process. It portrays the creation of value propositions as subtle processes that suppliers need to refine on an ongoing basis. In the strategic KAM planning process, the value proposition connects customer research, customer requirements and external opportunities in the marketplace.

Chapter 6, *Co-creating value with key customers*, outlines the complex and subtle relational processes that underpin the creation of new value with customers. It describes both the strategic and the tactical practices to align distinctive customer and supplier capabilities to co-create value.

Chapter 7, *The role of key account managers and KAM teams*, explains the crucial dimensions of a role that is becoming ever more encompassing, strategic and pivotal in making KAM work.

Chapter 8, *Measuring KAM performance*, addresses the principles and guidelines for developing appropriate measurement systems for KAM programmes, including metrics and the necessary inputs for these metrics.

Chapter 9, *Motivating, incentivizing and rewarding for KAM*, tackles the debate and practice of designing incentives and rewards for KAM, which are, by nature, different from those in sales. We explain how incentives need to be designed connected to the performance measurement systems in operation within the organization.

Chapter 10, *KAM and procurement: the buyer's perspective and value-based negotiation*, puts KAM in the context of some of the most crucial relationships, those that KAMgrs and directors have with the procurement function of customer organizations. We discuss high-level approaches to align negotiation and value-creating strategies.

Chapter 11, *International KAM*, outlines the practices and paradoxes inherent to managing key customers across countries, a key requirement for an increasing number of companies that deal with customers internationally.

Chapter 12, *The KAM framework*, focuses on 'bringing it all together', offering an integrated framework that allows KAM leaders to assess in detail the level of implementation of their KAM programmes. It also provides guidelines for supporting organizations in the change management effort associated with KAM as well as providing tools to facilitate the invigoration of existing KAM programmes.

We have written the book in a way that allows each chapter to stand alone from the rest. As in any other management text, we recommend you read the introduction first. Then the order you follow to read each chapter should be driven by your interest and the priorities of your KAM programme and your particular business context.

So whatever way you choose to read, we wish you a productive and informative experience.

Questions for managers

- In which ways are the behaviours of your customers changing? How do these changes affect your business?

- How can you leverage the power of new and digital technologies to redefine your relationships with key customers?

- How could your structures change to reflect new forms of value creation and value delivery?

- How will you ensure that the customers you nominate as 'key' have a similar relationship intent with you? That is, do they also consider you as a 'key' supplier?

- When re-evaluating your portfolio of key accounts, how do you manage internally the process of convincing a KAMgr that her/his customer is no longer a key account? And how do you manage the process of gradual divestment with the customer?

- Would you be prepared to share your key account plan with the customer it refers to? If so, what would you expect to gain? If not, what would be the reasons not to share these plans?

References

[1]   Pardo, C (1997) Key account management in the business to business field: the key account's point of view, *Journal of Personal Selling and Sales Management*, **17** (4), pp. 17–26.

[2]   Sharma, A (1997) Who prefers key account management programs? An investigation of business buying behavior and buying firm characteristics, *Journal of Personal Selling and Sales Management*, **17** (4), pp. 27–39.

[3] McDonald, M, Millman, T and Rogers, B (1997) Key account management: theory, practice and challenges, *Journal of Personal Selling and Sales Management*, **13** (8), pp. 737–57.

[4] Piercy, N F and Lane, N (2009) *Strategic Customer Management: Strategizing the sales organization*, Oxford University Press, Oxford.

[5] Jones, E et al (2005) The changing environment of selling and sales management, *Journal of Personal Selling and Sales Management*, **25** (2), pp. 105–11.

[6] Honeycutt, E (2002) Sales management in the new millennium: an introduction, *Industrial Marketing Management*, **31** (7), pp. 555–58.

[7] World Economic Forum (2016) The rise of emerging market multinationals: this is how they can become global industry leaders [Online] https://www.weforum.org/agenda/2016/12/emerging-market-multinationals/ [accessed 25 July 2017]

[8] Moncrief, W C (1986) Ten key activities of industrial salespeople, *Industrial Marketing Management*, **15** (4), pp. 309–17.

[9] Moncrief, W C and Marshall, G W (2005) The evolution of the seven steps of selling, *Industrial Marketing Management*, **34** (1), pp. 13–22.

[10] Davies, I A, Ryals, L J and Holt S (2010) Relationship management: a sales role, or a state of mind? An investigation of functions and attitudes across a business-to-business sales force, *Industrial Marketing Management*, **39** (7), pp. 1049–62.

[11] Montgomery, D B and Yip, G S (2000) The challenge of global customer management, *Marketing Management*, **9** (4), pp. 22–29.

[12] Ulaga, W and Eggert, A (2006) Value-based differentiation in business relationships: gaining and sustaining key supplier status, *Journal of Marketing*, **70** (1), pp. 119–36.

[13] Janda, S and Seshadri, S (2001) The influence of purchasing strategies on performance, *Journal of Business and Industrial Marketing*, **16** (4), p. 294.

[14] de Boer, L, Labro, E and Morlacchi, P (2001) A review of methods supporting supplier selection, *European Journal of Purchasing and Supply Management*, **7** (2), pp. 75–89.

[15] Marcos-Cuevas, J et al (2016) Value co-creation practices and capabilities: sustained purposeful engagement across B2B systems, *Industrial Marketing Management*, **56**, pp. 97–107.

[16] Sheth, J N and Sharma, A (2008) The impact of the product to service shift in industrial markets and the evolution of the sales organization, *Industrial Marketing Management*, **37** (3), pp. 260–69.

[17] Arnett, D B and Badrinarayanan, V (2005) Enhancing customer needs-driven CRM strategies: core selling teams, knowledge management competence, and relationship marketing competence, *Journal of Personal Selling and Sales Management*, **25** (4), pp. 329–43.

[18] Rackham, N and de Vincentis, J R (1999) *Rethinking the Sales Force*, McGraw-Hill, New York.

[19] Vargo, S L and Lusch, R F (2008) Service-dominant logic: continuing the evolution, *Journal of the Academy of Marketing Science*, **36** (1), pp. 1–10.

[20] Ballantyne, D and Varey, R J (2006) Creating value-in-use through marketing interaction: the exchange logic of relating, communicating and knowing, *Marketing Theory*, **6** (3), pp. 335–48.

[21] Frow, P and Payne, A (2007) Towards the 'perfect' customer experience, *Journal of Brand Management*, **15** (2), pp. 89–101.

[22] Prahalad, C K and Ramaswamy, V (2004) Co-creation experiences: the next practice in value creation, *Journal of Interactive Marketing*, **18** (3), pp. 5–14.

[23] Payne, A F, Storbacka, K and Frow, P (2008) Managing the co-creation of value, *Journal of Academic Marketing Science*, **36** (1), pp. 83–96.

[24] Heinonen, K et al (2010) A customer-dominant logic of service, *Journal of Service Management*, **21** (4), pp. 531–48.

[25] Grönroos, C and Ravald, A (2011) Service as business logic: implications for value creation and marketing, *Journal of Service Management*, **22** (1), pp. 5–22.

[26] Piercy, N and Lane, N (2006) The underlying vulnerabilities in key account management strategies, *European Management Journal*, **24** (2–3), pp. 151–62.

[27] Wiessmeier, G F L, Thoma, A and Senn, C (2012) Leveraging synergies between R&D and key account management to drive value creation, *Research Technology Management*, **55** (3), pp. 15–22.

[28] Brehmer, P-O and Rehme, (2009) Proactive and reactive: drivers for key account management programmes, *European Journal of Marketing*, **43** (7/8), pp. 961–84.

[29] Bastl, M (2011) An exploration of managers' openness and relationship transparency in a buyer-supplier relationship, Cranfield University, Bedford, UK.

[30] Speakman, J I F and Ryals, L (2012) Key account management: the inside selling job, *Journal of Business and Industrial Marketing*, **27** (5), pp. 360–66.

[31] Ojasalo, J (2002) Customer commitment in key account management, *Marketing Review*, **2** (3), p. 301.

[32] Ivens, B S and Pardo, C (2007) Are key account relationships different? Empirical results on supplier strategies and customer reactions, *Industrial Marketing Management*, **36** (4), pp. 470–82.

[33] Pilon, F and Hadjielias, E (2017) Strategic account management as a value co-creation selling model in the pharmaceutical industry, *Journal of Business and Industrial Marketing*, **32** (2), pp. 310–25.

[34] Eggert, A, Ulaga, W and Hollmann, S (2009) Benchmarking the impact of customer share in key-supplier relationships, *Journal of Business and Industrial Marketing*, **24** (3/4), pp. 154–60.

[35] Eggert, A and Ulaga, W (2010) Managing customer share in key supplier relationships, *Industrial Marketing Management*, **39** (8), pp. 1346–55.

[36] Workman, J P et al (2003) Intraorganizational determinants of key account management effectiveness, *Journal of Academic Marketing Science*, **31** (1), pp. 3–21.

[37] Jones, E et al (2009) Developing a strategic framework of key account performance, *Journal of Strategic Marketing*, **17** (3–4), pp. 221–35.

[38] Davies, I A and Ryals, L J (2014) The efectiveness of Key Account Management practices, *Industrial Marketing Management*, **43** (7), pp. 1182–94.

[39] Lambert, D M and Enz, M G (2012) Managing and measuring value co-creation in business-to-business relationships, *Journal of Marketing Management*, **28** (13/14), pp. 1588–1625.

[40] Jones, G et al (2015) Leading top performance in key account management, Cranfield School of Management, Bedford, UK.

[41] Andersen, S (2015) Key performance indicators (KPIs) of a strategic account manager, *Velocity*, **17** (1).

[42] McDonald, M, Rogers, B and Woodburn, D (2000) *Key Customers: How to manage them profitably*, Butterworth-Heinemann, Oxford.

[43] Davies, I A and Ryals, L J (2009) A stage model for transitioning to KAM, *Journal of Marketing Management*, **25** (9–10), pp. 1027–48.

[44] Zupancic, D (2008) Towards an integrated framework of key account management, *Journal of Business and Industrial Marketing*, **23** (5), pp. 323–31.

[45] Sengupta, S, Krapfel, R K E and Pusateri, M A E (2000) An empirical investigation of key account salesperson effectiveness, *Journal of Personal Selling and Sales Management*, **20** (4), pp. 253–61.

[46] Storbacka, K (2012) Strategic account management programs: alignment of design elements and management practices, *Journal of Business and Industrial Marketing*, **27** (4), pp. 259–74.

[47] Ryals, L J and Mcdonald, M (2008) *Key Account Plans: The practitioners' guide to profitable planning*, Butterworth-Heinemann, Oxford.

Note

1 The KAM Club at Cranfield School of Management has been running for 20 years and is Europe's leading centre of excellence and expertise in KAM. More information: www.cranfield.ac.uk/som/research-clubs/key-account-management-best-practice-club.

PART ONE
Re-engaging strategic customers

Adopting key account management

02

'What you choose also chooses you.'

KAMAND KOJOURI

When should we engage in key account management and how do we select the right customers?

Overview

The decision to adopt key account management (KAM) is really a strategic one that brings with it the commitment of specific resources, changes in the organizational structure, and most likely a shift in the company's culture in how to approach the business. Besides, in spite of the potential for KAM to make a supplier organization more profitable, this is not easy to achieve. There is evidence that a significant number of companies fail to charge a premium price to customers through KAM, compared to the price charged to customers that are not treated as key accounts [1]. Therefore, supplier firms need to carefully evaluate the convenience of adopting KAM and plan on how to do it.

The purpose of this chapter is to help companies assess the need for KAM and guide them in how to initiate the KAM process. A first decision has to do with whether or not a KAM approach to business is justified for a supplier company. Next, if the answer to the previous question is yes, the supplier has to define a mechanism to select key accounts. Once the customers with a 'key account' status have been identified, suppliers need to decide the kind and amount of investment they are willing to make in each key account relationship.

The need for KAM

A first question that suppliers need to answer is whether they need to implement KAM in their organization or not and, if yes, to what extent. This is of paramount importance given that adopting KAM typically requires a significant investment in resources that are idiosyncratic to specific customer relationships. Some examples of these are:

- the allocation of dedicated personnel to a key account, usually a key account manager (KAMgr) and a cross-functional team;
- training and skills development for customer-facing executives;
- the commitment of senior management time;
- the design of tailored products, services and solutions;
- the adoption of new technologies and communication channels.

In addition to these investments, KAM adoption normally requires the activation of some organizational changes to facilitate KAM implementation:

- developing a customer-centric culture;
- designing a new organizational structure;
- establishing new communication channels among functional areas;
- redefining performance metrics to incorporate customer-related aspects.

Therefore, suppliers have to make a thorough assessment of whether or not they need a KAM approach and, if yes, to what extent. With this purpose in mind, we propose a framework and a toolkit to inform these decisions. We posit that supplier companies must evaluate the convenience of KAM adoption through the assessment of three questions:

1 To what extent is our business concentrated on a few customers?
2 To what extent do our customers require a KAM approach?
3 To what extent can we create competitive advantages and differentiate through KAM?

Figure 2.1 shows the three main things a supplier company should consider when deciding on the adoption of KAM. These are depicted as thermometers, to highlight the fact that different levels in the measures will determine different actions.

Our business concentrates on a few accounts

A first and very common argument to justify the need for KAM is the fact that the supplier's sales revenues or profitability is concentrated around a few customers.

Figure 2.1   Assessing the need for KAM

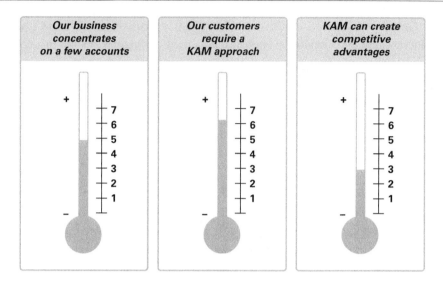

This is normally known as the *Pareto Principle* or 80/20 rule, where 80 per cent of the sales come from 20 per cent of the customers [2]. If this is the case, it would make sense to give more attention to those important customers. On the one hand, focusing on a few customers and providing extra care to these could be a sensible strategy to reduce the risk of losing a very important one, threatening the company's financial welfare. On the other hand, it is very likely that those very important customers will also be targeted as key accounts by other suppliers in the same industry. Therefore, a KAM approach might be the right tool to defend the supplier's current and future position in the market.

In addition to analysing the current business situation with customers, supplier companies must estimate the future business potential of customer relationships. The rationale for this is that it might be that today some customers are small in terms of the revenues they generate for the supplier, but they have a promising growth potential. The opposite could also happen with customers that, whilst today representing a large share of the supplier's revenues, are not expected to evolve successfully in the coming years. Consequently, a forward-looking perspective is needed to project the future level of concentration of sales and profits among customers. This requires, of course, significant knowledge about the critical market trends, as well as a sound understanding of the customers' business models and future perspectives.

Our customers require a KAM approach

There is ample evidence showing that procurement, both as a function and as a process, has experienced impressive development in the past few years [3]. This trend responds to the need for procurement to be strategic as a function and to assume a more significant responsibility in achieving the company's long-term profitability goals. One demonstration of this is the fact that executives involved in procurement increasingly have senior-level positions in their companies, a solid professional management background, and strong business acumen.

The decision-making unit or buying centre – ie the people and functional units involved in the organizational procurement process – is progressively more complex in terms of its needs and requirements. In addition, the influencers of the purchasing process are less visible to supplier companies, to a large extent due to the use of new technologies and social media. For example, influencers traditionally were easy to identify and, for the most part, belonged to the buying company; nowadays, influencers can be industry experts or even competitors of the buying firm that disseminate knowledge through social media. The use of new communication and business technologies has revolutionized several stages of the buying process. For instance, the identification of potential suppliers is increasingly reliant on the use of professional social networks such as LinkedIn. Likewise, in the suppliers' evaluation stage, many companies are following online discussion forums or blogs about the experience of different companies, with products and services offered by several suppliers. The following quote from the head of key accounts in a flooring company illustrates this trend in procurement and the role of social media.

The use of social media in procurement

'Make sure that you've got every last thing that a client could possibly ask for; if you haven't it's a mad scramble to familiarize yourself with whatever it is and adjust your offer to accommodate that thing. There's an increased pressure and I think some of it comes from the swell in the use of social media. I think it's now quite accepted that most folk are on LinkedIn, but increasingly more businesses are on Facebook and Twitter, and everything is moving at a very fast pace. There's a real urgency in the market…'. (Fleur Carson, Head of Key Accounts, Forbo Flooring Systems.)

In addition, the selection of eligible and preferred suppliers is becoming stricter in terms of the requirements a candidate must meet. For example, it is quite common for a retailer to establish a very rigorous application procedure for their suppliers, who have to make a strong case of why they should be considered as providers. The application process to become a supplier can sometimes take a long time and require several types of resources coming from varied sources. Furthermore, a number of companies are utilizing third-party procurement to reduce overall costs and to concentrate on activities that are considered core components of the business. Third-party procurement consists of outsourcing a significant part of the procurement activity (sometimes the whole process) to a company that specializes in it and does it for many organizations.

KAM can create competitive advantages

Whereas the two previous reasons for adopting KAM are of a reactive nature based on the situation faced by the supplier company and its customers, the third argument is, in its essence, proactive. The senior management of a supplier company may decide to adopt KAM if they see it as an opportunity to build sustained competitive advantages and differentiate from competitors.

A well-known approach to identifying and creating competitive advantages to support business strategy is the *resource-based view of the firm* [4]. It postulates that a firm is a bundle of resources and capabilities that can constitute a source of competitive advantage. For example, an engineering company may rely on its people as a key differentiating resource if employees are highly qualified, knowledgeable, and possess some unique technical skills that are hard to find elsewhere. Likewise, a bank may find a competitive advantage in the capability to adequately respond to customers' complaints; they may have developed a new system to communicate with customers and respond to complaints quickly and effectively. A useful tool to evaluate a specific resource or capability as a source of competitive advantage is the *VRIO* framework [5], which evaluates four aspects:

V Valuable

R Rare

I Imperfectly imitable

O Supported by the organizations

The practice of KAM should help suppliers to get closer to strategic customers, know them better, build rapport and trust and, consequently, become a business partner. In highly competitive markets, suppliers may find that an effective practice of KAM may constitute a source of competitive advantage. Some examples of resources and capabilities that can be built through KAM are:

- *Market knowledge.* Key accounts can be an extremely valuable source of market information that could help a supplier to react more quickly and effectively to new trends and unexpected events.

- *Quality of customer relationships.* Establishing an adequate KAM programme can help suppliers to build long-term relationships with key accounts by increasing customers' levels of satisfaction, trust and commitment with the supplier.

- *Co-creation of value.* A major trend in buyer–supplier relationships is the extent of value co-creation between the two companies; it is increasingly acknowledged that rather than the supplier defining the value to customers, both parties have to collaborate in the design and delivery of solutions and other forms of value. A KAM approach can facilitate this process by increasing the mutual understanding of each parties' business and needs, establishing the right communication channels, and creating a culture of collaboration.

A toolkit to assess the need for KAM

The questionnaire in Table 2.1 can help suppliers to evaluate their need for KAM. For each reason for adopting KAM there are four statements that need to be assessed, giving a number from 1 to 7, where 1 = strongly disagree and 7 = strongly agree. The total score for the 12 statements can go from 12 to 84.

In addition to evaluating the statements under each reason for KAM adoption, supplier companies can vary the weight assigned to each one (A, B, and C) to reflect their relative importance. So, for example, a small family company involved in the business of accounting services may assign a relatively higher importance to the company's business concentration (reason A), whereas a supplier of packaged consumer goods which is not a leader in its industry may assign a higher weight to customers' requirements (reason B).

Table 2.2 provides the template to assess the need for KAM. The first column to be completed comes directly from the template in Table 2.1 (Score A, Score B, and Score C). The next column is simply a conversion of the scores into percentages (%) to ease the interpretation. Finally, in the last column the supplier should include the weights assigned to each of the three reasons for adopting KAM.

There is really not a clear-cut decision rule or a threshold overall score/percentage that will determine whether KAM should be adopted or not, or to what extent. The availability of resources, the strategic priorities of senior management, the context of the specific industry, and the unique market conditions are some additional factors that suppliers need to consider. However, the guidelines summarized in Figure 2.2 can help suppliers to make a more informed decision (using the percentage overall assessment). The following four alternative outcomes result from the analysis:

Table 2.1 Template to assess the need for KAM

	Rate
A Our business is concentrated in a few accounts	**1=strongly disagree to 7=strongly agree**
1 Our current business in terms of revenues is highly concentrated in a few customers.	
2 Our current business in terms of profitability is highly concentrated in a few customers.	
3 Our future business in terms of revenues will be highly concentrated in a few customers.	
4 Our future business in terms of profitability will be highly concentrated in a few customers.	
Score A (1+2+3+4):	

	Rate
B Our customers require a KAM approach	**1=strongly disagree to 7=strongly agree**
5 Our main customers' procurement function is highly professional.	
6 The executives involved in purchasing at our main customers have ample experience and seniority.	
7 Our main customers' influencers are not always visible or known.	
8 Our main customers have very strict requirements to select their preferred suppliers.	
Score B (5+6+7+8):	

(continued)

Table 2.1 *(Continued)*

C KAM can create competitive advantages	Rate 1=strongly disagree to 7=strongly agree
9 Adopting KAM with our most important customers would enable us to have better market knowledge.	
10 Adopting KAM would enable us to jointly develop the right solutions with these customers.	
11 Adopting KAM with our most important customers would significantly enhance the quality of our relationship with them.	
12 Adopting KAM with our most important customers would help us to differentiate from our competitors.	
Score C (9+10+11+12):	
TOTAL SCORE (A+B+C):	

Table 2.2 Summary analysis to assess the need for KAM

Need for KAM categories	Assessment		Importance
	Score	%	Weight (%)
A Our business is concentrated in a few accounts			
B Our customers require a KAM approach			
C KAM can create competitive advantages			
OVERALL			100%

Figure 2.2 Evaluating the overall need for KAM

0%	25%	50%	75%	100%
NO NEED	**LITTLE NEED**	**ADOPT KAM**	**EMBRACE KAM**	
• Track it over time • Evaluate use of technology for efficiency	• Segment the market based on A, B, and C • Adjust offers to segments • Identify possible key accounts	• Select key accounts • Define KAM organization and investment • Meet key accounts' expectations	• Partner with key accounts • Align the organization • Co-create long-term value with key customers	

Overall need for KAM adoption

- *No need for KAM.* If the overall percentage is below 25, there is no need for KAM. However, managers are advised to keep track of this overall metric over time, as it may change due to the market dynamics.

- *Little need for KAM.* If the overall percentage is between 25 and 50, there is little need for KAM. Still, supplier companies may segment their customer base in terms of the relative size of the accounts, the procurement characteristics, and the potential to develop competitive advantages through a closer relationship with them. With this new segmentation approach, adjustments should be made to the current offers and value propositions to each resulting segment. Finally, it is desirable to identify possible key accounts that could be developed as such in the near future.

- *Adopt KAM.* If the overall percentage is above 50 but below 75, the suggestion is that supplier companies formally adopt key account management by selecting key accounts, defining the KAM organization, and deciding on the required KAM investments. At this stage, an important goal would be to meet key accounts' expectations in terms of the value being offered.

- *Embrace KAM.* If the overall percentage is 75 or more, supplier companies should embrace KAM. This means that suppliers should pursue partnership opportunities with some key accounts, with the purpose of engaging in value co-creation that will support a mutually beneficial long-term relationship. Together with this, the supplier company needs to secure the required internal organizational alignment across functional areas and hierarchical levels.

Selection of key accounts

Central to KAM is the assumption that customers that are part of a KAM programme are really *key*. Because KAM requires significant investment in customer relationships, suppliers need to be selective and focus on a small number of key accounts. In a way, key accounts are like close friends: how many intimate friends can you really have? With how many friends can you truly engage in frequent and deep communication, know them well, trust them and be trusted, be there for them when needed, and commit to a lifelong relationship of mutual support? The answer is straightforward: only with a few. However, it is common to find companies that claim to have more than 100 key accounts! How is this possible? What criteria are these companies using to select their key accounts? The quote from a senior management in KAM and expert in the shipping industry exemplifies the challenge of being careful in key account selection.

Selecting key accounts

'Another challenge is selection – selecting the key account who we believe has got the enduring capability to deliver value and the capability sets to match those is a never-ending discussion and process... we have to keep re-qualifying and revalidating and making sure that we are pointing a gun, if I could put it that way, towards the eight or ten key clients that are truly where we believe we should have sustainable, high-value relationships.' (Senior manager in KAM and expert in the shipping industry.)

One of the main difficulties that suppliers face in selecting key accounts is to define and follow a structured procedure for such a task. The following case study illustrates some of the challenges a company may face when trying to establish a procedure to select key accounts in a context where the common practice is that each sales executive individually defines the *key account* status of customers.

CASE STUDY   Selecting key accounts

An international industrial wood processing company decided to identify their key accounts to further develop business plans with each one. They invited the complete sales force to a meeting and asked each person to identify those customers that they considered *key* within the portfolio of their direct responsibility (based on geography and line of business).

With great conviction, each of the 17 sales executives selected three or four key accounts, making a total of 60. Then, each person was asked to explain why each of the identified customers was considered a *key account*. Interestingly, various dissimilar reasons emerged. For example, one executive selected a key account based on the size of the current business, and another one based on the trusting relationship they have had for many years. Yet another executive selected a key customer for being a prestigious company in the industry, and identified a second one for its growth potential.

In spite of the usefulness of this exercise, the managing director of the manufacturing company looked very worried, as he knew it was going to be a challenge to move forward with the key account selection process. On the one hand, they would have to reduce the total number of key accounts for the company, to be able to invest adequately in each one. On the other hand, they would need to agree on a procedure and a set of criteria to select key accounts for the company as a whole rather than doing it individually for each territory and line of business.

Given the strategic role of KAM, it is vital that the procedure for selecting key accounts be established by senior management, with the active participation of the people and business units involved in managing customer relationships; that is, a multi-level and cross-functional task is required. On the one hand, it is recommended that a combination of top-down and bottom-up approaches is followed. Senior managers are expected to define the company's strategic goals, which should guide the selection of key accounts. Likewise, executives that deal directly with customers or provide backstage support to them must provide relevant information about the customers' business context and market environment, and suggest relevant criteria to select key accounts. On the other hand, people from different functional areas (eg Production, Supply Chain and Logistics, and Finance) should be involved in this process, as they can offer information that is crucial for an adequate assessment of the customers that are candidates to be nominated as *key accounts*.

Selection criteria for key account status

The proposed framework for selecting key accounts is a three-stage process that evaluates customers that are candidates to obtain key account status, and focuses on answering the following questions:

1 Is this customer a very attractive one?

2 Does our company have a strong competitive position to deal with this customer?

3 Is this customer willing to co-invest in a *partnering* relationship with us?

The first two questions are addressed by adapting the GE-McKinsey framework [6] that evaluates a business portfolio and helps to prioritize the investment in different strategic options. In the case of key account selection, each candidate customer is first assessed in terms of attractiveness factors, to come up with a weighted score of overall attractiveness. Second, the competitive position of our company (similar to business strength) is evaluated for each candidate customer, to obtain a weighted score of overall competitive position. These two metrics are then combined to highlight the importance of *both* customer attractiveness *and* competitive position to select key accounts.

The third question is the most novel one for key account selection, and it was incorporated in the analysis after the consideration of recent trends in KAM that were captured through interviewing a group of senior executives. It became evident that nowadays effective KAM requires some sort of co-creation, co-development, and co-investment; therefore, it makes sense to consider this aspect as a third dimension for the key account selection criteria.

Stage 1: Customer attractiveness

A first and very intuitive aspect to consider when selecting key accounts is the attractiveness of customers. A number of factors can be evaluated to represent different sources of value for a KAM relationship. For example, a customer can be highly attractive in terms of demand stability or revenues. A customer can also be regarded as attractive if its culture is well aligned with that of the supplier. Looking forward, a customer could be deemed as attractive if it has a high growth potential, or if it could provide the supplier firm with access to new markets.

Figure 2.3 presents a practical matrix to classify customer attractiveness factors that could be used in the analysis. It includes a time-based dimension and a nature-based dimension, to represent factors that speak about the past, present or future, as well as those that refer to quantitative as well as qualitative elements:

Figure 2.3 Customer attractiveness factors

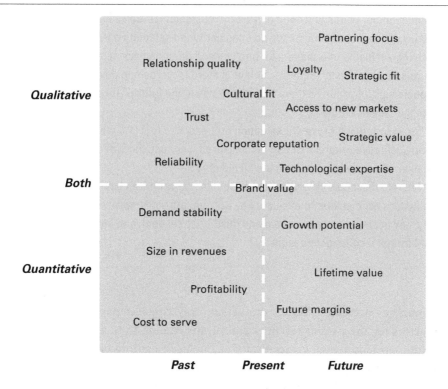

- *Time-based axis*: there are factors that speak to the past or present (eg demand stability, a trusting relationship), whereas some other factors are likely to relate to the future (eg growth potential, strategic fit).
- *Nature-based axis*: some attractiveness factors are quantitative (eg size in revenues, future margins) while others are qualitative in nature (eg relationship quality, partnering focus).

Previous research [7] suggests that a combination of quantitative and qualitative factors may offer a more comprehensive picture of how attractive a customer actually is. The following quotes by senior executives involved in KAM explain the need for this:

Selection of key accounts: quantitative and qualitative criteria

'Although quantitative criteria are very important to us, because they drive our key account selection process, qualitative criteria would make it more insightful. They would allow us to understand where the relationship is going, the collaboration/ partnership opportunities…' (Senior manager from the beverages industry.)

'For us, qualitative criteria are essential to evaluate the attractiveness of a key account. In our world, you need to trust the customer, perceive him as reliable and loyal; these are elements we do consider when selecting our customers. We exchange valuable information, technology and personnel so we need to assess all the relationship quality factors… In fact, if there is no room to develop meaningful relationships, how can I expect to make money in the future?' (Executive in KAM from the facilities industry.)

'So, in order to improve our selection process, I do feel that we should try to put some qualitative criteria that can be measured, because the outcome will be more reliable.' (Senior executive from the oil industry.)

'Share of business visions, cultural aspects, the values a customer promotes are factors we consider to evaluate key account attractiveness, since we believe they may improve our relationship and build trust, respect, and loyalty.' (Manager in KAM from the construction industry.)

Moreover, key account selection should not only consider past/present attractiveness factors (eg the current revenues and profits coming from a customer) but also some future perspectives. Financially, for example, estimations of a customer lifetime value would provide the supplier company with a forward-thinking view of customers as assets, which should inform the decision to invest in them as key accounts. *Customer lifetime value* is a methodology that estimates the future revenues and expenses coming from a customer relationship. Likewise, strategically a customer may be selected as key account based on its potential to develop future networks within an industry. The following comments by senior executives involved in KAM highlight this issue.

Selection of key accounts: past, present, and future perspectives

'I think that when you're selecting key accounts you again have to not to think about the here and now for today. I think, in terms of the selection criteria for key accounts, one has to take into consideration something that is future facing, be it your future pipeline, future advocates coming in to that space, whatever it might be…' (Louise Collins, Managing Director at Louise Collins Associates Limited.)

'If they haven't got the long-term vision, the chances are they're not going to be successful as a key account and they're probably not going to be that successful as a company in the medium to long term anyway, so it is probably not worth banging your head against a brick wall, trying to make them successful. And I would say, as a corollary to that, many organizations do have a real weakness for hanging on to customers based on their historic performance or their historic outlook...' (Richard Vincent, OEM Strategic Operations Manager, Hewlett Packard Enterprise.)

In summary, the recommendation is that suppliers choose a handful of factors (four to seven) to assess customer attractiveness, and look for a balance in terms of past/present vs future and quantitative vs qualitative focus. The specific factors to be considered will depend on the size, sector, and overall strategy of the supplier company.

Stage 2: Competitive position

The second stage for key account selection consists of assessing the competitive position of the supplier to deal with each candidate customer. Admittedly, it is very likely that a supplier's competitors will also be looking at the same customers as potential key accounts. Thus, if the company is not in a solid position to deal with such attractive customers relative to other suppliers in the industry, it may end up wasting valuable resources in a customer relationship that has little potential to be developed profitably over time.

Therefore, suppliers need to identify the competing factors (four to seven, ideally) that are relevant from the customer's perspective and assess them as objectively as possible, to support the decision on key account selection. The following list is not intended to be comprehensive, but shows examples of competitive position factors that supplier companies could use in the analysis:

- *Cost to serve*: it might be that a supplier company is in a better (or worse) position in this aspect relative to competitors. For example, if the company's geographical location is close to that of a customer, it may be able to serve this customer at a lower cost.

- *Customer knowledge*: it is very likely that competitors in an industry will have different levels of knowledge about specific customers; hence, those with higher knowledge are in a better position to succeed in a KAM relationship.

- *Corporate reputation*: this could be another relevant factor, especially in industries that operate in an international context (eg airlines industry), a highly regulated industry (eg financial insurance), or with strict safety standards (eg health sector).

- *Closeness to the decision-making unit*: supplier companies that have closer ties with those involved in the customer's purchasing process should have a higher chance of effectively managing that account.

- *Products and services requirements*: each customer will have a particular need in terms of the specifications for products and services, and a supplier may or may not be in the best position to meet those requirements, compared to other suppliers.

- *Logistics and delivery requirements*: in some industries the logistic capability is fundamental; suppliers with the capability to provide faster and flexible deliveries should be in a better position to compete and provide high-quality service to customers.

- *Technical expertise*: some customers may require very high levels of technical expertise from their suppliers, especially if they operate in a very high-tech and dynamic environment. It is possible that only a few suppliers will be regarded as technical experts in the field.

- *Culture of innovation*: it is likely that in highly innovative and dynamic industries, customers will value a culture of innovation when evaluating their suppliers.

Stage 3: Customer's willingness to co-invest

The third stage in selecting key accounts brings the customers' perspective on the extent to which they are willing to co-invest in a relationship with a supplier. Previous research on KAM has explored the importance of the customers' *strategic intent* and how its alignment with that of the supplier affects the practice of KAM [8]. The implication of this is that a supplier should find out whether a customer they are intending to treat as a key account is also looking at them as a *key supplier*. The question becomes: is this customer willing and interested in co-investing in a joint relationship and co-creating value?

The following quotes, captured during the interviewing of senior managers and experts in KAM and summarized in a recent research report on KAM trends and best practices [9], illustrate this issue:

Customer's willingness to co-invest in KAM relationships

'The criteria for key account selection will probably be less the size of the business, growth potential, level of influence, etc, and more the customer's ability and desire to partner. Supplier companies will need to ask themselves: what makes a desirable partner for our customers?' (Senior consultant on KAM in the healthcare industry.)

'With respect to selecting key accounts, the trend would be to complement some financial criteria with customers' willingness and readiness to co-invest. This signal of commitment may be critical to build sustained long-term relationships with key accounts.' (Executive in KAM in the professional services industry.)

'So the best partners are the ones who say, "We want to do this together, we want you to help us." I try to get people to look at the partnership from sufficient altitude, so that they can see it as though it was a single organization and then to ask themselves the question, "How would we do things if we were just a single organization?" If you can get people to buy in to doing things that way, you are genuinely doing co-development.' (Richard Vincent, OEM Strategic Operations Manager, Hewlett Packard Enterprise.)

A toolkit to select key accounts

The questionnaire in Table 2.3 can help suppliers to select their key accounts. For each of the three stages of the process there is a template that needs to be completed by senior executives, with the inputs and the active participation of the people involved in managing customer relationships, from different levels and functional areas in the organization.

Step 1: Customer attractiveness and competitive position factors

In the sections for *customer attractiveness* and *supplier's competitive position*, specific factors need to be incorporated and weighted based on their relative importance. Then, a score from 1 to 10 has to be assigned to each candidate customer, to reflect the extent to which each factor is present, with the meanings for the extreme values being 1 = 'very little' and 10 = 'very much'. So, for example, if a supplier includes 'revenue growth potential' as one of the customer attractiveness factors, then each candidate customer's attractiveness will be evaluated in terms of that criterion, using the 1–10 scale. Once this exercise is completed for all the relevant factors, a weighted score will be computed for each customer in the last row of that section in the table.

Step 2: Customer's willingness to co-invest

In the section for *customer's willingness to co-invest*, five questions are suggested to measure this aspect. If the supplier's senior management considers that all five are equally relevant, a weight of 20 per cent would be assigned to each one; these percentages can be modified to reflect differences in the relative importance of each question. Again, a score from 1 to 10 has to be given to each candidate customer, with the extreme values meaning 1 = 'very little' and 10 = 'very much'. A weighted score will be computed for each candidate customer.

Table 2.3 Template to assess key account selection

I. Customer attractiveness		Candidate customers for *key account status*					
Factors to measure it	Weight %	Cus_A	Cus_B	Cus_C	Cus_D	Cus_E	Cus_F
Factor 1	%						
Factor 2	%						
Factor 3	%						
Factor 4	%						
Factor 5	%						
Weighted average	100%						

II. Supplier's competitive position		Candidate customers for *key account status*					
Factors to measure it	Weight %	Cus_A	Cus_B	Cus_C	Cus_D	Cus_E	Cus_F
Factor 1	%						
Factor 2	%						
Factor 3	%						
Factor 4	%						
Factor 5	%						
Weighted average	100%						

III. Customer's willingness to co-invest

Factors to measure it	Weight %	Candidate customers for *key account status*					
		Cus_A	Cus_B	Cus_C	Cus_D	Cus_E	Cus_F
How willing is this customer to co-invest in a relationship with our company?	%						
How interested is this customer in co-creating products, services and solutions with us?	%						
How willing is this customer to co-develop a business strategy with our company?	%						
How likely is that this customer considers our company as a key supplier?	%						
How interested is this customer in establishing a partnering relationship with us?	%						
Weighted average	100%						

Step 3: Graphical representation and decision

Once the weighted scores have been computed for each customer on customer attractiveness, supplier's competitive position, and customer's willingness to co-invest, the results can be graphed. The matrix in Figure 2.4 can help managers to evaluate the criteria for key account selection, and it shows three elements through its axes and the size of the circles:

- *Customer attractiveness*: the scores for this dimension are shown in the vertical axis, on a scale from 1 to 10.

- *Supplier's competitive position*: the scores for this dimension are revealed in the horizontal axis, on a scale from 1 to 10.

- *Customer willingness to co-invest*: this dimension is captured through the size of each circle representing a customer in the matrix. Larger circles denote higher willingness to co-invest.

In the example presented in Figure 2.4 we find that the best candidates to obtain a 'key account' status are customers B and F. Customer B has high levels of both customer attractiveness and supplier's competitive position; however, it has a low

Figure 2.4 Evaluating the criteria for key account selection

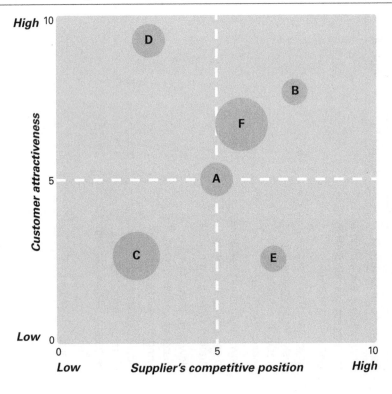

willingness to co-invest. Customer F, on the other hand, has a slightly lower score in customer attractiveness than customer B, and a more noteworthy lower score in supplier's competitive position; nevertheless, customer F has a high willingness to co-invest. Senior management in the supplier company can use this analysis to make a more informed decision on key account selection.

To effectively implement this tool, it is recommended that cross-functional teams in the supplier company discuss the selection criteria and the evaluation of each customer candidate. In addition, people from different hierarchical levels should also be involved: senior managers, middle managers, as well as the lower-level and operational staff who provide administrative support to customers. This 720-degree approach will contribute to a more comprehensive and realistic assessment. An interview with Louise Collins, Managing Director at Louise Collins Associates Limited, revealed interesting insights with respect to this aspect of key account selection.

Inputs of key account selection

'I think the issue is, it cannot just be done in a singular fashion. It's got to be done in a cross-functional fashion, where you've got that cross-functional challenge and you all sit down around the table and really thrash it out and say well ok, you know, you think that this account should be selected on the basis of these three criteria because whatever... Let's really discuss it and fine tune it. I think that's often something you simply give to key account teams; it's a given that these are your key accounts and therefore off you go! I think that needs to be done much more cross-functionally with good debate, challenge and discussion.

'I think we should improve the process of key account selection, because it is being done very much individually, or by a couple of people together, saying "how do we think this customer plays out?" We never go down to the point as a team of saying "this is definitely a key account, the weight of this criterion is 35 per cent...". That makes me feel arbitrary.'

To support this process, it is advised that some external perspective is brought into the analysis. By doing so, the supplier may prevent a potential lack of industry or market information, and reduce a possible 'internal' bias in the evaluation. In particular, it might be difficult to have an objective view of the supplier's competitive position with respect to each customer; hence, the use of objective data (eg industry reports, customer insights) and external advisors (eg industry consultants) in the process is highly recommended.

Key account selection can be challenging for suppliers facing highly heterogeneous markets, particularly those operating globally. The following quote from the Director of KAM Excellence at a global company, when asked about their key account selection procedure, illustrates this point. Interestingly, in addition to the geographic complexities of selling globally, there is an element related to organizational culture: in this case the selection of key accounts is done locally, and each market head has the freedom to choose key accounts and to define the selection criteria.

'Ah that's a fabulous question. So the answer specifically is no, because the challenge in that is far too great for me to even contemplate, in the sense that there's 54 European markets in which I operate. If I went to those markets' country managers and told them how to select their key accounts, it would not really be appropriate because they have the knowledge of the market; all I can do is create the awareness that they need to do it effectively and well.' (Geoff Quinn, Director of the Key Account Management Centre of Excellence, Pfizer Global Marketing.)

The KAM investment

Once the key accounts have been selected, the supplier has to determine the kind and amount of investment with respect to:

- each key account relationship;
- the overall KAM programme.

Investing in specific key account relationships

In the previous section we presented a framework for selecting key accounts. Let us assume, from the example provided, that the supplier decides to designate customers B and F as key accounts. Now the company needs to ask: *What specific investment do we need to make in each key account relationship?*

To respond to this question, the supplier needs to conduct a thorough analysis of each customer and project the expected joint business initiatives for the future. Once this plan is agreed internally (the KAM team, senior management, and all other relevant stakeholders), the supplier should discuss it with the customer and negotiate the conditions and the terms of the business relationship.

The following are possible types of KAM investments:

- *Organizational structure*: the allocation and recruitment of dedicated personnel to the key account. For example:
  - KAMgr, dedicated exclusively to this customer;
  - cross-functional team, to look after this customer and support the KAMgr;
  - senior manager as the executive sponsor of the customer to establish top-to-top contact and support the KAMgr and the KAM team.
- *People development*: the training and skills development of the personnel involved in managing the key account relationship. For example:
  - coaching programme for the KAMgr, to support his/her activities in front of people from various hierarchical levels in both the supplier and the customer;
  - training programme on customer-centricity for members of the KAM team coming from different functional areas;
  - technical training on the customer's business for all people involved in dealing with this relationship.
- *Solution to customer*: the adaptation of the offering to the customer in a way that is different from that given to customers that do not get the 'key account' status. For example:
  - designing tailored products and services for this customer;
  - offering special pricing and ordering conditions;
  - adopting new technologies to capture the needs of this customer;
  - using additional communication channels to support the day-to-day interaction with this account;
  - designing a unique plan for the delivery of products.
- *Other elements*: additional aspects that constitute an investment in the relationship. For example:
  - relocating a supplier's warehouse, to be closer to the customer;
  - launching a fidelity programme, to increase the instances of socialization with people from the key account;
  - conducting market research, to better understand the customer's business and market trends.

Table 2.4 provides a template that can be used by supplier companies to establish and communicate the KAM investments in each customer relationship. The template also indicates other aspects that are important for the implementation of this plan, such as the amount (£, $) of the investment, the timing for making it, and the request to be made to the customer.

Table 2.4   KAM investment in each key account relationship

Category	Description	Amount (£, $)	Timing	Request to customer

Investing in the overall KAM programme

Together with making specific investments in each KAM relationship, suppliers may need to develop initiatives that will support the KAM programme across all key accounts. This is what we refer as investing in the overall KAM programme, for example:

- hiring a consulting company to develop a customer-centric culture;
- developing a new system to manage customer complaints;
- reorganizing the layout of the offices to promote cooperation among functional units;
- redefining the performance metrics of the business to incorporate new customer-related indicators.

Conclusion

This chapter intends to guide supplier companies and managers in two major decisions. First, we provide some guidance on the decision about whether the company should adopt KAM as a strategic approach or not. Second, we propose a framework on how to select key accounts, based on their attractiveness, the supplier's competitive position, and the customers' willingness to co-invest in the relationship.

Questions for managers

- If we currently do not have a formal KAM programme, should we adopt one?
- How many key accounts can we realistically have?
- What are the specific investments that we need to make with customers that receive the 'key account' status?
- Which factors should we use to evaluate customer attractiveness?
- Which factors should we consider to assess our competitive position with each customer candidate to become a key account?
- Are we willing to establish a KAM programme with a customer that does not see us as a key supplier?
- Are there any investments that we will need to make for the overall KAM programme?

References

[1] Ivens, S and Pardo, C (2008) Key-account-management in business markets: an empirical test of common assumptions, *Journal of Business & Industrial Marketing*, **23** (5), 301–10.

[2] Koch, R (2017) *The 80/20 Principle: The secret of achieving more with less*, Nicholas Brealey Publishing, Boston MA.

[3] Paesbrugghe, B et al (2017) Purchasing-driven sales: matching sales strategies to the evolution of the purchasing function, *Industrial Marketing Management*, 62, pp 171–84.

[4] Grant, R (1991) The resource-based theory of competitive advantage: implications for strategy formulation, *California Management Review*, 33 (3), pp 114–35.

[5] Barney, J B and Hesterly, W S (2010) VRIO framework, *Strategic Management and Competitive Advantage*, pp 68–86.

[6] Coyne, K (2013) Enduring ideas: the GE-McKinsey nine-box matrix, *McKinsey* [online] https://www.mckinsey.com/business-functions/strategy-and-corporate-finance/our-insights/enduring-ideas-the-ge-and-mckinsey-nine-box-matrix

[7] Holt, S and Guesalaga, R (2016) Key account selection: identifying customer attractiveness criteria, *Cranfield KAM Best Practice Research Club* report (September), pp 1–59.

[8] Ryals, L and Davies, I (2013) Where's the strategic intent in key account relationships? *Journal of Business & Industrial Marketing*, **28** (2), pp 111–24.

[9] Guesalaga, R et al (2016) The future of key account management, *Cranfield KAM Best Practice Research Club* report (March), pp 1–16.

Building customer understanding and value planning 03

'Planning is an unnatural process; it is much more fun to do something. And the nicest thing about not planning is that failure comes as a complete surprise rather than being preceded by a period of worry and depression.'

SIR JOHN HARVEY JONES

How do we build an in-depth understanding of the customer's world and then translate this into future strategies that co-create value for both parties in the relationship?

Overview

This chapter looks at the importance of building an in-depth understanding of all aspects of a strategic customer's world and their future strategic direction. It is a fundamental part of the key account manager's role to develop an in-depth knowledge and understanding of their key account [1]. It is also a fundamental part of the role to develop a strategic account plan for a key account that has on average a three-year time horizon. In the past, key account planning was mainly driven by what the supplier wanted to achieve with a key account. Increasingly, however, organizations are moving to a customer-led planning approach that starts with understanding the customer's world first before then aligning the supplier's future strategies with the key account's strategies, in order to ultimately create competitive advantage and value for both parties. This chapter explores how to build an in-depth understanding of the customer's world and create value for both parties through taking a value planning approach to key account plans.

Building an in-depth understanding of the customer's world

Many business-to-business organizations and many key account managers (KAMgrs), when asked the question 'how well do you understand the world your customer is in?', will generally respond that they know them well. However, anecdotal evidence and our research over the years have shown that the opposite is normally the case, and many do not understand their customers in sufficient depth. It is also evident that even where attempts have been made to research and analyse customers, many organizations do not take a systematic approach to gathering the information or capturing it in a useful way. This is in contrast with what has been happening in the business-to-consumer world, where customer insight has become a flourishing business with a vast array of external consultancies and internal specialists all focused on this hot topic. Indeed, much has been written in the business-to-consumer context about how important customer/consumer insight is for key areas like new product development, research and innovation, market segmentation, marketing and advertising, and customer retention and loyalty.

Customer insight is about getting beyond the figures, facts and statistics that have traditionally driven marketing decisions and planning to really understanding the 'DNA' of consumers in terms of what really drives their decisions to purchase, or to remain loyal to a brand. By applying this approach, companies are trying to bring the consumer metaphorically, if not actually, into the boardroom. Companies usually combine a number of different channels in combination in order to collect their insight, including surveys, interviews, focus groups and loyalty cards. They are also increasingly using their online presence and other social media sites not only to test out ideas and gather insights on consumer behaviours and buying decisions but also to create personal experiences and products and services that are targeted directly to individuals.

The business-to-business world is lagging somewhat behind the consumer world in terms of gaining and managing customer insight. One challenge in business-to-business is that each key account is very different even if they are in the same or a similar industry sector, so gaining customer insight has to be approached on a case-by-case basis and even if there are resources to help the KAMgr it is still their responsibility to undertake the overall analysis. Another issue is how to really get into the DNA of what can be a highly complex, multi-function, multi-level relationship which generally has a number of people involved in the decision-making process who may also have different drivers in terms of their decisions. A further issue is that customers can be pan-geographic or even global, which presents further complexity for KAMgrs when trying to build up a coherent picture of the customer.

So how can business-to-business organizations improve their customer insight by drawing on some lessons from the business-to-consumer domain in order to try to build a much better and in-depth understanding of their customer's world?

We need to start by asking some questions:

- What do we need to do to better understand our customer's world?
- What aspects of the customer's world should we focus on?
- Where do we start?
- What questions do we need to ask?
- Where can I find the answers?
- How and where can I capture it?

Research vignette

Research undertaken at Cranfield [2] with KAM practitioners revealed that the least well executed part of many companies' key account plans was that relating to understanding the customer's world and their future strategies.

In order to help answer the first three questions and to provide an analysis framework, Holt (2003, updated 2016) developed the Wheel of Customer Understanding, shown in Figure 3.1 [3].

The nine key areas of customer understanding outlined in Figure 3.1 are based on research carried out with a number of different companies and their customers by Holt initially in 2003 and then revisited and updated in 2016 through interviews and feedback with delegates on Cranfield's Key Account Management Best Practice Open Programme. Initially interviews were carried out with over 50 people who were involved in strategic customer/supplier relationships. The important factor in the research was that half of those interviewed were the customers or clients, who themselves had identified that the most competent KAMgrs from their suppliers went out of their way to really understand the customer's business environment, opportunities and challenges. A senior partner in an international law firm supports this but also points out that in reality it is not always that easy: 'They must be the ones with the absolute understanding of the customer... this is easy to say but extremely difficult in practice.' The KAMgrs were then seen as being more effective at aligning the supplier's offering with the future strategic aims of the customer.

Figure 3.1   The Wheel of Customer Understanding [3]

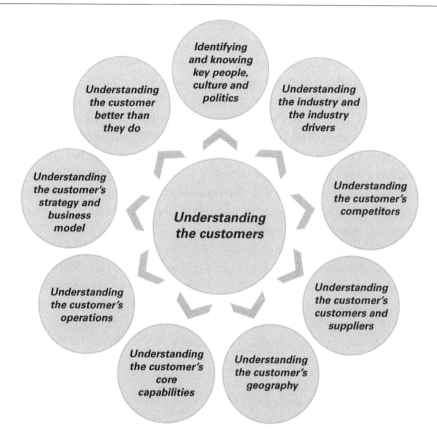

Voice of the practitioner

'The most successful key account managers for us are those who have really taken the trouble to understand our business, our challenges and even what is driving our customers. They are able to have a discussion with me about how they can help me with my competitive advantage and joint opportunities for both of us. This is miles away from the usual sell sell sell approach I get from other suppliers.' (Senior director, global engineering company.)

The next section looks at the nine components of the Wheel of Customer Understanding in more depth.

The components of the Wheel of Customer Understanding

Building up a picture of the customer using the nine components shown in Figure 3.1 is a logical approach to analysing the customer. Ideally, a KAMgr should start on the right-hand side of the Wheel by looking at the bigger picture or macro-environment, through looking at the *industry drivers* of the customer's industry They would then move on to analysing the micro-environment of the customer's competitor environment through looking at the *customer's competitors* and then the *customer's customers and suppliers*. This part of the analysis is largely focused on those aspects that are external to the customer and over which the customer has least control. However, there will be some things identified in the analysis that will be impacting the customer's business now and in the future for which they will have to devise strategies as to how they are going to respond in order to proactively manage these external pressures and opportunities.

The other six components are largely about those aspects that are internal to the customer and over which the customer has more direct control in terms of future goals and strategy. These are about building an understanding of the *customer's geography*, the *customer's core capabilities*, the *customer's operations*, the *customer's strategy and business model, understanding the customer better than they do* and finally the *key people, culture and politics*. Figure 3.2 represents the customer's world.

Figure 3.2   The customer's world

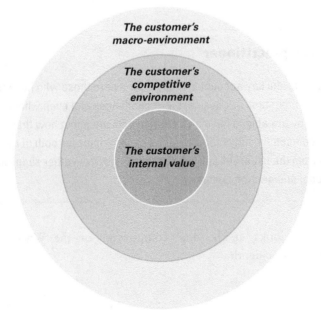

The nine key components of the Wheel are further explained below.

Step 1: Understanding the industry and industry drivers

This is not about just having an in-depth knowledge of the customer's industry, but also about identifying the wider competitive activities, emerging technologies, political pressures and changes going on in the industry and the economy; these are factors that can or could in the future impact either positively or negatively on the customer's business, over which they have little control.

Step 2: Understanding the customer's competitors

This is about analysing the customer's competitive environment and the impact on the customer of different types of competitor, both now and in the future. The competitors broadly fall into three categories:

1 Existing key competitors: these are industry competitors who are established in the market or industry and who are often offering broadly similar products, services or solutions. These are generally visible to all players in the market and should be the easiest to research.

2 New and emerging competitors: these are competitors coming in to the market or industry who may again be offering broadly similar products, services or solutions. However, they may also be taking a fresh and different approach to the market or bringing some new innovations including innovative ways of reaching different market segments. These are harder to research as there is obviously less available information on them.

3 Disruptive competitors: these are competitors whose products, services or solutions offer a completely alternative offering that in effect is a replacement for existing offerings. These can be 'black swans' and some industries have been completely obliterated by not noticing these replacement offerings until they have started to adversely affect and disrupt the existing market or industry.

It is also about understanding the customer's position in their market.

Step 3: Understanding the customer's customers and suppliers

This is about gaining an insight into what is driving the customer's customers, and also what is happening within their supply chains or networks. What pressures are the customer's customer putting on the supply chain and what changes might be happening in their world that will drive their behaviours in the future? It is the same with understanding future changes that might occur in the customer's supply chain.

Understanding the customer's customers

A leading UK financial services (FS) company had started to get complaints from their key accounts, who were either large IFA networks or partners like large retailers and building societies, about the complexity of their financial products and services. They felt the products were confusing for their customers (consumers and small businesses) and therefore many were discouraged from purchasing them. The innovation of the FS company had always been to develop new products and services and then to 'push' them onto the market. So with the help of their key accounts the FS company decided to do some direct research with their customer's customers, with the result that their next generation of products and services was completely different and far more attuned to the needs and preferences of the customer's customers. It also substantially differentiated their offerings from those of their competitors, which led to a huge increase for their business, but more importantly, for their key accounts. Customer satisfaction also rose highly among the customer's customers: a win all round!

Step 4: Understanding the customer's geography

This can be expressed, in the simplest terms, as knowing all the locations and countries the customer is operating in, and the relationships between them. Which countries are the power bases and where are the key decision makers located? However, beyond simple geography, it is also about, for example, having a knowledge of different political and economic situations in different locations, countries or regions and understanding how the customer handles business in different parts of the world.

Step 5: Understanding the customer's core capabilities

This is about really understanding what the customer's core capabilities or core competencies are, particularly in order to understand and identify how the supplier organization could match and enhance the customer's capabilities. Also identifying what are NOT the customer's core capabilities might identify areas they could outsource.

Step 6: Understanding the customer's operations

This is about knowing the customer's day-to-day operations and services in depth, again to identify where they have some strengths and where they may have some challenges.

Step 7: Understanding the customer's strategy and business model

This is a critical component which is about, for example, understanding the customer's business principles, business model, and future strategy and strategic direction. Having this 'big picture' and holistic view of the customer's strategy was seen as the most important factor among the original research respondents but was also the one of the nine components that KAMgrs felt they understood least well with regard to their key accounts.

Step 8: Understanding the customer better than they do

This was an unusual finding from the original research and was about the supplier's KAMgrs often being in a position to know and understand the customer's organization more broadly than the customer contact in the key account did. Some customers welcomed it as a way in which the KAMgr could add considerable value because they often had access to parts of the customer's organization that the customer contact didn't have. A note of caution, however: not all key accounts will be easy with this notion and some may see it as a threat. Customers also talked about the need for the KAMgr to put themselves in their shoes and to start thinking like them.

Step 9: Identifying and understanding key people, culture and politics

This is about knowing all the key people involved in the relationship in the customer's organization. It is not just about knowing who they are in terms of their position and job responsibility, it's also about identifying their personal drivers and 'knowing what makes them tick'. This is about the need to understand what a key contact in the key account's organization wants to achieve in terms of:

- their organizational objectives;
- their particular role/job objectives;
- their own personal agenda;
- their position and role(s) in the decision-making structure and their relative power and influence on the relationship vis-à-vis others.

Understanding the culture and politics of the customer's organization and the politics of the individual contacts is also important, as well as understanding the decision-making structure and power bases.

So it is a big task for a KAMgr to build up this picture of the customer's world. But what are some of the key advantages of building up this in-depth understanding and knowledge? Here is a summary of 10 of the advantages that have emerged from our research:

1 to provide a firm foundation for strategic customer-led key account planning;

2 to be able to demonstrate to the key account that you understand their world (and that you have taken the care and trouble to do so!);

3 to help the KAMgr to have more strategic and effective conversations with their key account, especially with senior people and the 'c' suite;

4 to identify current and future opportunities and challenges for the customer;

5 to identify current and future opportunities and challenges for your own organization;

6 to enable a proactive approach to the relationship with the key account rather than a reactive one;

7 to identify areas for co-creating value and collaboration with the key account;

8 to identify the knowledge and understanding gaps and plan on how to fill them;

9 to act as a basis for discussion and sense-checking with the customer and to facilitate joint future planning;

10 to become, as the KAMgr, the 'knowledge expert' about the customer.

The next section looks at the knowledge sources for KAMgrs in building up their customer insight.

Mini case: professional services

A major law firm decided to implement key client management but many of their key client partners were either sceptical or nervous about talking to individuals within the client who were senior people from the wider business rather than people from the client's internal legal team. A few partners did, however, decide they would be willing to try to have some business conversations with key people in the client and prepared themselves by carrying out a Wheel of *Client* Understanding analysis. The feedback they got from the clients was far more positive than they thought it would be, with one client, a major retailer, saying they 'had never had a lawyer express an interest in their business before'. The law firm went on to establish itself as a leader in strategic client management within the legal profession.

Tools and resources to build business-to-business customer insight

In order to build customer insight in a key account there are a number of tools and resources available to the KAMgr. Some of these will be obvious but some might be less so.

Strategy tools

KAMgrs can use the same strategy tools that many organizations use to analyse their world, and which help them to formulate their own future strategy. These can also be applied when analysing key accounts. These are tools such as PESTEL, competitive analysis, internal strengths and weaknesses analysis and SWOT analysis. There are also stakeholder and relationship mapping tools. These tools are explained in more detail later in this chapter.

Desk research

There is a lot of information available that KAMgrs can access to enable them to better understand their key accounts, including:

- the annual reports and accounts of the key account;
- analyst reports on the industry and competitors (these often contain PESTEL analyses, competitive analyses and SWOT analyses);
- online information resources (usually these require a subscription for access);
- the internet and company websites;
- trade organization websites and publications;
- newspaper reports and articles.

Personal research

The KAMgr needs to take on the role of a market researcher and do their own research both within the key account and within their own organization. They need to use their networks in the overall relationship to identify those people on both sides of the relationship who they need to effectively 'interview' to get insights across many of the nine components of the Wheel of Customer Understanding.

Other sources

Other sources of information can be company or industry events such as open days, conferences and award ceremonies.

Figure 3.3 shows the key tools and resources for each component of the Wheel of Customer Understanding.

Testing your understanding of the customer's world

One easy way to test your knowledge of the customer's world is to undertake a knowledge gap assessment (see Table 3.1) and score yourself as honestly as you can, scoring from 1–5, where:

Figure 3.3 The key tools and resources for completing a customer analysis

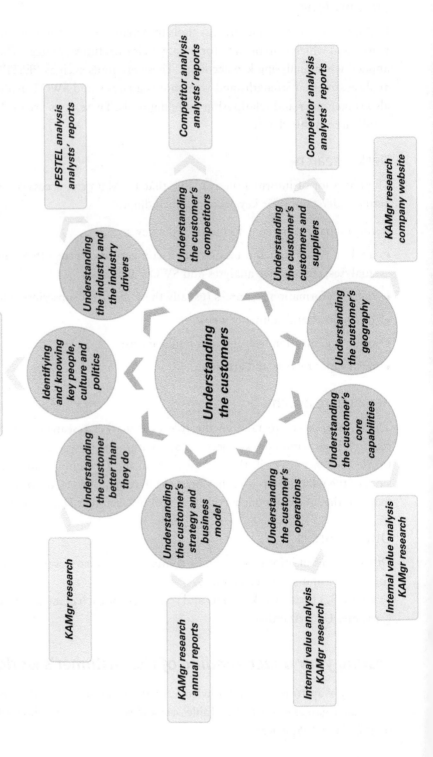

Knowledge Level 1: zero knowledge on this component.

Knowledge Level 2: some knowledge of this component.

Knowledge Level 3: average knowledge of this component.

Knowledge Level 4: good knowledge of this component.

Knowledge Level 5: excellent knowledge of this component.

You can also give yourself a score for where you would like to be in the future. It is not necessarily the case that you need to be at Level 5 across all the nine components; they won't be the same across all key accounts either. Each key account must be scored separately and in the appropriate way for that account. Once you have undertaken the knowledge gap assessment, you will be able to plan some strategies for how to plug the gaps (see Table 3.2).

The final test of how well a KAMgr really understands their customer's world is how well and to what extent the questions in Table 3.3 can be answered.

Having carried out a thorough analysis of the customer's world, the key account manager needs to capture and present the outputs of the analysis in a structured way. The vehicle for this is the key account plan.

Table 3.1 Testing your understanding of the customer's world

Component	Score now 1–5	Score future 1–5
Understanding the industry and industry drivers		
Understanding the customer's competitors		
Understanding the customer's customers and suppliers		
Understanding the customer's geography		
Understanding the customer's core capabilities		
Understanding the customer's operations		
Understanding the customer's strategy and business model		
Understanding the customer better than they do		
Identifying and knowing the key people, culture and politics		

Table 3.2   Planning how to 'plug' the knowledge gaps identified in the knowledge gap analysis

What I need to find out	What are my customer insight sources or resources?
1	
2	
3	
4	
5	
6	

Table 3.3   Questions to answer to demonstrate an in-depth understanding of a key account

Dimension	Key questions
Understanding the industry and industry drivers	• What are the PESTEL factors that are affecting my customer's industry? • Do I understand the industry they are in? Eg is it growing? Contracting? Consolidating? Outsourcing? Commoditizing?
Understanding the customer's competitors	• Who are my customer's key competitors? • Do I understand their competitive environment? • Do I know how my customer is responding to this environment and their challenges and issues?
Understanding the customer's customers and suppliers	• Who are my customer's customers? Eg what sectors/segments/geography are they in? • What is driving them/keeping them awake at night? • Who are the key players in the customer's supply chain? What is driving them?
Understanding the customer's geography	• What is the geographical scope of the customer's business? • How are they structured eg global, regional, country, local?

(continued)

Table 3.3   (*Continued*)

Dimension	Key questions
Understanding the customer's core capabilities	• What are the customer's core capabilities? • Where are the strengths and weaknesses in their core capabilities? • What are their key differentiators from their competition?
Understanding the customer's operations	• What are my customer's key operations? • Where are the strengths and weaknesses in their operations?
Understanding the customer's strategy and business model	• What are the key elements of the customer's business strategy for the next x years? • What are the customer's key objectives for the next x years? • Are there likely to be changes in management/focus/core capabilities etc? • Will they be growing, outsourcing, contracting, divesting etc?
Understanding the key people , culture and politics	• Who are the key decision makers with the customer? • What is driving them/keeping them awake at night? • What are the politics/power dynamics in the customer's organization?

Key account planning

'If a supplier has aspirations for building a relationship with a customer over time, then some kind of plan setting out a strategy for how this is to be achieved will be necessary' [4]. The structure of most key account plans is similar to the structure of many strategic marketing plans, with the obvious difference being that the key account plan is purely focused on one specific customer rather than on a segment of customers or the whole market.

Our research [2] has shown that key account planning is an important factor in the successful implementation of KAM. A study undertaken with members of the Cranfield Key Account Management Best Practice Club revealed that if a company successfully applied the elements, tools and practices of key account planning, then they also had a significantly higher chance of achieving a successful KAM implementation. This research further reinforced that of other researchers [5], who also found that the longer companies had been implementing KAM, the more importance they attached to key account planning. However, the Cranfield research also revealed that none of the organizations in the club scored their KAM plans very highly and many agreed that the most poorly completed part of the plan was that relating to their understanding of the customer's world. This is in spite of articles [6] and a seminal book [4] on key account planning.

The Value Planning Framework we use for key account planning starts with understanding the customer's world.

The Value Planning Framework

The Value Planning Framework (see Figure 3.4) was first presented by Davies and Holt in 2013 [7] and has its foundation in the KAM planning process developed by Ryals and McDonald [4]. However, it has been advanced and updated and now also includes customer-led value proposition development within the planning process.

The framework divides the planning process into five key sections:

- *Value insights:* this part of the process is all about analysing and understanding the customer's world. This is a critical factor for successful key account management (KAM).

- *Value opportunities:* having gained as much customer insight as we can, this part of the process looks at identifying the supplier's opportunities, responses and options in relation to the customer.

- *Value proposition:* the next step is for the value propositions for that customer to be created and developed. These need to be customer-led and focused on how we are creating value for the customer in terms of helping them to achieve their business goals rather than saying how wonderful our products or services are.

- *Value delivery:* this is about how we are going to deliver the value for the customer and how we are going to measure the success of the value creation both for the customer and for us.

- *Executive summary:* this is the last step in the planning process and is often a neglected and poorly executed part of the plan. However, as it is the vehicle by which a KAMgr gains senior management buy-in and support, it needs to be well presented.

Figure 3.4 The Value Planning Framework [7]

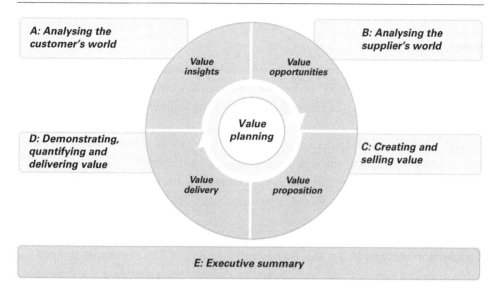

Figure 3.5 The Value Planning Toolkit [7]

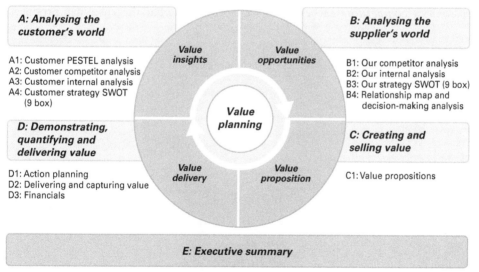

E1: Executive summary – overview

The Value Planning Toolkit

The Value Planning Toolkit (Figure 3.5) has a range of tools and techniques that enable a KAMgr to build a strategic key account plan for a key customer. Some of the tools will be familiar as strategy and marketing tools but they are linked together in a way that provides a logical flow for analysis of the customer and the subsequent plans and actions identified by the supplier.

Value insights

The best way to analyse the customer's business environment is to use the tools as shown in the 'value insights' section of Figure 3.5. This toolkit builds towards a customer 9-box SWOT (see Figure 3.9) and uses the following tools.

PESTEL analysis (A.1) This framework helps us to look at the customer's external macro-environment through understanding the *Political, Economic, Social, Technological, Environmental* and *Legal* changes that might impact our customer either now or in the future. We use it to identify the customer's future opportunities and threats (see Figure 3.6).

Competitor analysis (A.2) This framework (see Figure 3.7) enables us to examine the customer's external micro-environment through understanding the customer's competitive environment. This analysis looks at the future impact on the customer of changes to their existing competitors, any likely new competitors into the market, and any likely disruptive competitors (see also the section on *Understanding the customer's competitors* earlier in this chapter) for what the customer produces,

Figure 3.6　The six key topics of a PESTEL analysis

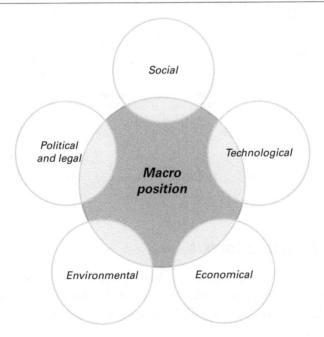

Figure 3.7   Competitor analysis model

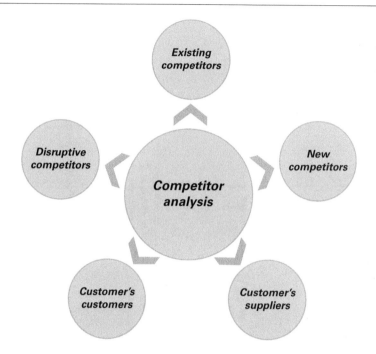

changes in the customer's supplier base and changes in the customer's customers. Again, we use it to identify the customer's future opportunities and threats.

Internal value analysis (A.3) This framework (see Figure 3.8) is used to look at the internal activities of a key account and acts as a checklist for identifying all the key activities undertaken by the customer that ultimately add value for their customers; it also identifies the customer's key support activities that are needed to run the business. We use the framework to identify the customer's key strengths and weaknesses in both the key activities and the support activities. Figure 3.8 shows an example of a manufacturing company. You need to identify all your key account's activities and then look at where their key strengths and weaknesses are internally.

9-box SWOT (A.4) Finally we use the 9-box SWOT analysis (see Figure 3.9) to put ourselves in the customer's shoes and think about the strategies that we think the customer should be pursuing if we were them. We use a 9-box SWOT as opposed to a 4-box SWOT, as this actively drives out top-level strategies and actions that the 4-box SWOT doesn't cover. Using the output from the three tools above we complete the SWOT by identifying:

Figure 3.8 The internal value analysis of a key account: identifying the customer's strengths and weaknesses

KEY ACTIVITY

Procurement and supply chain management

Manufacturing /research and development

Logistics and transport

Marketing and sales

Technical and after-sales support

SUPPORT ACTIVITY

Senior management

Strategic business planning

Human resources management

Information systems and processes

Company infrastructure

Internal value analysis: where are the customer's key strengths and weaknesses?

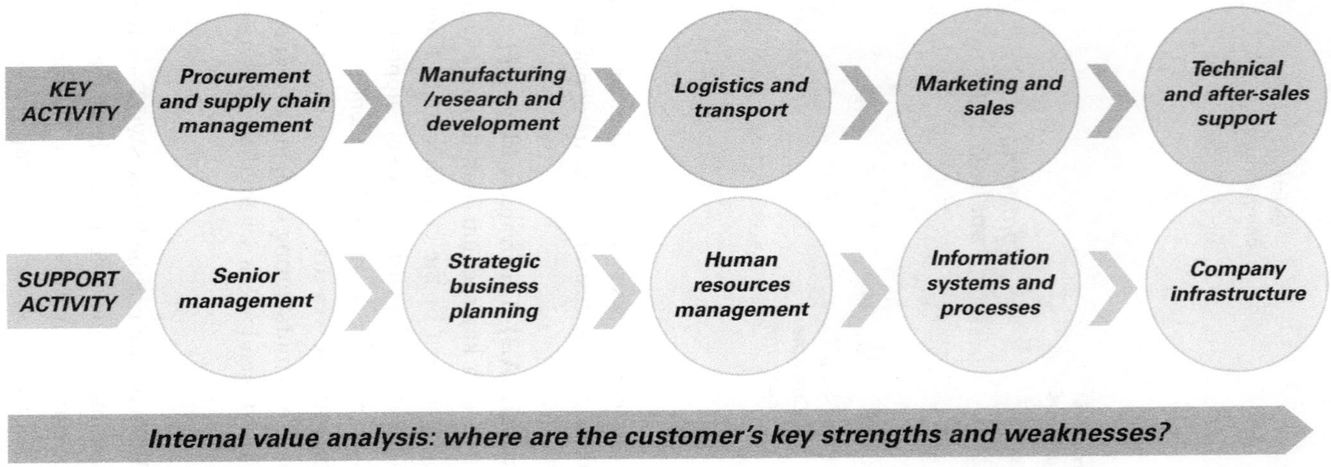

Figure 3.9   9-box SWOT

Customer's objectives	Key strengths	Key weaknesses
• • • •	S1 S2 S3	W1 W2 W3
Key opportunities O1 O2 O3	**Offensive strategies**	**Conversion strategies**
Key threats T1 T2 T3	**Utilization strategies**	**Defensive strategies**

- *Offensive strategies:* matching the customer's strengths with their opportunities. Does the customer have a key strength they can use to attack an opportunity? If so, what should they do?

- *Defensive strategies:* matching the customer's weaknesses and threats. Does the customer have a weakness that could make a threat even worse? If so, what can they do to lessen the impact of the situation on their business?

- *Conversion strategies:* matching the customer's weaknesses and opportunities. Does the customer have a weakness that could stop them from attacking an opportunity? If so, how can they convert the weakness to being neutral or even into a strength?

- *Utilization strategies:* matching the customer's strengths and threats. Does the customer have a strength they can utilize to lessen a threat? If so, what should they do?

Figure 3.10 shows the roadmap for how the tools fit together for the value insights analysis.

Figure 3.10 Linking the analysis tools to the 9-box SWOT

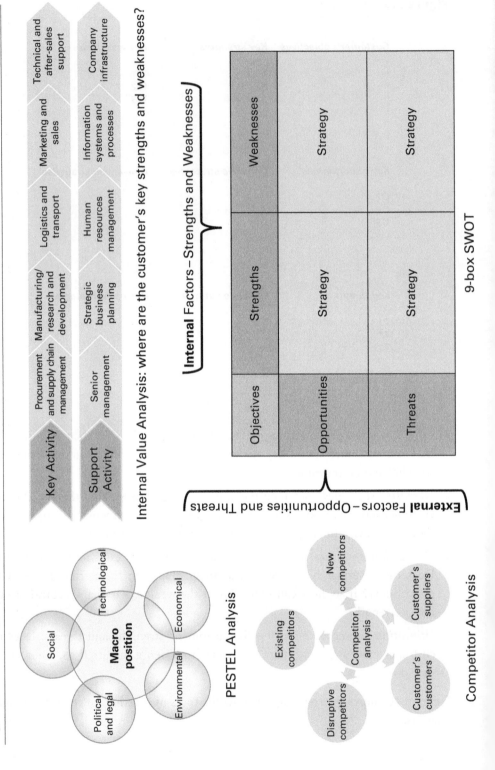

Internal Value Analysis: where are the customer's key strengths and weaknesses?

Internal Factors – Strengths and Weaknesses

9-box SWOT

External Factors – Opportunities and Threats

PESTEL Analysis

Competitor Analysis

Having built up our customer understanding and identified the customer's strategies we can then look at our opportunities, responses and options in relation to the customer.

Value opportunities

Using some of the same analysis tools we can now build our own SWOT and set of strategies and objectives that we will pursue with the customer and which form the basis of our planning activities. We do this by using the following process.

Analyse the customer's SWOT First of all we need to study and analyse the customer's SWOT that we have completed, to look for our opportunities and threats. Where can you help them? Is there a weakness or a threat you can help them overcome? Have they got any possible strategies that could be a threat or opportunity for you?

Your competitor analyses (B1) This brings in YOUR competitors and competitive environment and also YOUR customers and suppliers. Again, you are looking for your opportunities and threats with your customer in relation to your competitive environment.

Your internal analysis (B2) You need to carry out this analysis to identify your key strengths and weaknesses in relation to the customer.

Your 9-box SWOT (B3) Now you can build your 9-box SWOT and the set of strategies that you are going to implement over the life of the plan.

The whole planning process to this point is represented in Figure 3.11.

Relationship mapping and decision-making analysis (B4) The final piece of analysis in the value opportunities section is to undertake a mapping of the key individuals on both sides of the relationship including assessing the level of the relationship in terms of how positive or negative it is and the importance of the individual and their influence on the relationship. See also the section on *Identifying and understanding key people, culture and politics* earlier in this chapter and Chapter 4.

Having identified the objectives and strategies that we want to take forward with the customer we can then build our value propositions for them.

Figure 3.11 The roadmap for the key account planning process

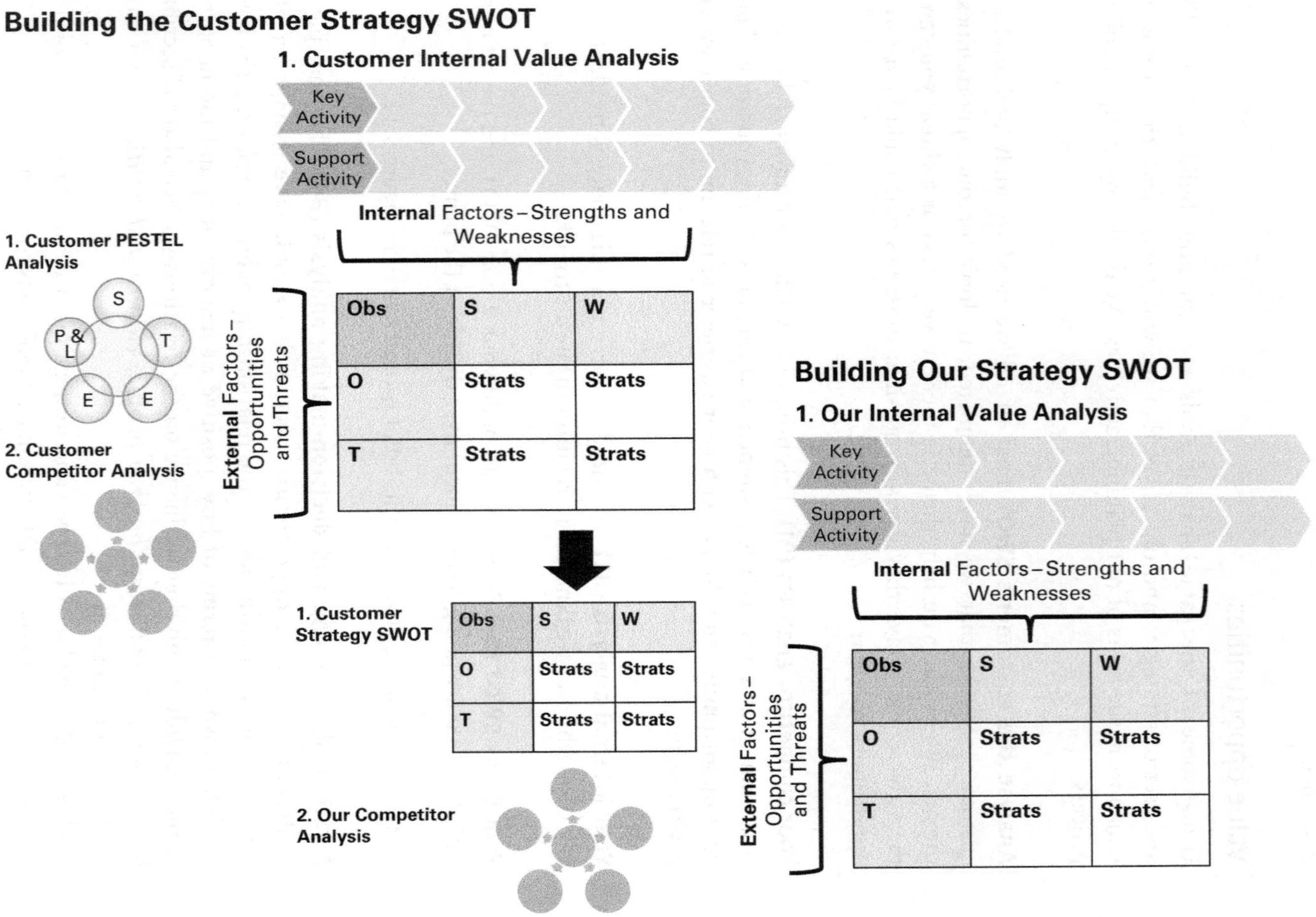

Building the Customer Strategy SWOT

1. Customer Internal Value Analysis

Key Activity

Support Activity

Internal Factors – Strengths and Weaknesses

Obs	S	W
O	Strats	Strats
T	Strats	Strats

External Factors – Opportunities and Threats

1. Customer PESTEL Analysis

2. Customer Competitor Analysis

1. Customer Strategy SWOT

Obs	S	W
O	Strats	Strats
T	Strats	Strats

2. Our Competitor Analysis

Building Our Strategy SWOT

1. Our Internal Value Analysis

Key Activity

Support Activity

Internal Factors – Strengths and Weaknesses

Obs	S	W
O	Strats	Strats
T	Strats	Strats

External Factors – Opportunities and Threats

Value propositions

This is the third section on the Value Planning Framework (C.1). Creating powerful value propositions is becoming a critical part of the KAMgr's role and is a major component of a best-practice key account plan. For how to develop compelling value propositions please see Chapter 5.

Value delivery

The final part of the value planning process is *value delivery*; this is all about how we are going to deliver the value for the customer and how we are going to measure success both for the customer and for us. There are two main elements in this section:

Action planning (D.1) An implementation plan needs to be formulated for operationalizing the key account plan. The action plan that is developed for the customer must contain all the key activities to be undertaken by the supplier to deliver the value that has been promised. Some of these actions might be short-term or milestones to longer-term goals and strategies. Remember that the key account plan should be working to a three-year time horizon. The action plan, usually on a spreadsheet, needs to include columns as follows for each action or milestone that needs to be completed:

- the key actions;
- the owner(s) of each action;
- the other functions, divisions or teams that are involved for each action;
- the resources needed to complete the action;
- measures of progress as appropriate;
- the KPIs used to measure the completed action;
- the date the action is due to be completed;
- the date the action was completed.

The development of the right KPIs to measure all aspects of the plan are vital in ensuring the value is delivered as planned. There are a number of questions we can ask:

- How do I know if my KAM efforts are effective?
- How do I measure each action?
- How do I know if I am creating value for my customer?

- How do I measure my success?
- Do I need more than one KPI to measure an action or strategy?

In order to measure effectively we also need to look at metrics from the viewpoint of both the customer and the supplier, hence the inclusion of D.2 below in the plan. There are a wide variety of metrics that suppliers can use to measure the success of their value delivery, and there is more on metrics for KAM in Chapter 8.

Delivering and capturing value (D.2) This final part of the plan captures the value gained by you and your key account from the completion of the actions and the delivery of the overall strategies. You need to record the date the action or overall strategy was completed and the value that was obtained for both parties in the relationship.

Financials (D.3) Last but not least we need to make a projection of the financial outcomes of the plan. Usually this would be for a three-year time horizon.

Executive summary

The last part of the plan is the executive summary. As already stated above, this is often poorly presented and can often be too long. If the KAMgr wants to grab the attention of senior management then the executive summary needs to be focused. The best way to construct it is to confine it to one page using the four main section headings for the format:

- value insights;
- value opportunities;
- value propositions;
- value delivery.

How good is your key account plan?

So you have produced a three-year, forward-looking key account plan based on our Value Planning Framework. But how good is your plan? How do you measure up to best practice? The assessments in Tables 3.4 and 3.5 give you a template against which to judge your plan. Table 3.4 is about assessing the value insights part of your plan and Table 3.5 covers assessing the other three sections. There is also a last line in Table 3.5 that asks you to make an assessment of the overall plan.

Table 3.4 Assessing the value insights section of your key account plan

Plan element	5	4	3	2	1
Customer PESTEL	Comprehensive and effective use of tools. Deep understanding of customer's external macro-environment.	Significant and effective use of tools. Illustrates main points of customer's external macro-environment.	Some use of tools. Elucidates key issues facing customer in their external macro-environment.	Little use of tools. Weak understanding of the customer's external macro-environment.	Little or no use of tools. Poor understanding of the customer's external macro-environment.
Customer competitor analysis	Comprehensive and effective use of tools. Deep understanding of customer's external micro-environment.	Significant and effective use of tools. Illustrates main points of customer's external micro-environment.	Some use of tools. Elucidates key issues facing customer in their external micro-environment.	Little use of tools. Weak understanding of the customer's external micro-environment.	Little or no use of tools. Poor understanding of the customer's external micro-environment.
Customer internal value analysis	Excellent and coherent analysis. Deep understanding of customer's strengths and weaknesses.	Good and coherent analysis. Good understanding of customer's strengths and weaknesses.	Adequate and somewhat coherent analysis. Adequate understanding of customer's strengths and weaknesses.	Poor and sometimes incoherent analysis. Poor understanding of customer's strengths and weaknesses.	Very poor analysis. Very poor understanding of customer's strengths and weaknesses.
Customer SWOT	Strategies clearly stated. Targeted. Consistent with objectives.	Strategies clearly stated. Targeted.	Strategies clearly stated.	Strategies simply stated.	Strategy not stated, and/or stated strategies are outcomes or actions.
Relationship mapping	Excellent and coherent analysis.	Good and coherent analysis.	Adequate and somewhat coherent analysis.	Poor and sometimes incoherent analysis.	Very poor analysis.

Table 3.5 Assessing the value opportunities, value propositions and value delivery sections of your key account plan

Plan element	5	4	3	2	1
Our competitor analysis	Comprehensive and effective use of tools. Deep understanding of our external micro-environment.	Significant and effective use of tools. Illustrates main points of our external micro-environment.	Some use of tools. Elucidates key issues facing us in our external micro-environment.	Little use of tools. Weak understanding of our external micro-environment.	Little or no use of tools. Poor understanding of our external micro-environment.
Our internal value analysis	Comprehensive and effective use of tools. Deep understanding of our internal strengths and weaknesses.	Significant and effective use of tools. Illustrates main points of our internal strengths and weaknesses.	Some use of tools. Elucidates key issues facing us in our internal strengths and weaknesses.	Little use of tools. Weak understanding of our internal strengths and weaknesses.	Little or no use of tools. Poor understanding of our internal strengths and weaknesses.
Our SWOT	Strategies clearly stated. Targeted. Added value for customer. Consistent with objectives.	Strategies clearly stated. Targeted. Added value for customer.	Strategies clearly stated.	Strategies simply stated.	Strategy not stated, and/or stated strategies are outcomes or actions.
Value propositions	Future focused, well defined and very compelling.	Well defined and compelling.	An understandable proposition but not that compelling.	A weak proposition that is not compelling.	Poorly expressed and not at all compelling.

Value delivery	12-month development plan. 3-year major action. Matched with strategy. Thorough measurement framework.	12-month development plan. 3-year major action. Matched with strategy. Focused measurement framework.	12-month development plan. Limited measurement framework.	Short-term action. Measurement is just sales targets.	Short-term action. No control mechanism.
Overall	Excellent understanding of KAM planning. Complete and coherent. Addresses key issues. Appropriate emphasis. Focused and clear. Creative.	Good understanding of KAM planning. Mostly complete, some visible coherence. Addresses key issues. Clear.	Acceptable understanding of KAM planning. Essential components. No significant contradictions or omissions.	Weak understanding of KAM planning. Significantly incomplete or incoherent.	Little or no understanding of KAM planning. Incomplete and/or includes major contradictions.

Ten pitfalls to avoid in key account planning

1 The key account plan is seen as belonging to the KAMgr.

2 The KAMgr does the plan on their own.

3 Senior management show no interest in the plans.

4 The plans are done once and never looked at again.

5 The plans are too short-term and transactional.

6 The plans are not regularly reviewed or updated.

7 The plans are all about the supplier with little demonstration of customer understanding.

8 The KAMgr keeps the plan 'close to their chest' and doesn't share it.

9 The planning process is seen as a box-filling exercise.

10 In the worst-case scenario, nobody owns it!

How do I keep my key account plans live?

One of the major challenges that many companies report is that of keeping key account plans *live* and current. How can such plans be used as *working documents* and *drivers of account strategy*, rather than just as a record of activity, or worse, as a repository of information that is completed and then never looked at again. Some ideas we have seen for keeping plans live are:

1 *Factoring in regular reviews* of the plan by the KAMgr and the key account team. These can be done monthly or quarterly and the plan should be updated as necessary with irrelevant stuff being deleted. If it is done only once a year then it is likely to become a victim of planning inertia.

2 *Use it as the team glue* for building the key account team. The plan needs to be developed with the team rather than solely by the KAMgr. This should result in better team buy-in and better responsibility for delivering the plan for the key account from the whole team.

3 *Make it accessible* through having the plan on, for example, an intranet system, or having a team room for the key account, where all those involved in the key account team can access the plan. This is especially important when key accounts are pan-geographic and the account team is spread across a number of countries across the globe.

4 *Presentations to senior management* are a powerful way of keeping plans live and strategic. It isn't just the fear factor for KAMgrs who do not wish to present an inadequate plan to their senior managers that makes this powerful, it is also important in order to keep senior managers up to date with developments in the customer portfolio. It also allows senior managers to see where they may need to leverage customer relationships, where they can help with future opportunities, and where they may need to take remedial action.

5 *Involving the customer* through a joint planning activity is a powerful way not only to develop the plan but also to keep it live. Again, regular reviews with the customer will keep it current and on track.

6 *Linking to the organization's business plans and planning cycle* is also a good way to ensure the key account plans are live and contributing to the overall future strategy of the business.

You don't need to do all of these things, but even one of them will increase your chances of keeping the key account plan alive and well and, most importantly, driving the strategic relationship forward.

CASE STUDY   Successful key account management with EMCOR UK

As a leading facilities management (FM) provider, EMCOR UK is responsible for some of the most regulated, secure and technically challenging workplace environments in the world. KAM is a critical factor in EMCOR UK's continued success and growth.

Background

An influx of new FM market entrants since 2005 has resulted in increased buyer choice along with commoditized FM procurement and buyer behaviour. Faced with these challenges, EMCOR UK recognized the need to move away from traditional FM approaches and place customers at the centre of their business strategy. This meant reshaping the business, developing a customer-centric business model, and creating a 'people first' culture. A deep understanding of the needs of customers is key to retention, and to achieving sustainable business growth. KAM offered a proven approach that clearly aligned with the core business strategy and facilitated the following goals:

- placing customers at the centre of the business;
- improving sales returns across each service capability;
- differentiating from the competition in a crowded market;

- engaging all employees in developing and delivering cutting-edge customer solutions;
- creating a networked best practice community across the business.

EMCOR UK approached Cranfield University to help build a KAM learning and development programme for customer-facing management and executives as well as KAMgrs. Over 200 employees have since gone through KAM training in less than 10 years.

As part of their strategic planning process, EMCOR UK developed a bespoke KAM Management System to support application, planning and implementation. This is aligned to the British Standard (BS11000:2010) framework for Collaborative Business Relationships – which is now an International Standard (ISO44001:2017).

To further support KAM, EMCOR UK invested in the development of advanced information management IT solutions, enabling account managers to make high-level, customer-focused recommendations and tactical decisions backed by high-quality data.

A company-wide approach

Account managers and a variety of functional support teams all take part in the programme; it is also a key element of succession planning. Integrating KAM across the entire workforce ensures seamless support for customers from account planning and objectives to action plans.

The fusion of people, knowledge, systems and process enables account managers to analyse multiple customer and competitor data sets, provide detailed insight, and make data-driven decisions based on a deep understanding of the customer.

> Key account management for us is all about understanding our customers and the challenges they face, so that we can build better service solutions that enhance the customer experience as well as addressing new market challenges.
>
> Christopher Kehoe, Group Executive Director, EMCOR UK

EMCOR UK's KAM development programme with Cranfield also covers the behaviours and competencies needed to deliver world-class KAM. Exchanging information freely, learning from each other, accepting change, responsibility, accountability and trust all complement the company's diversity, sustainability and collaboration agenda.

Insights Discovery; a psychometric tool based on the psychology of Carl Jung, is also built in. This helps individuals better understand themselves (emotional intelligence and self-awareness), understand others and how they like to communicate, and make the most of workplace relationships.

Building a rich and detailed understanding of customers

Account management teams use KAM to understand buyer and customer behaviour and motivations, develop a deeper understanding of wider markets and competition, and develop opportunities to innovate with new products, services and alternative approaches.

EMCOR UK utilize their growing customer knowledge portfolio to align operations and build resilience across the entire lifecycle of workplace services, capabilities and the extended supply chain. This actively connects the customer vision with EMCOR UK expertise, creating long-term sustainable benefits for all stakeholders.

> As our world becomes ever more complex, we are constantly refreshing and improving the learning and development experience for our KAM teams, dynamically responding to ever-changing global customer demands by building new solutions which support our collaboration, diversity and sustainability agenda.
>
> Christopher Kehoe, Group Executive Director, EMCOR UK

KAM is also used when engaging with new opportunities. The Business Development team utilize it as part of their opportunity evaluation approach with new prospects, thereby demonstrating an in-depth understanding of the customer's world and their future opportunities and challenges. Specifically showing how EMCOR UK can help achieve goals has proved to be a tender-winning strategy.

Measurement and control

Systematic review of account performance keeps the account management strategy alive. EMCOR UK uses its own KAM Maturity Measurement Tool (MMT) to align critical success factors against five pillars of maturity. As an ISO27001 certified business, the company can safely share customer knowledge and insight across its organization and extended supply chain. This allows teams to connect, rapidly solve customer problems and add value. Taking advantage of Big Data and analytics is increasingly critical to account managers too, enabling them to solve problems and use data to deliver new customer experiences.

EMCOR UK's Strategic Key Account Management Board sets direction and objectives, ensuring that collaboration systems and KAM are working effectively for all stakeholders, driving value, and facilitating continuous improvement and performance excellence.

EMCOR UK is on the Board of the Institute of Collaborative Working (ICW) and was instrumental in developing the new International Standard for Collaborative Working, ISO 44001:2017. It was the first FM Company to adopt the British Standard (BS11000) and was one of the original six companies worldwide to achieve certification to the new International Standard (ISO 44001) in April 2017.

> We used much of our strategic key account planning process and the performance metrics of our key accounts over a five-year period to demonstrate that we had met the requirements of ISO 44001. We also demonstrated how we integrate ISO's new high-level structure across all of our other standards, building business excellence and organizational resilience.
>
> Jeremy Campbell, Director of Business Development, EMCOR UK

How KAM has made a difference for EMCOR UK

- Everyone in the organization is involved in either planning or executing account objectives and actions.
- Senior board members are visible in the KAM planning and learning process.
- Account maturity and risk are measured.
- Integrated team rooms, standard templates, toolkits, support information and training applications all support KAM planning.
- Collaborative working is now a demonstrable core value.

  Key account management has been instrumental in helping EMCOR UK to identify and win new customers as well as providing the framework to deliver first-class customer service and operational excellence.

  Jeremy Campbell, Director of Business Development, EMCOR UK

Conclusion

This chapter has given an overview of how important it is for KAMgrs to really understand their customer's world and has provided some practical tools and techniques for building this understanding. We have also looked at the importance of having strategic key account plans that take a long-term approach to planning around the key account relationship. The Value Planning Framework provides a best-practice approach to key account planning and the accompanying toolkit provides a practical and logical framework for building a strategic account plan. We have also provided an assessment tool for judging the efficacy of your key account plan.

Questions for managers

- Do you feel you have appropriate processes in place to really develop in-depth understanding of your customer's world and their future strategic direction?
- Can you access the right resources to undertake the Wheel of Customer Understanding analysis?
- How well do you think you really understand your key account?
- What is the role of key account plans within your KAM programme?
- Do you have a planning template that is used by all KAMgrs in your organization?

- Do your key account plans have at least a three-year time horizon and are they regularly updated?
- Does your key account planning start with analysing the customer's world?
- Have you assessed how good your key account plan is?

References

[1] Woodburn, D and McDonald, M (2011) *Key Account Management: The definitive guide*, 3rd edn, Wiley, UK.

[2] Gonçalves, J (2015) *Key Account Planning Best Practice*, Cranfield MSc Thesis.

[3] Holt, S (2003) *Global Account Managers: Just what do they do?* Cranfield KAM Club Report, Cranfield School of Management, Cranfield University.

[4] Ryals, L and McDonald, M (2008) *Key Account Plans*, Butterworth-Heinemann, UK.

[5] Davies, I and Ryals, L (2009) A stage model for transitioning to KAM, *Journal of Marketing Management*, 25 (9/10), pp. 1027–48.

[6] Ryals, L and Rogers, B (2007) Key account planning: benefits, barriers and best practice, *Journal of Strategic Marketing*, 15 (2/3), pp. 209–22.

[7] Holt, S and Davies, M (2013) *The New KAM Planning Framework*, Cranfield KAM Club Toolkit Series 1, Cranfield School of Management, Cranfield University.

Developing customer relationships

04

'I'm lucky in having found the perfect partner to spend my life with.'

SARA PARETSKY

How can we build and develop successful long-term relationships with key accounts?

Overview

To most companies, the development of long-term customer relationships is critical for effective key account management (KAM). Admittedly, supplier companies may have key accounts with a transactional approach to business (eg based on specific opportunities to win a big deal or contract). Still, the greatest potential for strategic KAM rests on the development of long-term relationships with customers. The continuity of a supplier–customer relationship usually brings positive outcomes, such as revenues, profitability, market knowledge, and new business opportunities.

The purpose of this chapter is to explain the relevance of customer relationships and provide some recommendations on how to successfully develop key account relationships. First, we explore the nature of buyer–supplier relationships and the implications for KAM. Then, we provide some suggestions on how to build and develop mutually beneficial long-term customer relationships.

Buyer–supplier relationships

Types of buyer–supplier relationships

Suppliers and buyers can have various types of relationships, based on two dimensions [1]:

- *Situation of dependency/power.* This refers to the level of dependency that each party (supplier and buyer) has in a business relationship, and it is mainly driven by the level of each party's power. A typical measure of power is the level of concentration of the business of both parties. For example, a retailer can be in a powerful situation if the purchases from a specific supplier represent a small portion of its total purchases but a large portion of the supplier's sales. This would be a case of power imbalance. However, if both the buyer (retailer, in this example) and the supplier have a similar dependency on the counterpart, we consider it a balanced-power situation. Additional elements could influence the situation of dependency in buyer–supplier relationships, such as access to strategic market/industry information, a leading position in the use of new technologies, access to specific customer segments, etc.

- *Transactional versus relational.* This is really a continuum as there are many possible degrees of 'relationalism' in a buyer–supplier relationship. At one extreme, the two companies may have a purely transactional relationship, where they exchange products and services and seek payoffs in each transaction. Other relationships evolve into long-term collaborative exchanges, where relational norms are established and complex roles between buyers and sellers emerge. In a relational exchange the two parties are willing to cooperate and commit to a continued relationship over time.

Figure 4.1 depicts these two dimensions with the resulting types of buyer–supplier relationships for different levels of *dependency/power* and *transactional vs relational* situations. The first dimension (X-axis) goes from 'Supplier dependency' to 'Buyer dependency'; the middle section is 'Mutual dependency', with a balanced power between the supplier and the buyer. The second dimension (Y-axis) goes from 'Discrete transactions' to 'Relational exchanges' with different combinations of transactional and relational components. The following types of buyer–supplier relationships are identified:

- *Vulnerable supplier.* The supplier is in a high-dependency position relative to the buyer, and they have a transactional approach to their business relationship. The buyer has the option to use that higher power to gain some benefits, whilst reducing those of the supplier.

- *Vulnerable buyer.* The buyer is in a high-dependency position relative to the supplier, and they have a transactional approach to their business relationship. The supplier has the option to use that higher power to gain some benefits, whilst reducing those of the buyer.

- *Inviting buyer.* The supplier is in a high-dependency position relative to the buyer, and they have a relational approach to their business relationship. The buyer is willing to collaborate with the supplier, in spite of having a more powerful position.

Figure 4.1   A typology of buyer–supplier relationships

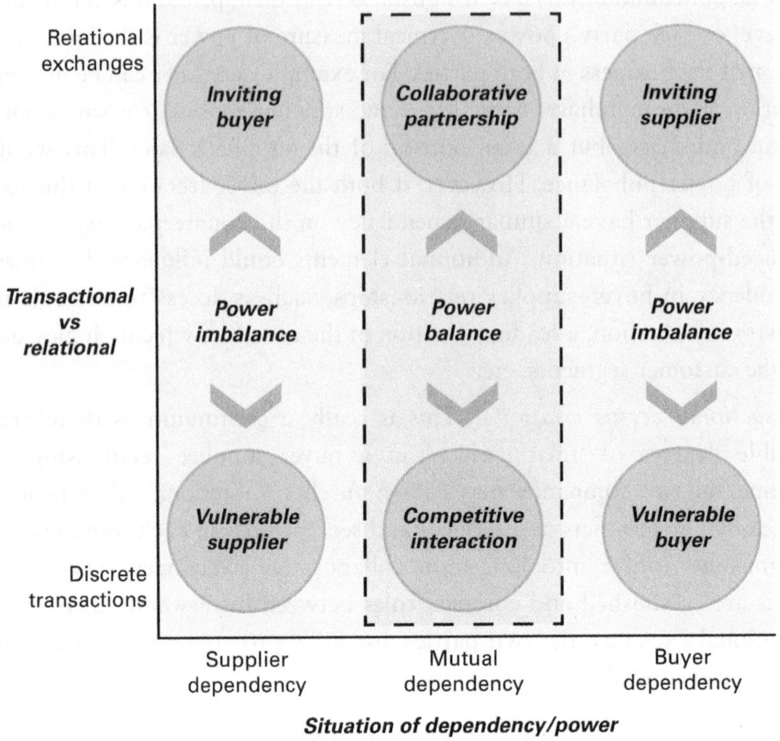

Situation of dependency/power

- *Inviting supplier*. The buyer is in a high dependency position relative to the supplier, and they have a relational approach to their business relationship. The supplier is willing to collaborate with the buyer, in spite of having a more powerful position.

- *Competitive interaction*. There is a mutual dependency between the supplier and the buyer, and they have a transactional approach to their business relationship. They are inclined to compete for the benefits whilst reducing those of the counterpart, ending up in a win–lose situation.

- *Collaborative partnership*. There is a mutual dependency between the supplier and the buyer, and they have a relational approach to their business relationship. They are inclined to collaborate for the shared benefits, looking for a win–win solution.

Using this typology with your key accounts

Step 1: Understand the potential benefits and risks of being in a certain position, and take actions that support the exploitation of the benefits and the reduction of the risks.

For example, if a supplier is in the position of 'vulnerable supplier', it may want to look for ways to reduce its own dependency (eg by broadening the customer portfolio), increase the buyer's dependency (eg by offering custom- ized solutions), or persuade the buyer to have a more relational approach (eg by highlighting the benefits of collaboration and/or investing in the relationship beyond specific transactions). Alternatively, a supplier could be in a comfortable 'inviting supplier' position with a key account. The question becomes: should this supplier use its power to reap the benefits of that relationship whilst the buyer loses out, or should this supplier, instead, avoid the use of its power and favour further collaboration with the buyer even if this drives the relationship into one of mutual dependency?

Step 2: Establish a goal of where you want the relationship with the key account to be in the future, with a specific definition of the required timings and actions to be implemented.

Ideally, the supplier and the buyer will discuss and agree where they want to take their relationship over time. To illustrate, a supplier may currently have a 'competi- tive interaction' type of relationship, which is based on mutual dependency but with little or no engagement in relational exchanges. The supplier may invite the customer to develop their relationship towards a 'collaborative partnership' that could help both companies grow their business.

The trend towards collaborative, long-term buyer–supplier relationships

A major trend is the growing importance of collaboration between suppliers and buyers and a preference for long-term relationships with fewer customers (or suppliers) rather than short-term contracts with a large number of accounts (or suppliers) [2]. The idea of continuity in these relationships has gained acceptance as a way to grow profits through reduced discretionary expenses and higher customer retention, and to increase the likelihood of survival by being less vulnerable to competitors' actions [3].

The process of moving from a transactional relationship into a relational one is complex and takes time, as it is driven by the development of interpersonal ties. Thus, the economic exchange between a supplier and a buyer is not entirely rational, as it is influenced by the existing social ties within the network of people involved in the relationship between the two companies. This idea is nicely illustrated by the following quote from experts in strategic management [4, p. 980] about buyer–supplier relationships:

...develop over time from a state characterized by arm's-length relationships to relationships based on adaptation and trust.

Figure 4.2   The dimensions of relationship quality

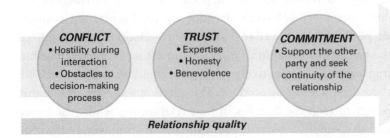

Characteristics of successful buyer–supplier relationships

How can you tell when a buyer–supplier relationship is good? Previous research has identified a number of characteristics of successful relationships, such as the continuity of the relationship, the overall satisfaction, and the levels of mutual trust and commitment.

In this chapter, we focus on *relationship quality* as a critical indicator of success in buyer–supplier relationships. It is an assessment of the present state of the relationship between the two parties and of the expectations of how this relationship will evolve. As illustrated in Figure 4.2, we consider the following three dimensions of relationship quality: conflict, trust, and commitment.

Conflict

Conflict is tension between a supplier and a buyer due to real or perceived differences, which can often generate hostility during the interaction, create obstacles in the decision-making process, and lead to the distortion or withholding of information, among other behaviours [5]. A high level of conflict negatively affects the quality of the relationship between a supplier and a buyer; therefore, it is often called *dysfunctional* conflict. An example of this is represented in a quote from a divisional director of national accounts in the industrial safety sector, who acknowledges that sometimes conflict is created by doing things in a way that does not align with the way the customer does things.

Conflict in buyer–supplier relationships

'I think in terms of what we try to deliver to the customer, we are sometimes restricted by our desire to sort something out for a customer or work in a particular way that may go against what the business might want to do and therefore you can get some conflict.' (Nick Davies, Regional Sales Director at Arco Ltd, industrial safety sector.)

However, a certain level of conflict between parties is not necessarily a bad thing, as it can boost productive discussions and lead to creativity, innovation and adaptation. When disagreements are focused on how to work together and achieve common goals, conflict can be beneficial in provoking open discussions that bring new insights and knowledge. This is called *functional* conflict.

In KAM it is expected that a certain amount of conflict will be present between the supplier and the buyer, both in the day-to-day interactions and during major negotiations or joint planning. The challenge is to find the right balance, avoiding behaviours of dysfunctional conflict that prevent the two organizations from trusting each other but, at the same time promoting discussions that allow disagreements of the functional conflict type, to support the joint discovery of opportunities, the solution of problems, and the co-creation of value.

Trust

Trust is the willingness to rely on an exchange partner in whom one has confidence [6]. It is a belief and an expectation about the supplier (or buyer) based on the exchange partner's expertise, reliability, and intentionality [7]. It can reduce the perception of risk associated with engaging in a business relationship (eg acting opportunistically to increase one's own benefits at the expense of the other party). In addition, a trusting relationship should increase the confidence that short-term problems and iniquities will be resolved over a longer period of time. Likewise, mutual trust between the supplier and the buyer can reduce transaction costs in the relationship by lessening the need to formalize every agreement between the two companies. Finally, both companies should be more willing to make idiosyncratic investments in the relationship if there is a high level of trust.

The challenge of building customer trust

'There's a lot of cynicism and the biggest hurdle to overcome with the customer is trust. As you know, it takes a long time to build trust, and we have a very long track record of destroying it. Our biggest hurdle with customers really is to build that trust, build sustainable partnerships with them, to help them build sustainable health care systems.' (Global Head of KAM Excellence, pharma industry.)

Trust is extremely important in building long-term KAM partnerships between the supplier and the buyer. As the above quote from the pharmaceuticals company indicates, building customer trust is critical but also very difficult; it can take a long time and, unfortunately, it can be destroyed easily and rapidly.

The definition of trust adopted in this book reflects two components:

1 Trust in *credibility*: the extent to which the buyer (or supplier) believes that the counterpart has the knowledge and expertise to perform effectively, and is professional, reliable and honest.

2 Trust in *benevolence*: the extent to which the buyer (or supplier) believes that the counterparts have goodwill towards each other, showing intentions and motives that are beneficial to the supplier (or buyer).

To illustrate, in a very competitive industry you may find that several suppliers are very similar in terms of their credibility with buyers, but then there might be some important differences in terms of their benevolence towards customers. This may trigger the buyer's preference and loyalty to certain suppliers only.

Commitment

Commitment is the desire to develop a stable buyer–supplier relationship, a willingness to make short-term sacrifices to maintain the relationship, and a feeling of confidence in the stability of the relationship [8].

A committed relationship should not only demonstrate the intentions to maintain continuity in the exchange, but also the behaviours associated with that purpose. One case of this is the investment in idiosyncratic resources; for example, a supplier company may develop a new information system to adjust to the business operation of a particular customer.

KAM involves, by its nature, the investment of unique resources in customer relationships and the adaptation of some elements of the selling process; for instance, an organizational structure with a dedicated key account manager (KAMgr) and a KAM team, the manufacturing of products with tailor-made features, or an exclusive treatment in the payment conditions. However, it is not uncommon to find supplier companies where their managers claim to have key accounts, but without making any idiosyncratic investment; this is probably a mistaken idea of what KAM really is.

Drivers of relationship quality

How can suppliers and buyers improve their relationship quality? We suggest that the four factors presented in Figure 4.3 are essential.

Shared values and goal congruence It is more likely that a supplier and a buyer will commit to a relationship if the two companies share similar values and goals. This resemblance can act as a facilitator for the mutual creation of value and the development of ties that go beyond the individual ones, to create collective ones [9]. Suppliers and buyers may have different goals, and this may generate conflict, distrust and, sometimes, opportunistic behaviour. Therefore, having goal alignment and

Figure 4.3 Drivers of relationship quality

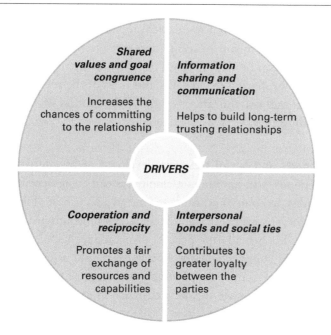

shared values facilitates the establishment of social norms of acceptable behaviour and reduces uncertainty.

Information sharing and communication The exchange of information between suppliers and buyers is essential for building long-term relationships, as it demonstrates norms of equity and fairness and can even prevent unethical behaviour [10]. The willingness to share information is a signal of trust in the benevolence of the counterpart. Likewise, fluent communication is key, either face to face or through technological means, as a senior manager in the industrial safety sector indicates.

The importance of communication

'So in terms of key account management, we have to make sure we're relevant in the future – that face-to-face communication is still relevant. And if you're dealing with somebody who doesn't want that, we've got the technology that allows us to sit behind a desk but still contact and deliver the important messages that we need to for our business.' (Nick Davies, Regional Sales Director at Arco Ltd, industrial safety sector.)

Cooperation and reciprocity A buyer–supplier relationship exists, inherently, because both companies need each other and are mutually dependent on the access to resources and capabilities that are critical for their business. Thus, a bilateral relationship emerges as a means to secure necessary resources, and cooperation is an important mechanism to achieve that [11]. Both companies need to show reciprocity and fairness in sharing the benefits and costs of the relationship, as well as in the way they act and collaborate throughout the process of value creation and relationship building.

Interpersonal bonds and social ties The development of interpersonal relationships and social bonds with key contact employees can bring benefits such as faster approvals, flexibility in communication, and better conflict resolution. As a senior consultant in KAM explains below, interpersonal relationships are critical for KAM implementation, and it is really the process of planning that supports relationship building between the supplier and the buyer. Relational and social ties between customers and suppliers contribute positively to customer loyalty and can sustain an ongoing relationship in spite of the occurrence of events that reduce customer satisfaction [12].

The role of interpersonal bonds

'I've seen that myself in both organizations I've worked in latterly, where they thought it's all about the plan, we've got to get the plan done. And then there's the stark realization that comes when they realize it's not about the plan, it's about the planning process and talking to people and the building of relationships right across the organization.' (Ralph Baillie, KAM Consultant.)

To assess these four drivers of relationship quality, an option is to conduct a survey, ideally with people from both the supplier and the buyer. The following sample statements can be used for that purpose.

Survey on drivers of relationship quality

With respect to the relationship between your company and (name of supplier/buyer), please indicate the degree to which you agree or disagree with the following statements by circling the number that best reflects your perception, on a scale from 1 to 7, where 1 means 'strongly disagree' and 7 means 'strongly agree'.

Shared values and goal congruence:

- Our attachment with this supplier/buyer is based primarily on the similarity of our values.
- What this supplier/buyer stands for is important to us as well.
- We and this supplier/buyer share each other's goals to a big extent.

Information sharing and communication:

- We are willing to share proprietary information with this supplier/buyer.
- We frequently exchange relevant information with this supplier/buyer.
- The quality of communication between this supplier/buyer and us is very high.

Cooperation and reciprocity:

- We generally cooperate with this supplier/buyer in several ways.
- We always reciprocate to this supplier/buyer when they do something valuable for us.
- The relationship with this supplier/buyer is highly collaborative.

Interpersonal bonds and social ties:

- We have close personal relationships with people from this supplier/buyer.
- This supplier/buyer and our company have established strong social ties.
- We get along well with people from this supplier/buyer.

Developing successful relationships with key accounts

As discussed in the previous section of this chapter, buyer–supplier relationships can be of different types, contingent on the level of dependency and the transactional versus relational nature. In the context of KAM, two questions arise:

1 What types of buyer–supplier relationships should be represented in successful KAM?

2 How can suppliers develop these KAM relationships, and what are the critical success factors?

Previous work on KAM indicates that, over time, key account relationships usually evolve from an exploratory phase into more collaborative and extensive stages: basic, co-operative, interdependent, and integrated [13]. In our framework, the expectation is that key account relationships will develop towards a *collaborative partnership*, where there is mutual dependency and a relational type of exchange. Likewise, a successful KAM relationship should have high levels of relationship quality; as previously discussed, this should be the result of aligning the values and goals of the two companies, promoting information sharing and communication, fostering cooperation and reciprocity, and building social ties and interpersonal relationships.

We now elaborate on three analytical elements that are fundamental to support the development of successful key account relationships:

- *Customer journey*: the mapping of each key account's journey, identifying the critical stages, challenges, touchpoints, and experience factors.

- *Decision-making unit*: the analysis of the individuals, groups, and entities that participate in the organizational buying process.

- *KAM organization*: the supplier's structure for KAM, including the role of top managers, the KAMgr, the KAM team, and other people who interact with the customer.

Figure 4.4 presents a framework for how to develop relationships with key accounts. First, we illustrate with a cone the expected evolution of customer relationships from *transactional* to *relational*, together with the advancement towards a situation of *mutual dependency*. It is expected that a 'vulnerable' type of relationship will evolve into an 'inviting' type, towards a 'collaborative partnership'. Likewise, in successful KAM, the 'competitive interaction' type of mutual dependency relationship should evolve into a 'collaborative partnership' type by means of moving from a transactional to a relational business approach. Second, we depict with rings along the cone the drivers of *relationship quality* as vital conditions and processes that will support

Figure 4.4   Developing relationships with key accounts

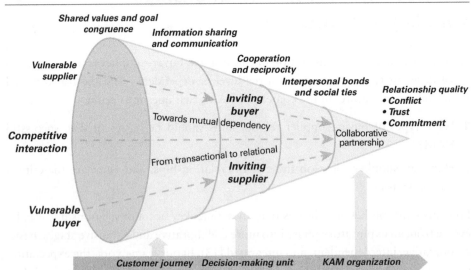

the transition toward a collaborative partnership: shared values and goal congruence; information sharing and communication; cooperation and reciprocity; and interpersonal bonds and social ties. Third, we represent with arrows at the bottom three analytical elements that should facilitate the development of successful key account relationships: customer journey; decision-making unit; and KAM organization.

Customer journey In order to develop successful key account relationships, supplier companies need to have a clear understanding of the customer journey, which refers to the complete purchase cycle and dynamic process over time across multiple touchpoints that build customer experience [14]. The following quote from a senior executive in KAM illustrates suppliers' need for much more detailed customer journey mapping given that buyers are increasingly relying on social media and other online tools to support their purchasing process at various points of the journey.

Mapping the customer journey

'... more and more of our customers are really looking to serve their needs online before they get into a face-to-face relationship. You know that's certainly bringing with it the need for us to understand that customer journey and undertake customer journey mapping in a lot more detail than perhaps we have done in the past.' (Max Walker, Commercial Leader, Strategic Key Accounts Group at 3M United Kingdom.)

Customer experience is holistic and multidimensional in its nature, as it includes the customer's cognitive, emotional, sensory, social and spiritual responses. Although this conceptualization was initially developed for customers as 'consumers', it is still relevant in the business-to-business context: business relationships are really *business-to-people*, and customer experience is closely linked to people's reactions.

The 'touchpoints' represent any type of direct or indirect contact between the supplier and the customer along the customer journey, for example, a pre-sale meeting between the supplier and the customer. Another touchpoint might be when a customer uses social media to search for potential suppliers. A third example could be the presence of both supplier and buyer at an industrial trade fair.

A customer journey has broadly three main stages (Figure 4.5):

- *Pre-purchase*: includes the recognition of needs, as well as the search, consideration, and evaluation of alternatives.
- *Purchase*: involves the decision making on a specific choice, the ordering and payment, as well as other considerations for the purchasing process itself.

Figure 4.5   The customer journey

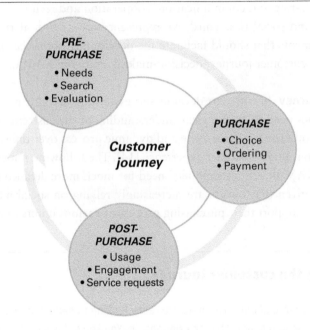

- *Post-purchase*: contains the usage/consumption of products, services or solutions, the request for additional information or services, and the engagement with the supplier's offering through a variety of possible actions or behaviours (eg recommending the supplier, sharing the usage experience with other companies, etc).

In each of the three stages of the customer journey there will be certain touchpoints between the supplier and the key account, and some of these will be more critical than others in terms of how much they influence customer experience. Therefore, a first goal is to identify all relevant touchpoints and assess their relative importance within the entire customer journey.

A second goal is to identify the experience factors that are most critical for each touchpoint. So, for example, in a pre-sale meeting with the customer (touchpoint), an important customer experience factor could be the extent to which the supplier demonstrates knowledge of the customer's business. Importantly, customer experience goes beyond the traditional cognitive appraisal of a service, to incorporate emotional elements that have been shown to affect customer loyalty [15].

Next, the supplier should evaluate its level of influence in those experience factors, as this will indicate the extent to which the company can make meaningful changes to improve customer experience. For instance, an online auction conducted by a customer usually leaves little control to the suppliers that participate, whereas a company visit by the customer to the supplier's factory constitutes a touchpoint where the supplier has a very high level of influence. If things go wrong in the latter, the supplier company should be able to get enough feedback from the customer and act in a way that prevents a similar failure in the future.

Importantly, supplier companies need to adequately measure customer experience at each meaningful touchpoint and in relation to all relevant experience factors. The specific methodologies to measure customer experience are beyond the scope of this book; a good starting point may be the book *Measuring Customer Experience* by Dr Phil Klaus [16]. Having the measures of customer experience, the supplier will be able to evaluate its performance at each touchpoint and in relation to each experience factor. From there, actions to improve customer experience should be undertaken, particularly on aspects with a high level of influence. On the other hand, for those touchpoints or experience factors with a lower level of influence, the supplier could look for ways to either increase their influence or reduce the relative importance of the touchpoint or experience factor. For each touchpoint the supplier must:

1 identify the experience factors that mostly affect the customer's experience;

2 evaluate the supplier's influence to affect the customer's experience;

3 evaluate the supplier's performance in each experience factor;

4 suggest how to measure customer experience (eg survey, interview);

5 suggest what to do to improve customer experience through those experience factors.

The following example presents an overview of how this process could work at a steel manufacturing company.

Customer journey: an example of how to apply it

A steel manufacturer wants to analyse the customer journey of a key account, a major automotive company. For the pre-purchase stage, the following touchpoint is identified: the main UK industry trade fair:

1 *Identify the experience factors that mostly affect the customer's experience*:
- the availability of relevant information about suppliers in a credible and timely manner;
- the opportunity to meet senior management from the supplier companies.

2 *Evaluate the supplier's influence to affect the customer's experience*: the level of influence is high, as the supplier can plan its participation in the trade fair with anticipation and bring to the event the relevant people and the right information.

3 *Evaluate the supplier's performance in each experience factor*: the supplier's performance is currently low (a score of 2 in a 1–5 scale) because they have not been able to secure this customer's access to their Chief Sales Officer during the past two fairs. In addition, several technical questions from the customer have not been answered during the previous events, but only a few weeks after.

4 *Suggest how to measure customer experience (eg survey, interview)*: the steel company (supplier) could send a brief online questionnaire to the customer's key contact personnel within five days after the event, to ask about their experience in relation to the two identified experience factors.

5 *Suggest what to do to improve customer experience through those experience factors*: the supplier could explore with their key account the extent to which they require the presence of a top manager, and the reasons for that. They could then coordinate the calendars of their top managers ahead of time to make sure that they meet with people from this key account, whilst supporting these senior executives with the information they need to make those meetings productive.

Decision-making unit

The effective development of key account relationships also requires a good assessment of the decision-making unit (DMU) within the buying company. The DMU – also called the 'buying centre' – is represented by all the individuals, groups, business units, functional areas, and other entities that participate in the organizational buying process.

The roles in the buying process

There are several roles within the DMU, which on some occasions are concentrated in a few people or units, and in other situations are spread among several or many people or units. The following roles, depicted in Figure 4.6, have been identified [17]:

- *Initiator*: recognizes the need, opportunity or problem that leads to considering the purchase of a product, service, or solution.
- *User*: uses or works with the product, service or solution, and normally has a say in determining the specifications that the offering must have.
- *Influencer*: influences the decision by providing inputs on the requirements and/or alternatives available. This role is usually related to technical expertise.
- *Gatekeeper*: controls the flow of information among the members of the DMU, and often influences the extent and means of communication between the supplier and the customer.
- *Decider*: makes the final decision on the purchase, by having formal authority or other sources of power.
- *Controller*: determines the budget for the purchase and other restrictions (usually of a financial nature).

Figure 4.6   Decision-making unit: roles in the buying process

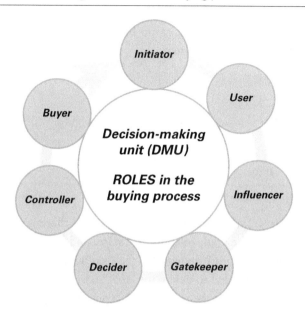

- *Buyer*: makes the purchase and leads the ordering process; people in this role usually have some power in selecting suppliers and determining some conditions for the deal, such as the payment terms or timings for the delivery of products and services.

The need to have a good GRASP of the DMU

In KAM, it is extremely important to have good knowledge of the customer's decision-making unit and the goals that the supplier company needs to accomplish with each of its members. Also, closeness to the DMU and the development of ties of influence are fundamental for a beneficial long-term relationship.

To analyse the DMU, we propose the GRASP approach, which stands for: Goal, Role, Appeal, State, and Power. Each member of the DMU needs to be assessed using the five aspects of GRASP, as described in Table 4.1.

Table 4.1   The *GRASP* approach to DMU analysis

G	Goal	What are our goals and action plans with respect to this DMU member?
R	Role	What are the roles that this member plays in the buying process?
A	Appeal	What is appealing to this DMU member about the offering and buying process?
S	State	What is the state of our relationship with this member of the DMU?
P	Power	What level and source of power does this DMU member have?

Example of the GRASP approach Let us think of an industrial manufacturer of machinery that decides to analyse the DMU following the GRASP approach. Table 4.2 shows how this assessment could be done. In this example, the relevant members of the DMU are the following:

- Purchasing Manager;
- Chief Engineer;
- Finance Director;
- Technical team;
- Chief Executive Officer (CEO);
- CEO's personal assistant.

As indicated in Table 4.2, for each member of the DMU there is a GRASP analysis, that is, an evaluation of the goal, role, appeal, state, and power. It is recommended to leave the 'goal' element until the end, as the examination of the other elements provides inputs that are needed to define the 'goal' aspect.

In addition to the GRASP analysis, the supplier should have a deep understanding of the buying process: the overall procedure, how decisions are made, the means and frequency of the communication flows among DMU members, the timings for the different stages of the buying process, etc.

Procurement trends to keep in mind

Procurement has evolved tremendously in the past few years. The DMU has become more complex, involving a larger number of people and even individuals outside the buying organization, incorporating new technology tools in the buying process (eg social media) and raising the bar in terms of suppliers' requirements to be eligible as such. As an example of these trends, a senior manager from a services company provides an interesting quote that stresses the evolution of the purchasing function into one with a higher decision-making power.

The evolution of procurement

'...guys are buying in a much more tender-driven away, a much more regimented way. We're seeing the buyers that procurement departments raise in their power and decision-making authority... we're expecting more robust emphasis on due diligence buying processes, particularly from the large, more complex deals that we do.' (Senior executive in the services sector.)

Table 4.2 Example: Application of the *GRASP* approach

		Purchasing Manager	Chief Engineer	Finance Director	Technical Team	Chief Executive Officer (CEO)	CEO Personal Assistant
G	Goal	Position ourselves as a reliable and flexible supplier	Demonstrate quality of our product and explore need for post-sale services	Translate the quality of our machine into financial savings to be generated	Recover from a bad brand image and provide evidence of reliability	Obtain a top-to-top meeting with our CEO to present our company	Keep bonding and obtain information about the buying process
R	Role	Buyer Influencer	Initiator User Decider	Controller Decider	Influencer	Decider	Gatekeeper
A	Appeal	Efficiency in buying process Flexibility in delivery	Performance Quality of images	Price of purchase Obsolescence Profitability	Product specifications Safety	Return on investment Functionality	Internal recognition Socialization
S	State	We have a close and good relationship with her	No previous interaction with him	He is a close friend with one of our team members	They had a bad experience with our brand in the past	She knows very little about our company	She gets along with our key account manager
P	Power	She shortlists suppliers and establishes payment conditions	High decision power and well respected among peers	Not so powerful in affecting the decision; little time in the company	High influence with the Chief Engineer, based on their expert knowledge	High hierarchical power in the organization	She manages the agenda of the CEO and is a very trusted PA

KAM organization

The development of key account relationships requires the right structure and organization, as well as top management involvement. Similarly, the KAMgr has a critical role in facilitating the coordination and the discussions with people from the customer and also internally. Depending on the stage of the buyer–supplier relationship, it may be desirable that several people from the supplier company interact directly with a number of people from the key account.

Top management support

The involvement of senior managers in KAM is critical to achieve supplier performance and to build long-term customer relationships. Top management support is needed for structural adjustments and relational capability development to facilitate KAM implementation [18]. Senior managers must spread the supplier's cultural values by showing consistent actions. Top management involvement in aligning the goals of various functional areas and creating a customer-oriented culture can enhance the quality of the relationship between suppliers and strategic accounts [19].

The following list indicates some of the main activities top managers should be involved with, to adequately support KAM implementation:

- selecting key accounts;
- recruiting KAMgrs;
- setting strategic goals for the key accounts;
- supporting activity planning and implementation;
- promoting customer knowledge utilization;
- empowering the KAM team;
- enabling resource allocation;
- making direct customer contact when needed;
- facilitating the access to top executives in the buying organization;
- establishing social contact with the customer through top-to-top encounters.

Within the supplier firm, senior executives have a fundamental role in promoting a customer-centric culture. They must align the goals and procedures of the different functional units to provide a service of excellence to key accounts and build long-term relationships (see following quote by a KAMgr in the forestry sector).

In spite of the importance of top management involvement in KAM, there is a risk of senior executives being too involved in business aspects that should be managed by the KAMgr and the KAM team. If senior executives are not well informed about the specifics of the customer relationship and business interaction, active involvement of senior managers could, in fact, damage the relationship with the customer whilst also upsetting the KAMgr (see quote by a KAMgr in the printing industry).

The role of top managers in KAM

'It is so hard to convince people in production about the importance of meeting customers' requirements, that we need top executives to intervene. (KAMgr, forestry sector.)

'Our VP of sales doesn't really know what is going on with the customer on a daily basis, and in some meetings that is so evident that customers get upset... and that can hurt the relationship with our company because we lose credibility.' (KAMgr, printing industry.)

The role of the key account manager and interaction with the customer

The KAMgr has a critical role in developing customer relationships. They should be the main (and sometimes the single) point of contact with the customer, and internally orchestrate the support from different functional areas. It is critical that the KAMgr be able and willing to talk at every level within the key account and also within the supplier company. Also, given the increasing importance of KAM, in many companies the KAMgr must have a senior-level position in the company. The purchasing function has become more strategic and the key influencers in the decision-making unit are usually in high-level positions.

Admittedly, there are many possible ways to configure the supplier's organizational structure for KAM, and a detailed analysis of these options is beyond the scope of this book. However, it is important that supplier companies organize interactions with key customers using a multiplicity of contacts. We suggest that KAMgrs establish the following links.

Internally (within the supplier company):

- Direct and frequent interaction with the members of the KAM team, to effectively manage the relationship with customers and deliver high value.
- Direct links with all departments, to provide and receive inputs about key accounts and encourage collaboration and frequent communication.

- Direct access to top management and at least indirect contact with the c-suite, to have a clear understanding of the company's strategy, inform senior executives about some specifics of the relationship with key accounts, and request their support when needed.

Externally (with the customer):

- Direct and close contact with the purchasing manager as the main point of contact, to coordinate all relevant aspects of the relationship and to request the inputs from other functional areas and from senior management in the buying organization.

- Direct connection with other areas as needed, such as Supply Chain, Finance, and Trade Marketing, to obtain up-to-date information and to establish interpersonal bonds with the different stakeholders.

- If possible, some direct contact with top management, or at least indirectly through the purchasing manager, to communicate the strategic value that the supplier company can provide to the customer.

Figure 4.7 shows a diagram of a possible mapping of the expected relationships between a supplier and a key account.

Figure 4.7   Relationship links between the supplier and a key account

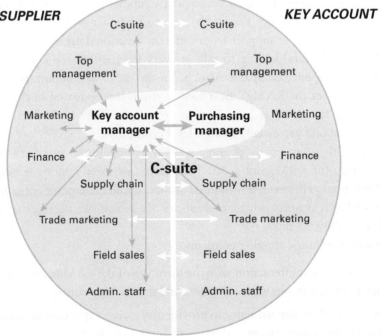

CASE STUDY AND INTERVIEW Developing a successful customer relationship

We present a case study of how a business-to-business service company has developed, in four years, a successful relationship with a key account. Several of the elements previously discussed in this chapter resonate with the story of this company.

The company – referenced here as SAF, 'Service Advisory Firm' is a leading financial and business advisor providing assurance, audit, tax and advisory services.

This case study focuses on how SAF has developed, over the last four years, a successful relationship with one strategic account: a construction company named simply as CS ('construction support') for confidentiality reasons. The client is a property, residential, construction and support services group. The information is provided by the senior account manager of this client, who kindly agreed to be interviewed.

SAF has a strategic account programme with clients from different sectors. Each account has a relationship lead who is responsible for growing the relationship through co-creating solutions and delivering value. For each strategic account, the relationship lead is supported by a team composed of a strategic account manager and a group of professionals that provide technical support and market insight.

In 2013, SAF was asked by CS to tender for a large piece of work. They didn't win but through the process SAF was able to position itself as a service provider with a different view and perspective to those of its competitors. As indicated by the senior account manager:

> We provided them with a different picture, inviting them to try something different... you don't know if you don't try... and gave the client some experience and insight to show why working with us would give them a fresh perspective to stimulate change.

Importantly, the tendering process allowed SAF to get a much better understanding of the culture of CS, how they like to be communicated with and what the key issues were for them. It also enabled SAF to build credibility with CS's senior management team. As explained by the senior account manager:

> Sometimes potential clients are unclear of our capability to handle complex projects. To counter that perception and grow the knowledge of our firm we position ourselves as a credible and fresh alternative to our competitors.

Following that tender the relationship with CS has evolved very successfully. Importantly, it has been nurtured at different levels across both organizations. SAF has continued to develop the relationship with the senior management team through the relationship lead, whilst the senior account manager and wider account team have built and maintained relationships with middle management across CS's core divisions. This top-down and bottom-up approach has a number of advantages in terms of connecting the dots and ensuring consistency of messages at all levels. For example, when the account lead has meetings with the c-suite he can feed back what the SAF team are seeing and hearing across CS's divisions. This also works the other way around. This process enables SAF to build trust and gain integrity across the client, positioning themselves as a trusted advisor and 'critical friend'.

Another key for success has been the fact that SAF provides this client not only with technical expertise but also with market insight. As explained by the senior account manager:

> The customer has a very strong presence in the public sector, and our knowledge of this sector and procurement processes is strong. As a result we've been able to connect them not only with our insight, but with our wider sector network as well.

Through having a great understanding of CS, SAF engages in areas that will provide value and mutual benefit. They focus on the things that are really important to CS and have expanded the services offered to the client in terms of both breadth and value. The number of relationships has grown, and continues to develop all the time, as SAF identifies new people at CS that they can engage in broad business conversations with. The senior account manager reflects on the state of the relationship with CS by saying:

> With this client, we are at the point of the relationship where we are comfortable taking ideas to them to stimulate their thinking. Our people enjoy working with CS and we continue to look for areas to collaborate.

The story of this strategic account relationship is an evolving one; the challenge for both is to continue being relevant to each other, bringing and sharing new ideas and initiatives. To that end, SAF needs to be aware of the trends in CS's sector and core business, to anticipate which will be their main challenges in the future.

Conclusion

This chapter provides an overview of how to develop customer relationships in the context of KAM. A first step is to understand the types of buyer–supplier relationships that could be established, as well as the characteristics of successful long-term relationships. In KAM, it is expected that relationships with customers will evolve into collaborative partnerships with high levels of relationship quality. Several processes support the achievement of this purpose, including goal alignment, information sharing, cooperation, and interpersonal ties. In addition, suppliers need to analyse the customer journey and the decision-making unit, whilst establishing an appropriate organizational structure for implementing KAM.

Questions for managers

- What type of buyer–supplier relationship do we currently have with each of our key accounts?

- How do we evaluate the quality of the relationship with each key customer, in terms of conflict, trust and commitment?

- What can we do to transition into a collaborative partnership with our key accounts?

- Do we have a clear understanding of the customer journey, its key touchpoints and experience factors?

- Do we have a good GRASP of the decision-making unit of our key accounts?

- What can we do in terms of KAM organization to support the development of customer relationships?

References

[1] Tangpong, C et al (2015) A review of buyer-supplier relationship typologies: progress, problems, and future directions, *Journal of Business & Industrial Marketing*, **30** (2), pp 153–79.

[2] Charterina, J, Basterretxea, I and Landeta, J (2016) Types of embedded ties in buyer–supplier relationships and their combined effects on innovation performance, *Journal of Business & Industrial Marketing*, **31** (2), pp 152–63.

[3] Bowman, D (2014) Evolution of buyer-seller relationships, in *Handbook of Strategic Account Management: A comprehensive resource*, pp 277–92.

[4] Andersson, U, Forsgren, M and Holm, U (2002) The strategic impact of external networks: subsidiary performance and competence development in the multinational corporation, *Strategic Management Journal*, **23** (11), pp 979–96.

[5] Menon, A, Bharadwaj, S G and Howell, R (1996) The quality and effectiveness of marketing strategy: effects of functional and dysfunctional conflict in intraorganizational relationships, *Journal of the Academy of Marketing Science*, **24** (4), pp 299–313.

[6] Moorman, C, Zaltman, G and Deshpande, R (1992) Relationships between providers and users of market research: the dynamics of trust within and between organizations, *Journal of Marketing Research*, **29** (3), p 314.

[7] Ganesan, S (1994) Determinants of long-term orientation in buyer–seller relationships, *Journal of Marketing*, **58** (2) pp 1–19.

[8] Anderson, E and Weitz, B (1992) The use of pledges to build and sustain commitment in distribution channels, *Journal of Marketing Research*, **29** (1) pp 18–34.

[9]   Cuevas, J, Julkunen, S and Gabrielsson, M (2015) Power symmetry and the development of trust in interdependent relationships: the mediating role of goal congruence, *Industrial Marketing Management*, 48, pp 149–59.

[10] Eckerd, S and Hill, J A (2012) The buyer–supplier social contract: information sharing as a deterrent to unethical behaviors, *International Journal of Operations & Production Management*, 32 (2), pp 238–55.

[11] Kim, K K et al (2010) Inter-organizational cooperation in buyer–supplier relationships: both perspectives, *Journal of Business Research*, 63 (8), pp 863–69.

[12] Woisetschläger, D M, Lentz, P and Evanschitzky, H (2011) How habits, social ties, and economic switching barriers affect customer loyalty in contractual service settings, *Journal of Business Research*, 64 (8), pp 800–08.

[13] McDonald, M and Rogers, B (2017) *Malcolm McDonald on Key Account Management*, Kogan Page Ltd, New York.

[14] Lemon, K N and Verhoef, P C (2016) Understanding customer experience throughout the customer journey, *Journal of Marketing*, 80, pp 69–96.

[15] McColl-Kennedy, J R et al (2015) Fresh perspectives on customer experience, *Journal of Services Marketing*, 29 (6/7), pp 430–35.

[16] Klaus, P (2014) *Measuring Customer Experience: How to develop and execute the most profitable customer experience strategies*, Springer, New York.

[17] Johnston, M W and Marshall, G W (2016) *Sales Force Management: Leadership, innovation, technology*, Routledge, Abingdon.

[18] Gounaris, S and Tzempelikos, N (2014) Relational key account management: building key account management effectiveness through structural reformations and relationship management skills, *Industrial Marketing Management*, 43 (7), pp 1110–23.

[19] Guesalaga, R (2014) Top management involvement with key accounts: the concept, its dimensions, and strategic outcomes, *Industrial Marketing Management*, 43 (7), pp 1146–56.

PART TWO
Developing winning offerings

Creating compelling customer value propositions 05

'The aim of marketing is to know and understand the customer so well the product or service fits him and sells itself.'

PETER DRUCKER

Question: What techniques can be used to develop innovative customer value propositions and offerings?

What is a customer value proposition?

The customer value proposition is possibly the most critical component of the strategic KAM process, for one simple reason: this is how value is presented to the customer and this is what they buy. In the strategic KAM planning process, it connects with and will develop to be more compelling on the back of strong customer research, which enables greater consideration and understanding of what is critical to the customer.

The value proposition is effectively an executive summary of what is being offered to the customer. As such, it should be short, concise, well written and focused on explaining a considerable amount of information in two or three paragraphs. Figure 5.1 shows how the value proposition connects with the wider customer offer. Whilst the offer is very detailed and explains the nuances and critical components of what will be provided, the value proposition summarizes this in a very commercial and high-impact manner. It is exactly like an iceberg. The visible aspects of the offer sit in the value proposition, which should appear at the front of any presentation, document or discussion. It is the piece that focuses the supplier/customer conversation.

Figure 5.1   The customer value proposition

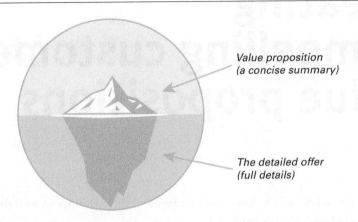

The offer sits beneath this. Once the customer is 'hooked' by the promises in the value proposition, and they can see some advantage in progressing talks with the supplier further, then discussions will proceed to the offer. This will be a more detailed, technical and explanatory document. To avoid getting lost in the weeds, always stay focused on the content of the value proposition.

The following definitions are provided to differentiate KAM value proposition and the supporting offer:

> A value proposition summarizes an improved future scenario offered by a supplier to its key account. It describes products, services and the relationship ethos that will be provided, and supports this position with evidence to demonstrate how these value promises will deliver a sustainable competitive performance.
>
> Adapted from *Infinite Value* [1]

> The key account offers details all of the components that will be delivered by the supplier to make the value proposition promises become reality [1].

These definitions help with understanding the concepts of value proposition. The rest of this chapter describes practical means to start thinking about value and constructing value propositions.

Linking innovation and KAM

Innovation runs through the veins of a value proposition, since there should be a focus on supplying and emphasizing a unique set of products, services and relationship ethos that both satisfies customer needs and beats the competition. The pace of change in today's environment means that suppliers can no longer rely on a portfolio of brands and high-performing products. Whilst these are essential as a foundation for the key account offering, there needs to be a continual assessment of what is important to the customer and what will add value to their business. Strategic planning and researching the customer is part of this activity, but at some stage the development of new creative ideas will have to be introduced. The other alignment between innovation and KAM comes from the supplier perspective. Organizations select and position a key account (usually) by assessing future potential growth, which will only come from the customer buying additional products and services. The key account manager (KAMgr) is tasked to find this growth and establish areas where investment should be applied. Growth will come from two areas: first, the customer may grow organically and the supply of products and services will grow on the back of this customer activity; and second, the value proposition that the customer buys. KAMgrs cannot simply hope for additional growth coming from the customer – they need to proactively develop and demonstrate new sources of value that the customer will buy. This is innovation, but it is innovation generated by the KAMgr (not the broader R&D department who are focused on more general products).

When faced with the challenge to 'innovate', many professionals assume that there is a significant amount of time and investment required, because it is usually the domain of long-term product teams. However, innovation can come from a range of opportunities and techniques, which can be classified as shown in Figure 5.2.

Tweak innovations are simple amendments to small things. They are often easy to introduce but have impact on the customer because they are important; for example,

Figure 5.2   KAM innovation (and how it powers value)

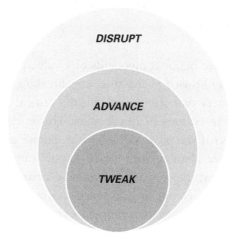

changing the way that invoices are raised (or the frequency) or altering customer support from Monday–Friday to 24-hour dedicated support. These are relatively easy to implement and demonstrate a focus on customers' 'needs'.

Advance innovations take the foundation of what the customer sees as the supplier's competitive advantage and builds on this to really maximize the value. Advance innovations take more effort and investment, but they can pay back significantly; for example, developing a product packaging so that it is bespoke for the customer. Introducing new materials, humidity barrier pouches or specific printing designs are all examples of where additional equipment and investment may be required; however, the customer sees the benefits and pays for them. One organization that produced contract pharmaceutical products implemented a dedicated production line and staff to ensure product supply for a key account customer. This was not a different product, but it was an example of adapting the manufacturing process to advance benefits for a critical customer.

Disrupt innovations do usually involve new products or services. Many organizations are looking to introduce 'advanced services' and 'total solution' packages to customers. These essentially require a different business model for the supplier, but they can disrupt and change entire industries. Key accounts are very well positioned to benefit from advanced services, since they have complex operations and consequently can offer alignment for these more sophisticated value propositions.

KAMgrs need to be mindful of the need to create new innovations, which is a different skill set from traditional sales and account management. Being able to gain alignment between their own organization and the customer organization to generate innovative new ways of working is a major differentiating skill for a successful KAMgr.

Components of a compelling customer value proposition

Figure 5.3 shows the three major components of a value proposition, to provide a practical process that can be used to construct one. Breaking down the elements will help to remove the mystery that often surrounds this critical component of KAM.

The leading tip is the customer's future state. This is the description of what the customer can expect if the proposal is bought. Future state should talk in the language of the customer, aligning with issues that are important to the customer and the strategic goals that they pursue. It should be written in a way that is exciting but realistic, believable, compelling and timely. Most importantly, this opening section should be describing things that competitors probably cannot deliver. Always be mindful that if you are offering something that one or more competitors are also

Figure 5.3   Three main components of a customer value proposition

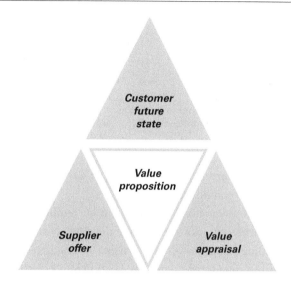

offering, your opportunity to negotiate more favourable fees and terms diminishes. As soon as professional buyers sense an opportunity to play off two suppliers a potential commoditization supply position can result. Of course, you must be realistic; not everything that you supply will be unique. But there should be elements of your value proposition where you add unique value. Focus on these areas.

The customer future state sets the proposition in action. The next step is to have a solid description of how this future state will be achieved; this is the 'nuts and bolts' of the offer. This is the 'how' and the 'what' components of the value proposition, and must be credible, robust and supported with evidence. You are supporting your value promise with practical details and gravitas.

The final element of a value proposition is the commercial appraisal. Discuss at a high level what it will cost the customer to buy the offer and what the payback will be (and why it is such good value).

The following sections provide tools and techniques to help with the construction and development of each of these elements.

Defining customer future state

The future state is the leading paragraph of a compelling value proposition. This statement should be totally focused on the customer's world, and should punch at the strategic and operational issues that key decision makers, in their environment, will recognize as advancing and improving the things that are important (valuable) to them.

Figure 5.4   The five sources of value

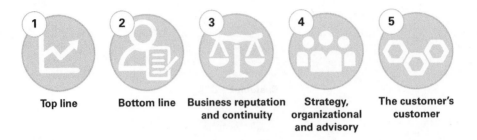

| Top line | Bottom line | Business reputation and continuity | Strategy, organizational and advisory | The customer's customer |

Figure 5.4 shows the five sources of value that capture the areas that describe future state; each is described here, with examples.

Top-line value. Customers have businesses that require income. This comes from the sales and marketing efforts that they develop to supply to their customers. Examples of a value proposition that drives top-line growth with a customer include: helping them to understand a new market; helping to sell more products by improving sales effectiveness; improving market access/channels; or assisting with joint promotional campaigns. If the customer is non-profit (for example a hospital trust) the value proposition could describe ways to help them secure a bigger budget, since this is effectively the top line for that type of operation.

Bottom-line value. Any organization must manage costs to maximize profits. Examples of bottom-line value include saving costs, minimizing waste, maximizing recycling, reducing energy bills and reducing labour. Significant value can be derived through understanding a customer's business and helping them to run more efficiently.

Business reputation and continuity. This value can be described using the acronym HSSEQ. This describes the increasingly essential business behaviours of Health, Safety, Security, Environmental and Quality. Organizations must operate within government and industry guidelines. This can be complex and costly, but failure to comply could destroy the business through legal fees, fines and possible total loss of brand value. Consider VW and the engine emissions scandal, BP and the Horizon oil platform disaster, and almost the entire banking and investment sector (10 years on from the 2008 credit crisis). Capturing these value activities can be business critical.

Strategy, organizational and other advisory. Businesses engage management consultants on a regular basis. They provide strategy, HR, supply chain, marketing and advice in all other aspects of business. As a supplier with considerable expertise in certain specific and aligned markets, what is stopping this source of value being offered as a very credible alternative?

The customer's customer. The fifth source of value considers value from the perspective of the consumer. The previous four sources are aimed at 'business to business' value; the consumer is a different concept. Most value starts here, since it is those consumers who buy products in volume that businesses serve by working together in supply chains. Value here resides in human needs: food, drink, shelter, health and wellbeing, social belonging, financial aspects, education and advancement, and community. Thinking of your own personal needs and requirements will help you to uncover value sources for the wider consumer community.

These five sources of value are useful when considering how your value proposition will have impact and be compelling for the customer. It is advisable to build a model that provides content and ideas against each one. As more value propositions are developed, and as more key accounts are managed, this database can be updated and will become increasingly valuable as a source of information.

Expanding your offer to the customer

Given that this is typically the stage on which many suppliers choose to focus when selling ('we have an A–Y product that does A–B things'), it is surprising how organizations can stumble and forget the incredible breadth and width of things that they can and do offer to key customers. This part of the value proposition statement will remind you of the things you have in your toolbox and armoury.

Figure 5.5 shows the marketing mix '7P' model. This is a widely adopted and very useful tool to consider the elements of an offer to a market. In this case, our market is a 'segment of one', since it is a single key customer. The model originally was described as the '4P' marketing mix, but it was expanded some 15 years ago to reflect the increasing shift towards services-based businesses. The original 4Ps are product, place, price and promotion. The expansion to 7Ps embraces people, process and physical evidence. These are now explained in more detail:

Figure 5.5   Expanding your offer to the customer

- *Product* (and service) is the foundation of the value proposition. These are the tangible and intangible things that the customer requires.

- *Price* is the fee that the customer pays to receive goods and services. It is also the complete suite of commercial aspects that wrap around this price, and could include things like rebates, credit terms, service level agreements, distribution fees and contracts.

- *Place* refers to the channels and locations where the supplier reaches and connects with the customer. This could include distribution channels, web-based mechanisms, direct selling and being based directly in the customer operations (implanted).

- *Promotion* is the way a company communicates what it does and what it can offer the customer. It includes branding, advertising, PR, corporate identity, social media outreach, sales management, special offers and exhibitions. Promotion must gain attention, be appealing, send a consistent message and provide the customer with a reason to choose your product rather than someone else's.

- *People* represent your entire organization. Of course, the commercial, technical and supply people that the customer interacts with regularly should be emphasized, but the calibre and professionalism of the supporting teams also demonstrate the strength of your business. As a key account, they should be able to access and interact with your people. As a concept, it is useful to remember that as you shift towards a service-based offering your 'people become your product'.

- *Process* is the way that you describe and structure the way that complex things will be made to happen, seamlessly and without drama. For some customers, a well-constructed process will provide assurance that you are a credible supplier to do business with. Some industries audit and make processes an essential part of the offer, for example pharmaceutical, aerospace, financial and food. Compliance and traceability are essential parts of their business. As a supplier, you need to work to the same high standards.

- *Physical evidence* is a strange phrase but it is used to enable professional services organizations to describe their business. Legal, accounting, consulting and construction design firms have no tangible products; they deliver value through expertise and by having exceptional people. Physical evidence exists in offices, websites, qualifications, endorsements and industry awards. Published articles and books also serve to make the 'intangible tangible'.

Supplier organizations are advised to take this 7P model and adapt it for their business. Build the model so that it has details under each section that fit the value you offer.

Quantifying customer value

The closing statement of a customer value proposition provides the financial justification and/or customer investment metrics that can be used to demonstrate that your offering is commercially viable and attractive. It should use metrics that are important to them and, if possible, demonstrate rate of return.

This closing section should seal off the value proposition. In many ways, it might be the first part that the customer looks at (how often do we go straight to the price page of any brochure, proposal or quote?). And yet the beauty of a well-structured value proposition is that it starts with customer impact statements that are intended to engage the buyer and let them see that this will help them achieve their business goals.

The final justification should pick out high-level measures that are important to the customer. These might include:

- the programme fee/price;
- estimated payback period;
- time to install/generate results;
- comparing the fee against existing spend (for example, this package will cost 30 per cent more than your incumbent supplier, but will generate cost savings of more than twice the total programme fee).

Other measures that are very effective in the closing statement of a customer value proposition are the critical performance measures (CPIs) with which you propose to demonstrate the value that will be generated once the programme starts. These should link to the five value sources, and will have a greater impact if they are measures that are important to the customer today. Examples might be:

- top-line value CPIs (*sales/quarter, market penetration, budget growth, consumer satisfaction*);
- bottom-line value CPIs (*reduced scrap rates, reduced employment costs, reduced energy costs*);
- business reputation and continuity value CPIs (*eliminate employee accidents, reduce rejects due to quality issues*);
- strategy value CPIs (*complete China entry study within six months*);
- customer's customer value CPIs (*conduct a consumer buyer behaviour study in Norway in six months*).

Remember, these metrics capture the essence of the customer value proposition. You need to discuss these with the customer during the negotiation stage of the sale. As value propositions become more complex, the measures that they drive become more complex as well. It is obvious that the supplier cannot make the examples shown above a reality in isolation; there needs to be a joint commitment.

Of course, the ownership and real effort sits with the supplier. As such, these metrics should be fundamental to demonstrating that the programme works. The customer must see that the supplier has done its job. In short, 'they trusted us to deliver our value promise, and we have'.

Products and advanced services

Professor Theodore Levitt was a Harvard Professor of Economics, who wrote a pivotal paper titled 'Marketing Myopia' [2]. The paper is regarded as classic and of significant importance because it proposed that, rather than emphasizing and talking about features of the products they were trying to sell, organizations should discuss how well the offer they provided met customer needs. Levitt coined a phrase after the paper was written to further articulate this point: 'People don't want a quarter-inch drill, they want a quarter-inch hole.' This is a solid observation. This book has emphasized the need to understand the customer and develop strategies around the specific needs that are discovered.

There really is nothing earth-shattering about Levitt's paper. It was well received and won him a McKinsey award – in 1960! This is a point to reflect on. Thinking, acting and communicating in terms of the customer business (and not simply selling what you offer) is often talked about, but rarely done. This is a significant difference for KAM. If you are building a unique offer, it must resonate with the customer; that means talking in their language.

It can be observed that today, almost 60 years after 'Marketing Myopia', there is a shift that is forcing business into a position whereby suppliers must provide value for the customer. This shift is coming from technology in its many forms. In their book, *Absolute Value* [3], Simonson and Rosen describe a new model now used by consumers to quantify the value of things they purchase. They argue that there are three factors that now influence a consumer when selecting goods and services:

- *marketing* – the information that sellers send to the market in the form of advertising, brand positioning and promotions;

- *prior preferences* – the consumer draws on their own personal history and experiences when buying;

- *other people* – this is a critical emerging influence, where consumers take the views of other consumers and seek advice (good and bad) about the things they are buying.

Figure 5.6 Technology accelerates advanced services

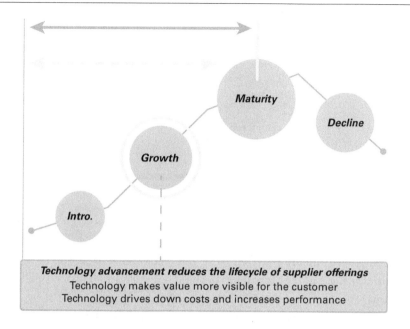

Technology advancement reduces the lifecycle of supplier offerings
Technology makes value more visible for the customer
Technology drives down costs and increases performance

This latter trend is firmly in place and has shifted value power to the consumer. No matter how hard organizations advertise and 'transmit' messages to the market, if consumers are dissatisfied they will report it and 'tribes' of like-minded users will gather around and comment, positively and negatively, about the supply offering.

This has an impact on many things. For suppliers, it means that they must deliver good products that are competitively priced and stronger than the competing offerings. It also means that the length of time a new product or brand can enjoy as 'market leader' is reduced. Figure 5.6 shows a product life-cycle chart. Historically, organizations might have enjoyed several years from a new product entering a market. Competitors would eventually bring comparable products to market, but there was a respectable period for suppliers to generate income before this happened.

Today, this period can be reduced to months. Even Apple, the biggest organization in the world, has to bring new versions of its iPhone and iPad to market at least once a year. Two factors drive this: first, consumers expect better products (and voice their opinions, as proposed by *Absolute Value*). Second, technology is moving forward at an exponential rate, with the speed and capability of processors rapidly advancing, whilst the cost and size grow smaller and availability becomes greater.

To compound this, with these cheaper and more powerful technologies, the Internet of Things (IoT) is rapidly emerging and bringing a connectivity that suppliers can use to monitor and track the use of their products in operation, often globally. Technology is a phenomenon of the 21st century. It can be argued that

Figure 5.7   Integrating KAM and advanced services

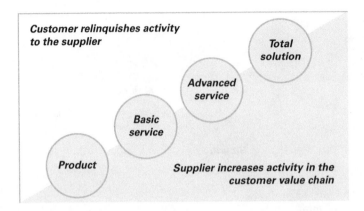

we are still in the infancy of the capability of the internet and those technologies that both empower and are powered by it. But against this backdrop of threats and opportunities, what can KAMgrs do to develop stronger and more compelling value propositions?

One response is to develop innovative value propositions by wrapping services around the foundation core products. Sometimes known as 'servitization', it can also be described as 'advanced services' and lends itself perfectly to KAM (it can be argued that 'advanced services' cannot exist with a key account/key supplier type of relationship).

Figure 5.7 shows how a supplier can integrate into the customer operations by increasing the level of service they provide. As each step advances, the supplier takes a bit more activity away from the customer, and the customer relinquishes activity to the supplier. We could take the example of a pharmaceutical equipment supplier:

- *Products* – this is a range of processing, blending, drying, packaging and labelling machinery. The supplier could provide these pieces of equipment to customers who wanted to implement and operate them themselves.

- *Basic service* – the supplier could provide the equipment but also provide validation and commissioning support at the implementation stage.

- *Advanced service* – the supplier could offer a package whereby the machinery is maintained and calibrated over its entire operational life. With the use of remote sensors and the IoT, there could be a 24-hour/7-day-per-week monitor and evaluation package provided.

- *Solution* – the supplier could provide the equipment, install and validate, maintain and operate. This allows the pharmaceutical customer to focus on their value-adding activities (developing and marketing innovative new drugs) and relinquishing the manufacture of products (a lower value-adding activity) to the equipment supplier.

The advanced service package is becoming a very popular and established phenom-enon. Organizations have been changing their value propositions because of more advanced, reliable and cost-effective technologies. For example, Rolls-Royce aero engines can offer 'power by the hour'. Sensors are installed in engines and, if the customer chooses, Rolls-Royce can track the performance of the engine whilst it is in operation all over the world. The information is collected at the Derby headquar-ters and reports are sent to the airline operator before the aircraft lands, advising if repairs and maintenance are required.

JCB and Caterpillar operate similar advanced packages. They can monitor equip-ment in use (literally in the field) and inform staff, should maintenance be required. The sensors also track equipment, should it be stolen.

This use of technology is one aspect of the advanced service offering. Of course, there are several other aspects that require managerial and relationship design. This is where KAM is an essential component.

Interview with Professor Tim Baines, Head of ASG (Advanced Services Group) and Eleanor Musson, Senior Partnership Manager ASG

The Advanced Services Group is a centre of excellence at Aston Business School, Aston University in the UK. They provide education, training, research and a global network of like-minded professionals around advanced services and servitization. ASG work with global manufacturers and technology innovators to develop services-led strategies, and are a leading organization in the advancement of service-based value propositions.

Q. Why do you think AS is gaining in popularity? Why is it attractive to suppliers and customers?

Manufacturing is experiencing one of the most turbulent periods in its history. Faced with competition from both low-cost competitors and new high-tech disruptors, traditional manufacturers have to radically innovate the way in which they compete if they are to thrive. Meanwhile, the appetite of consumers and businesses in the most developed economies for product ownership is declining relative to their consumption of services.

Q. How would you define advanced services?

A particular type of business model – an *advanced service* business model – is being adopted to meet this challenge. With this business model, the emphasis changes from being focused on the sale of products to delivering a capability within the customer's business operations. These business models exploit digital technologies and the design authority of the manufacturer, and can lead to benefits such as locking out competitors, developing sustainable revenue streams and stimulating growth.

There are four components to the business model:

- customer value proposition: what you will do for the customer and the outcome they will receive;
- value creation and delivery system: the resources, processes, organizational structure and partnerships needed to develop and deliver the value proposition;
- value capture mechanism: how you will get the benefit and revenue from what you do;
- competitive advantage: how you will be better than your competitors at doing what you propose.

Within an advanced service business model, the customer value proposition is to support the customer's business (rather than simply supporting a product). The proposition is to support the assets, processes and even the business model of the customer.

Q. Do you think that suppliers that are providing AS offerings manage to generate a good financial return?

Yes. Companies like Rolls-Royce make around 50 per cent of annual revenue from advanced services. This business model can help to both win new customers and lock in existing ones for longer contracts or increase the amount of business done with them.

Q. What sort of things do suppliers need to do to ensure they develop and operate profitable programmes?

Delivering these services successfully is a complex undertaking. An organization that adopts advanced services as its overall strategy will go through significant change in terms of staffing and skills, facilities and processes, operations, use of data etc.

A few key points to get started are:

1 Get to know your customers better, and learn about the customer's own customers: service offerings should help your customer to become more successful in their own operations and grow their own business.

2 Understand the services business landscape: work out the potential market and the level of costs and risk involved with offering advanced services.

3 Benchmark what others are doing: well-established advanced services offerings exist in a range of industries; find out what these manufacturers have done, and how and why it is successful in order to help generate your own ideas.

4 Ensure existing products and services are fit for purpose: you cannot deliver advanced services if your existing products are not reliable and your current services offerings (eg spare parts and maintenance) are not responsive.

5 Understand your value network: delivering services is different to delivering products; you need to understand which existing partners you should and shouldn't work with.

Example of a customer value proposition

It is useful to have a simple model that will act as a guide to build a customer value proposition. Figure 5.8 provides this framework. It pulls together all the aspects covered so far in this chapter and can be used by practitioners and KAMgrs as a 'step-by-step guide'.

Step 1: Describe the customer future state. Refer back to the five value sources discussed earlier in the chapter and use them as a guide to determine the opening value future state. Remember, this should be impactful and reference things of importance to the customer.

Step 2: Supplier offering. Refer back to the 7Ps model and think about ways in which you will deliver value. Additionally, Figure 5.7, which illustrates the KAM integration and advanced services model, is useful here; it can help you to brainstorm and build your KAM business model.

Step 3: Evidence and credibility. This requires case studies and references to past examples where you have implemented similar models. This will be stronger if you have examples in the customer's business (maybe in other countries or operating units). Also consider examples from similar industries – it will resonate with the customer more.

Step 4: Value appraisal. Refer to the section on quantifying customer value. Be as precise and compelling as possible. These are the components that will need to satisfy general managers, finance and legal (with your organization and the customers) so be careful regarding your value proposition claims!

Figure 5.8 Customer value proposition construct process

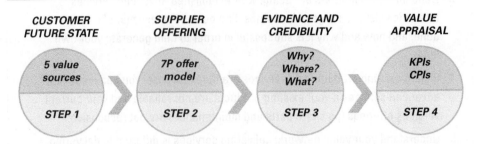

CUSTOMER FUTURE STATE	SUPPLIER OFFERING	EVIDENCE AND CREDIBILITY	VALUE APPRAISAL
5 value sources	7P offer model	Why? Where? What?	KPIs CPIs
STEP 1	STEP 2	STEP 3	STEP 4

The following case study shows an example of a customer value proposition. This must be anonymized, but it reflects a real-life situation. The supplier was a manufacturer of controls and energy efficiency equipment. They supplied products and services to large customers via a network of distributors and control panel builders. Historically, this relationship had become strained, and to improve matters the supplier decided to select a small number of key distributor organizations which they felt were strategically positioned, technically superior, professionally organized and of the correct mindset.

The example value proposition was what they pitched to a large distributor 'customer' with whom they wanted to develop a stronger relationship.

CASE STUDY Your sustainable growth from our partnership

We understand and appreciate your aspiration to have a secure and sustainable business whilst operating in a challenging, changing and competitive marketplace. Your goal to be recognized as a premium control systems provider will give you a competitive advantage, and we would like to be a key enabler of your transition and future. We conservatively estimate that we can raise your annual turnover by (15–20 per cent) per annum, whilst improving operating profit by (5–10 per cent). These targets could be achieved within an 18-month time-frame. This performance is underpinned by our working together in partnership to deliver value to 'end-user' customers.

To enable these results, we can offer you membership of the Strategic Partner Programme. This is aimed at enterprises that we recognize as strategically placed to promote our products and services, whilst also having a cultural fit. The programme focuses on four key pillars:

1 *Sales growth:* we will help you win more business.

2 *Operating efficiency:* we will help you to run a more profitable business.

3 *Quality systems*: we will provide systems to make your operations compliant and secure.

4 *Strategic and management support*: we will provide advice and support as your organization expands.

The programme has already been in place with selected organizations for some three years, achieving significant results with participating partners. This past performance gives us the confidence that we can now extend this package across Europe and the United States to selected organizations. We will invest resources, systems, equipment and training programmes; in return, we request a more strategic working alliance with you, to drive growth with our mutual customers.

To track the impact of the programme on your business, there will be several measures that capture your effort and time investment against the business improvements that you receive. These KPIs can be demonstrated but are linked to the four strategic pillars listed above.

Effective value propositions follow the guidelines that have been discussed throughout this chapter. This is a good example of how a carefully constructed proposition can only follow on from a lot of research, strategic thinking and intent.

Ten tips to create a compelling customer value proposition

1 Remember! A well-researched and carefully constructed strategic KAM plan will always provide the critical foundation components to a compelling customer value proposition. It can be argued that the value proposition is the most important aspect of KAM (since this is what the customer ultimately buys), but in the absence of KAM you will struggle to build a strong proposition.

2 A unique customer value proposition is essential in KAM. With smaller customers, a more generic/vanilla offer is acceptable (this is the only cost-effective way to serve large numbers of smaller-value customers), but KAM demands a unique approach, and this requires innovation. Draw on the wider capability of the organization. Include typically 'non-sales' professionals – they have tremendous insights, experience and ideas.

3 Stronger value propositions are those that meet more strategic customer challenges. To understand these challenges, this often means having conversations with more senior executives and possibly board members. 'Different conversations

with different people' is a mantra that is often used in KAM – these conversations lead to deeper insights and consequently stronger ideas and value propositions.

4   Describing a future state for the customer should be the leading section of the value proposition. This should focus on value benefits and gains for the customer. The five sources of value should be considered: top line; bottom line; business reputation and continuity; strategy organizational and advisory; and finally, the customer's customer (the consumer). Really stretch your understanding of what the customer values – use these five sources of value to discuss value.

5   It is not uncommon for suppliers to forget the tremendous breadth and depth of the things that they provide today, and what they could provide in the future. It is strongly recommended that the 7P model be adopted (and adapted) to suit your business. Use it to brainstorm and think about new things that could be supplied. Always recognize the value to the customer that every component of your offer provides.

6   If the supplier does not capture the value they provide to the customer, the customer will not buy – why should they? Be careful to split the high-value-adding critical value measures from the plethora of lower-key value measures. These should feature in your value proposition, along with investment return and fee estimates.

7   It is almost certain that an innovative value proposition will take an existing bundle of products and enhance this offering with a set of services. In so doing, the supplier will integrate more deeply into the customer business. There are a range of service options, from base services right through to advanced solution packages. Quite often, the simpler and less advanced options provide more benefits for both parties. Be mindful that delivering a solution to a customer is a completely different business model to delivering a product.

8   Keep an eye on your competitors (they will be looking to eat your lunch). Competitive advantage comes from two measures: meeting and exceeding customer expectations, and surpassing competitor offerings. If you are blind to your competitors and the strength of what they supply, how can you compete with them?

9   Deliver what you promise. It is very dangerous to sell something to a customer and then fail in its delivery. In the scramble to develop something compelling and unique, innovation techniques can produce some fantastic ideas. Make sure that your wider organization is aware of what you have promised (key members may be less than willing to support the delivery of the new offering).

10 Keep your value proposition sharp and well written. Make it punchy and use language that resonates with the customer. A good tip is to start with bullet points and drawings. Test these 'concepts' and when everybody is happy, bring in the copy-editors.

Interview with Andrea Clatworthy, Head of Account-Based Marketing, Fujitsu

Andrea is a leading practitioner and thought leader in the field of Account-Based Marketing. Her 2017 presentation to the Cranfield KAM Best Practice Club on ABM was one of the best-received sessions and has set the pathway for many KAM organizations to start considering how they can integrate ABM into their own organizations.

Q. What is Account-Based Marketing (ABM) and how do you use it to create value for your customers and Fujitsu?

ABM is a strategic approach that coordinates relevant marketing and sales efforts to open doors and deepen engagement at specific accounts. Or to put it another way, treating one customer as a market in its own right. Working closely with the account team the ABMer can, taking lots of insight from all sorts of sources, including what the account team already knows about the customer, help define the right story and messages that are relevant to the customer – a compelling value proposition – and then with a well-thought-through integrated marketing communications campaign, ensure the right message gets to the right person at the right time. The three key measures we use are Relationships, Reputation and Revenue: enabling the right positioning (reputation) with the right stakeholders (relationships) means that marketing can help support the revenue objectives of the organization, which is generally the definition of value for any selling organization. Typically we find that if we get the first two Rs right, the third comes along. Using this approach also ensures we are only taking things that are relevant to the customer. Because we've done our research and determined what is important to them, we are adding value by helping them with things they need, even if they don't quite know they need them yet, and when that happens it can reduce the length of the sales cycle too.

Q. What sort of success have you had implementing ABM?

ABM is about developing the account, by 'shifting left' and engaging with the customer well before they have come out to market with their requirements. We know the way customers buy has changed significantly over the past few years, so we need to respond to that. We've found this approach is so successful that we cannot keep up with the demand for ABM from the business, and indeed also for Deal-Based Marketing, which uses the same approach as ABM but for when there is a sniff of an opportunity, or deal, in play. Great ABM naturally gives rise to DBM; however, we are getting demand for DBM on accounts which are not in the ABM programme, because the bid teams see the value in it as well. At Fujitsu we've influenced approximately 60 per cent of the pipeline with ABM and DBM, with 2 per cent of the marketing resource.

Q. Do you think KAM and ABM work together well? What are the key lessons to get them aligned and effective?

Yes! They work very well together especially when the KAM and the ABMer operate as peers, and the objectives of each align. There needs to be an open and honest working relationship, with the account team including the ABMer as part of the team, and the ABMer being confident enough to challenge thinking and assumptions, to be the marketing and communications expert, and often to act as the Voice of the Customer. Some 'skin in the game' plays a role here too, and the way I enable that is that Marketing pay for the resource – the ABMer – and the account pays for any activity that requires spend. This maintains the peer relationship and avoids either party 'chucking stuff over the wall', or the ABMer being treated as an extra admin resource or the provider of PowerPoint, pens and parties. When the collaboration works brilliantly, and at strategic level, the KAM and the ABMer become the driving force together for the account. I have one ABMer who is called 'the boss' by one of her KAMs. On the flip side, I have seen KAMs that are inexperienced or unsure of their stature and strategy reject ABM as interfering in their kingdom, so picking the right account and the right KAM is just important (right horse and right jockey) as assigning the right ABMer.

Final thoughts

1 In many ways, the customer value proposition is the most important aspect of KAM. If the key customer is truly 'a market segment of one' and demands a unique offer, then the development of a high-impact value proposition is critical. Ultimately, the customer buys the value proposition, not a KAM plan.

2 KAM often draws on strategy, planning, project management and a systems approach to doing business. These things are all relevant, but in the absence of creativity and innovation, nothing new will evolve. Innovative customer value propositions need creativity and new ways of thinking to establish attractive offerings for the customer.

3 To enable this creative thinking, there has to be a wide and broad-thinking KAM team. Insights in input need to come from supply chain, manufacturing, finance and R&D. The establishment of a committed and engaged KAM team is critical to enable creative idea generation when building new KAM value propositions.

4 The planning cycle described in this book aligns value proposition and KAM perfectly. All value propositions start with a deep understanding of the customer, and stage one of the KAM planning cycle captures the strategy of the customer. KAM and innovation align perfectly – they don't conflict.

5 Strong customer value propositions describe a 'future state' that will improve their business world. The more relevant this is (will it help them achieve their strategic goals and objectives?) the more likely the customer is to buy the offer. Relationships and trust at a higher organizational level help to increase the level of potential value impact (and hence a stronger value proposition).

6 There are five sources of value that suppliers can use to improve the future state of the customer: top line; bottom line; business reputation and continuity; strategy organizational and other advisory; and the consumer (the customer's customer). Dropping your price is not a source of value!

7 Many key account value propositions develop by adding service packages around a core platform of products. These 'Advanced Service Programmes' can add significant value to the customer and the supplier, but they are a different business model. We see KAM as a vital management activity to enable advanced services, and advanced services as a critical element in the KAM toolkit.

8 One of the biggest complaints from KAMgrs is that they struggle to get support from managers from other departments and functions. To address this challenge, Account-Based Marketing is emerging – a means of allocating marketing professionals to key accounts when there is a strategic need to boost thinking and research power. ABM is an exciting new aspect of KAM, and it's highly probable that it will continue to develop in the future.

9 That said, if we look at one of the strongest sectors that practises KAM, the consumer packaged goods industry (organizations such as P&G, Unilever and Mars), they have huge dedicated teams that work for just one customer (such as Wal-Mart). They have Account-Based Marketing, Supply Chain, Finance, Manufacturing and even HR. ABM is exciting, but some industries have practised the idea for decades (it is simply leveraging resources to meet customer potential opportunity).

10 Ultimately, building a KAM plan and developing innovative customer value propositions rests on the shoulders of the KAMgr. It cannot be overstated (again) that high-impact key account programmes need high-calibre individuals to make a lot of complex things happen (and generate value for both the supplier and the customer).

References

[1] Davies, M (2017) *Infinite Value: Accelerating profitable growth through value-based selling*, Bloomsbury, London.

[2] Levitt, T (1960) Marketing Myopia, *Harvard Business Review*, 38, pp 24–27.

[3] Simonson, I and Rosen, E (2014) *Absolute Value: What really influences customers in the age of (nearly) perfect information*, Harper Business, New York.

Co-creating value with key customers   06

'Whatever you can do, or dream you can, begin it. Boldness has genius, power and magic in it.'

J W VON GOETHE

How can your company engage with key customers to define practices to co-create value in ways that each organization alone could not?

Overview

In the previous chapter, we outlined the components of a value proposition and ways in which value can be quantified. In this chapter, we go deeper into analysing the joint supplier–customer processes that underpin value creation. We conceptualize value co-creation as a capability that is built through the focused engagement of both the supplier and the customer organizations and individuals.

Foundations of value co-creation: value in exchange vs value in use

Value co-creation is an overarching theme that captures the evolution of organizational entities towards the development of a higher relational orientation and deeper interaction between suppliers and some of their key customers [1]. In business-to-business markets there is a recognized shift in the locus of value creation from simple 'exchange', that is the value is inherent in the product, to 'value in use', whereby value is created in the process of utilizing the product or service to a particular end. Value cannot be circumscribed to the consumption of units of output any more, but is seen as a process of interacting in ways to produce a holistic experience [2].

Value in use may be created prior, during and after the purchase [3], hence value resides not in the object of consumption, but in the experience of consumption [4]. Another dimension is 'value in the experience' as the lived experiences of value that extend beyond the current context of service use to also include past and future experiences and customers' 'broader life contexts' [5].

Value co-creation therefore extends beyond the present interaction between a producer and a customer, and includes also past and future experiences and expectations. Service providers need to understand the customers' continuously emerging experience beyond individual interaction episodes, as well as their activities with other actors to facilitate value co-creation [3].

Value in use is realized through more nuanced, and subtle factors than value in exchange. For instance, in the context of industrial and manufacturing companies these may include [6]:

- organizational competences of the supplier;
- employee competences;
- customer orientation;
- network competences.

For value co-creation to emerge, the roles of producers and consumers must shift, allowing the interfaces amongst actors to connect and integrate their resources [7]. Customers create value for themselves when using the resources offered by a supplier firm, whereas firms can develop opportunities to co-create value with customers by creating possibilities for interaction during the use of goods and services [8].

Unilever Food Solutions: co-creating inspiration for your customers

Unilever Food Solutions (UFS) is a global provider of food products and ingredients aimed at creating solutions that help chefs and food service professionals in their jobs. UFS operates in 65 countries worldwide, directly employing 5,400 people, including 2,600 salespeople and 150 chefs, all sharing a 'passion for food'. Despite the complexities of the food service market and its decline in mature markets through the global economic recession, UFS has maintained a stable position in a highly competitive environment by recognizing that food service has increasingly become a commoditized market with a growing number of alternative brands for professional use. The company prides itself in being a customer-centric organization, that is, rather than just a food product manufacturer, a solutions provider, committed to adding value to the catering industry through engaging with its clients in purposefully defined culinary developments. They realize this mission by sponsoring key industry events, helping customers with recipes and ideas for food preparation and presentation, food costing analyses, and working with chosen channel partners to provide customers with the best possible solutions for their food preparation processes.

UFS aims to offer its customers 'inspiration every day', helping them succeed in their own businesses through its developmental interaction capability. To address this purpose, UFS re-energized its offering by developing a comprehensive suite of services. These include three core areas: first, 'Your Guests', aiming to inspire food operators to understand more about their guests and their behaviour when eating out; second, 'Your Menu', encouraging food professionals to design nutritious and healthy meals, but at the same time creating profitable menus; and third, 'Your Kitchen', providing operational insights to optimize kitchen processes, helping chefs to work smarter rather than harder [9]. Drawing on a wealth of knowledge of food operations, consumers and markets, UFS co-creates solutions in its interaction with customers (co-diagnosis, co-ideation and co-design), which help food service businesses to become more effective and competitive. UFS's chefs are a key element of the customer service strategy and their expertise is offered as part of a total value proposition. Overall, UFS sales and culinary teams are instrumental in implementing the firm's aim of purposeful engagement with customers to identify how to meet key challenges in food service such as quality, effectiveness of kitchen functions, taste, originality and food safety.

UFS marketing and sales teams work together with key customers' marketers and food operations staff to co-design concepts and co-ideate new solutions. These concepts typically include a combination of branded products, merchandise and equipment. Altogether, these aim to offer the end consumer an enhanced experience, and the operator new opportunities to grow its revenues in the food [10] and beverage [11] categories. Overall, differentiated value propositions are co-created for different types of customers, aiming to be consistent with the company's overall customer management strategy.

As an example of its interaction capability and co-ideation practices, UFS prides itself in its ability to listen to its customers and consumers. Award-winning marketing practices [12] and new products have often come from its engagement with network partners that allow an in-depth understanding of the consumer and meaningful customer insights. Applying the latest technologies, the company co-creates products that provide consumers with a unique experience [13]. Product innovation is at the heart of what the company does. In particular, there is a marked emphasis on co-designing product innovations that significantly increase consumers' wellbeing, whilst reducing environmental impact. For instance, the company reported that 61 per cent of its products met salt levels equivalent to 5g per day, and the total waste per ton of production was reduced to 4.77 kg (from 6.48 kg) [14].

Understanding consumer and customer needs is a key driver for product innovation at Unilever. Bi-annually, UFS releases the World Menu Report [15]. This document contains research into consumers' eating habits globally. It is recognized that eating habits have changed substantially over the last few decades, with increasing concern for the nutritional aspects of food, but without compromising the enjoyment and pleasure of food tasting. In particular, the latest report indicated an overwhelming need for consumers to be provided with more information about the food they are eating when out of the home. As a result, UFS is developing ways to raise awareness and increase transparency about food ingredients. As the report recognizes, 'Chefs have the power to change the health of our world. And restaurants, shops, canteens, schools and cafeterias along with food service providers all need to be part of the solution' [16].

Innovation in business-to-business contexts does not just come from product innovation. It is widely acknowledged that sustainable competitive advantage can no longer be achieved just by improving existing products. As in other sectors, food service has seen the surge of service solutions, part of which is the co-creation of value and the adoption of a partnership approach with the customer [16]. UFS has been pioneering innovative offerings and ways of working collaboratively that have become 'best practice' in food service.

Hence, value creation can occur within at least three spheres: the provider, the customer, and the joint sphere created in their interaction. In addition to the customer being an independent value creator [17], value is co-created in the joint sphere by empowering the customer to integrate and use other actors' resources into their own processes. Often wider networks of B2B actors can also be involved in the process, for example by 'mediating' value creation [18]. This way, the boundaries of the joint sphere are expanded, enabling a broader interaction platform and engendering new value co-creation opportunities.

Practices and capabilities for value co-creation

Value co-creation with key customers requires the development of a set of practices across the supplier and the customer organizations. We understand a practice as 'a routinized type of behaviour' comprising skills and knowledge, and manifested in the way organizations and individuals work, understand and interrelate in a social context [19]. Practices can be claimed to be *routinized ways of doing* performed by individuals involved in key account relationships, underpinned by specific *capabilities*. These provide stability and continuity to the organization, allowing the co-creation of value over time [20], [21].

In turn, we see capabilities as embedded, sustained and habitual patterns that become the foundation for competitive advantage. Capability is generally defined as a set of 'skills and resources which enable the company to achieve superior performance' [22] in a way that is almost impossible for competitors to mimic [23], [24]. Because of their dynamic nature, capabilities enable the organization and its network of actors to match resources to the changing needs in the environment [25]. We characterize capabilities as the integrative mechanisms that provide the coherence and integration of practices so they result in value co-creation. In this sense, capabilities allow the 'whole' (value co-creation) to emerge, becoming more than the sum of

Figure 6.1   Interaction capabilities for value co-creation

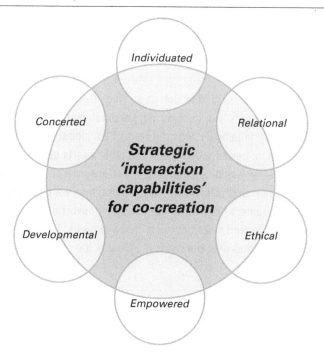

the 'parts' (practices). In other words, capabilities provide the background for the assembly and integration of firm-specific assets into clusters, allowing the realization of value co-creation.

Existing research identifies six strategic 'interaction capabilities' that enable an organization to co-create value by facilitating the reciprocal integration of resources across customer and supplier organizations [26]:

1 *Individuated* interaction capability refers to the identification of a customer's expressed and latent needs, processes and the value sought by these customers [27].

> An example of individuated capabilities is Amazon; its systems analyse search and purchase patterns in order to offer individuated suggestions and purchase recommendations [26].

2 *Relational* interaction capability is the cultivation of social and emotional ties between the parties and empathic interaction with the customer decision makers and key individuals [28].

3 *Ethical* interaction capability manifests by enabling fair and reasonable customer processes, avoiding opportunistic behaviour, so that trust emerges to govern the relationship between supplier and customer.

4 *Empowered* interaction capability enables the customer to influence the relationship agenda and the conception and delivery of value.

> About a decade ago, Nike decided to shift its strategy from being a sportswear brand to becoming the enabler of customized, personal experiences through the 'Customer Decides' initiative. It was the start of the global sportswear manufacturer betting on personalized boots and other sports gear.
>
> Nike CEO Mark Parker explained then that 'The Consumer Decides is one of Nike's 11 maxims that really define who we are and how we compete as a company. Today, consumers have never held as much power as they do today. They have more choices and more access to those choices. They connect and collaborate with each other over the world. ... Clearly, the power has shifted to consumers'.

5 *Developmental* interaction capability builds the knowledge, competence and learning necessary for resource integration.

6 *Concerted* interaction capability is the ability to coordinate and involve the customer in value-creating activities that take place across departments and the wider network of actors [26].

Microsoft and AstraZeneca's collaboration in drug discovery simulation provides a good example of concerted interaction capabilities. These two companies are involved in a collaboration to develop the so-called 'drag and drop' computer modelling of key signalling pathways in cancer cells. This approach has the potential to drastically reduce the need for traditional laboratory experiments to bring personalized treatments to patients and to increase the effectiveness of drug development by focusing the research on the cell targets that matter most. The joint effort has enabled the development of a computer tool called the Bio Model Analyser (BMA), a simulation tool being used to predict drug effects on cancer cell signalling pathways.

 Jonathan Dry, principal scientist and global strategy lead (Bioinformatics, Oncology, Innovative Medicines and Early Development) at AstraZeneca claims, 'We [AZ] contributed the big data sets and knowledge about the signalling pathways in order to fine-tune the models, and Microsoft brought the software expertise. They captured the relationships between proteins in a pathway to build the model and run the simulation. We were then on hand to validate the results of simulations with our laboratory data.' [29]

These joint capabilities are the ones that enable supplier organizations to achieve a service-dominant orientation and to jointly realize value with their customers. How they relate to the various co-creation practices is still a fertile area of scholarly and practitioner work [30].

 Table 6.1 presents a set of practices that firms exhibit when engaging in value co-creation with key customers.

 There are a growing number of examples of firms engaging in value co-creation practices with key customers. For instance, the provision of complex offerings in advanced technologies such as aerospace and professional (eg management consultancy) requires elements of 'co-diagnosis': actors collect and organize information for collaborative use [31] in order to 'co-diagnose' their need to facilitate offer development and, if necessary, its re-design [32], [33], [34].

 Organizational innovation processes are driven by co-creation practices like co-ideation, co-valuation, co-design, co-testing, and co-launching. These practices can be seen as intertwined stages during which actors co-create value. In addition, a customer's role in quality assurance relates naturally to value co-creation practices in B2B markets, ie to evaluate the emergence and outcomes of an offering [34].

Table 6.1   Co-creation practices and underpinning capabilities

Co-creation practices	Underpinning capabilities
Co-diagnosis. Collecting and organizing information for collaborative use *Co-ideation.* Generating and suggesting ideas, communicating and sharing, engaging *Co-evaluation.* Commenting and selecting ideas	*Connecting* Mobilization of social connections and networks across the supplier, the key account(s) and their ecosystems
Co-design. Developing concepts and knowledge *Co-testing.* Prototyping and improving the offering, giving feedback *Co-launching.* Creating and managing information, advertising, marketing, and diffusing information	*Developing* Production of co-created product-service offerings.
Embedding. Developing rules, norms and standards	*Reinforcing* Organizational practices related to the design of institutions and structures to capture and retain value created

Figure 6.2   Co-creation capabilities and practices

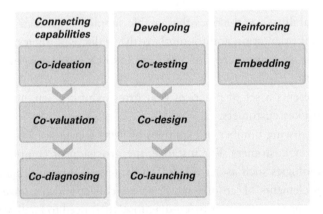

In the event of unexpected results, both customer and seller can be involved in service recovery resulting in positive consequences for the development of the relationship, including diminishing risk perception for future cooperation and clearer roles followed by better value co-creation potential [35], [36]. In certain contexts value co-creation among actors in service systems [37] becomes institutionalized, that is, embedded in the company's systems and ways of working.

We integrate these practices into a framework of three core capabilities (Connecting, Developing and Reinforcing) to develop a more complete view of value co-creation.

Rolls-Royce: co-creating value through advanced services

The Rolls-Royce Group is a global business with customers in more than 120 countries and a workforce of 55,000 committed to the vision of 'better power for a changing world'. Rolls-Royce provides power systems and services for civil aerospace, defence, marine and energy markets [38]. The company is widely known in the aerospace industry for TotalCare®, an innovative offering that consists of a menu of original equipment and related services. Rolls-Royce provides a comprehensive suite of services including full engine overhaul and a number of engine reliability improvements, all under Rolls-Royce specialist maintenance capabilities. Add-on services include technical records management, engine transportation, spare engine support, additional overhaul coverage and the option for the customer to initiate specialist line maintenance. The customer-driven approach and the slightly different service levels across different customers make TotalCare® highly customizable and adaptable to customer needs.

The development of TotalCare® was driven by interest from key customers such as American Airlines to be offered 'on the wing' service contracts [39]. Additionally, the threat of third parties that entered the aftermarket parts business compelled Rolls-Royce to further develop new service offerings which have, over the years, proved highly successful. TotalCare® developed further into providing engine health monitoring, a service that captures engine performance data in real time using the Aircraft Communications Addressing and Reporting System (ACARS). The data is then transmitted from the aircraft to Rolls-Royce service centres by radio or satellite, enabling Rolls-Royce to detect potential anomalies quickly and to predict and plan urgent or future engine repairs. Over the years, the focus of TotalCare® has gradually shifted to 'no remote site issues'; in other words, preventing the costly breakdowns in remote locations that result in major expenditures in terms of flying engines out for refit and significant costs for airlines as a result of network disruption [40], [41], [42], [43]. TotalCare® and other advanced services represent more than 50 per cent of Rolls-Royce's civil aerospace revenue today.

For customers, TotalCare® means enhanced predictability, durability, efficiency, reliability and maintained asset value. Customers achieve higher levels of predictability in terms of operational performance, reducing unplanned shop visits. Rolls-Royce has a huge amount of data on engine performance that enables the company to quickly detect variance and address potential non-conformities. TotalCare® also enables increased cash-flow predictability since customers can opt in to the process of paying by the hour of engine operation, aligning the interests of both Rolls-Royce and the customers. In order to realize these benefits, deep engagement with the customer and a clear understanding of the purpose and operational model of the airline are required. Very close customer collaboration is realized, underpinned by Rolls-Royce's 'empowered' and 'concerted' interaction capabilities to ensure in-depth understanding of the airline operations, network structure and asset (ie aircraft) utilization regimes. TotalCare® packages are designed knowing how the airlines operate their aircraft in order to gain efficiencies. A factor that affects engine lifecycle is the way that airline pilots fly. Rolls-Royce adopts an 'engine life' approach to service contracts and encourages pilots to manage the use of thrust in ways that enhance engine durability. In an effort to employ its co-diagnosing practices, a Flight Operations Advisor (FOA) from Rolls-Royce works closely with airlines and spends time with pilots, advising them on more efficient flying methods that also help to reduce fuel burn. Lastly, value is co-created well beyond the product, since modern equipment under TotalCare® maintains higher resell value [40].

TotalCare® as a co-created and integrated service offering is constantly evolving. Rolls-Royce has developed sophisticated processes and capabilities to better understand airlines' interests. Frequent internal events called the 'Voice of the Customer' allow customer teams to visit Rolls-Royce and to spend time with various parts of the business, including Sales, Marketing, Service Operations and Engineering, to share their experiences with Rolls-Royce teams and vice versa. This helps build mutual organizational understanding and to focus on providing specific operational benefits. Overall, the provision of TotalCare® brings about a fundamental shift from emphasizing the transaction (new engine sale) to a long-term, risk-sharing, value co-creating partnership.

These capabilities form three overarching dimensions. First, the first set of practices relate to facilitating connections and mobilizing networks [1], which we label *connecting*. Such practices ideally take place on a continuous basis and include sharing and circulating knowledge and ideas not only about the offering, but also about the relationship, markets, and resources. Second, the operational practices that are tightly related to the emergence of co-created offerings [30] are labelled *developing* [44]. These practices include the creation of material objects and artefacts that demonstrate and realize elements of the co-created value offering. Third, *reinforcing* practices are embedded across the connecting and *developing* practices by continuous coordination, ie the design of institutions and structures to capture and retain the value created [45]. The categories presented in Table 6.1 do not need to happen in a linear order but may take place simultaneously and continuously.

> Xerox creates value with strategic accounts leveraging respective (customer/ supplier) strengths. Their approach to co-innovation brings together ethnographers, material scientists, technologists, etc to scope and deliver co-innovation not just for new service generation, but also to identify relevant innovation at the level of supply chain networks, business models, etc [46].

Value co-creation as purposeful engagement

Following the outline of practices and capabilities for value co-creation, we present a grounded model grouping of value co-creation practices and underpinning capabilities. This makes the process of value co-creation more tangible and thus applicable to B2B organizations that may be pursuing value co-creation in their business contexts. We present a conceptualization of three higher-order categories (Connecting, Developing and Reinforcing) to organize and make sense of co-creative practices by bringing them together with the strategic organizational capabilities necessary to achieve them: concerted, individuated, relational, ethical, empowered, and developmental (see Figure 6.3).

The actual processes of co-creation require high degrees of interaction across levels, from the individual to the organization. Co-creation is associated with an increasing blurring of boundaries across actors operating in a network that is held together throughout by high levels of trust, as well as social and emotional ties.

Best practice companies in value co-creation employ the individual co-creative practices in different ways, resulting from their diverse industries. We see commonality in the high level of engagement of their network partners and the role of this engagement in the co-creation process. For example, Bekaert, a world market and technology leader in steel wire transformation and coating technologies, uses co-creation as a means to develop tangible products, through interaction with already established customers.

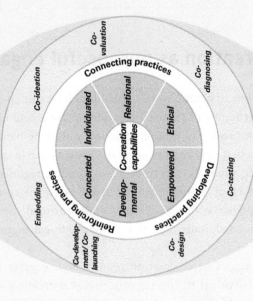

Figure 6.3 The value co-creation framework

Another example, SAP, co-creates knowledge and new solutions not only by involving customers, but also by deliberately inviting a number of different partners from their ecosystems such as universities or governmental groups. This results in a co-creative process with a pronounced emphasis on connecting and institutionalizing. We argue that these differences in practice focus do not mean that one approach to co-creation is more successful than the other. In our experience, the practices identified above and the capabilities that they emerge from can be combined and realized in different ways, while still leading to the co-creation of value.

A key phenomenon of 'compelling events' lies at the heart of the co-creation capability development process. These events act as catalysts for renewed collective action towards co-creation to fulfil the stakeholders' needs and expectations. For instance, Rolls-Royce (see box above) faced an unexpected demand (ie an opportunity) from a key customer, American Airlines, to provide engine-related services to reduce complexity and to increase predictability. SAP initiated their approach to engage key players in their markets with the first major acquisitions of software companies like Steeb and CAS. Unilever Food Solutions realized that increasingly commoditized markets with an explosion of distributor-own brands (DOBs) would quickly diminish their growth, unless a fundamental programme to 'reconnect' with buyers and a fully revised offering were developed and implemented in collaboration with customers.

Not all business organizations respond equally to 'compelling events', suggesting the notion of 'co-creation readiness' as an ability to first sense and seize [47] opportunities for value co-creation and second, deploy the necessary capabilities to build strong relationships to enable the sustaining of co-creation. We argue that not all organizations may have an organizational culture and social capital to enable the fruitful adoption and development of co-creation practices.

High levels of interaction in networks, strong connections, collegiality and trust are necessary but not sufficient conditions to co-create value in B2B systems. Suppliers and key accounts need to *purposefully engage* in practices such as co-design and co-launching. For instance, purposeful engagement enables high-risk technology developments at SAP and the formulation of new-generation jet engines services at Rolls-Royce by galvanizing a collective willingness to mobilize the resources to co-create value in a context of ever-evolving ecosystems and complex technologies. In fact, some of Rolls-Royce's new engines and existing engine improvement programmes with customers span decades. The integrated IT suites that SAP is able to offer are the result of consolidation, integration and redeployment efforts over years. Unilever Food Solutions' service campaigns to co-create menus, and to implement more efficient meal preparation procedures, is implemented owing to the company's tradition of deeply engaging with chefs, buyers of food and beverages and owners of outlets in their food service operations.

We argue that *purposeful engagement* becomes an overarching mechanism that connects organizational capabilities, practices and resources across stakeholders within the B2B system in a way that creates value over protracted time frames. *Purpose* emerges as a widely shared view of the expected outcomes from a co-creating endeavour, facilitated by common technical knowledge. Purpose reveals itself as an important underpinning driver of co-creation, particularly in complex industrial systems, where technologies are constantly evolving and the materialization of a product or a service happens in the medium or long term.

The cases in this chapter reveal how common purpose is facilitated by similar professional cultures and identities. Chefs from Unilever Food Solutions share insights with chefs from food service operators. Engineers from Rolls-Royce scope and assess new developments and address aero-engine issues jointly with airline and aircraft manufacturers' engineers. IT consultants from SAP share an in-depth understanding of information technologies, and customize through demanding configurational activities the systems that will help deliver the customer's business goals. Across the cases, there is a consistent theme: the high level of appreciation between the organization's technical and professional communities. Common purpose is often facilitated by agreed mechanisms to share the risk and the benefits of co-creation, particularly when substantial investments are needed.

Engagement is manifested as the individual actors' interest in the co-creation enterprise and demonstrated by their contribution to practices such as co-ideation, co-valuation, co-diagnosing, through to co-launching. Engagement is also evidenced by a party's openness to consider possibilities and an uncompromising quest to push the 'possible' so it became 'feasible' within complex technologies and highly interconnected B2B systems.

Conclusion

The adoption of co-creation practices through implementation of specific organizational capabilities has a number of implications for managing key accounts, as well as sales organizations. First, the value proposition, traditionally originated by the supplier, now resides in the interface and interaction between key players in the network. Thus, the approach of 'communicating value' needs to be refocused into efforts to facilitate sustained purposeful engagement. Managers can achieve this by designing and agreeing flexible contracts containing outcome-based agreements [48] that encourage alignment and realization of common goals.

Second, new forms of risk and benefit sharing need to be defined, particularly when risk is either higher or more unpredictable than the potential value created within one organization only. Third, the implications of an increasingly servitized and co-created marketplace for sales forces are profound. Conventionally, sales forces were deployed when services or products had been developed by a supplier organization. In complex service offerings, sales forces may be needed even before the solution exists. Sales professionals will be required to engage with customers to co-create the service, and then employ a concerted interaction capability to engage various functions across the supplier organization to deliver it [49], [50].

Industrial sales forces, therefore, will in many contexts have to become more aligned and in some cases integrated with R&D, operations and supply chain functions. Since customer value is created 'in-use' [51], salespeople will have to adopt a proactive and collaborative approach with customers to fully understand their needs and requirements, using methods other than the traditional customer needs analysis. Because customer knowledge may become more critical than product knowledge, business relationships will still fundamentally underpin B2B exchanges and will transcend traditional exchanges to become complex dynamic interactions with customers and other network members. These trends will challenge the conventional notion of the role of salespeople to move from 'selling' to 'co-creating' [52]. Finally, managers need to foster collective (ie across actors) social capital that facilitates alignment and compatible cultural meanings [53]. Social gatherings, interpersonal relationships, games, teamwork exercises, off-site away days and the like will contribute to create the 'social fabric' that underpins meaningful relations conducive to value co-creation.

Interview with Jesús Gómez, Sales Director at Mondelēz International

Mondelēz International Inc (NASDAQ:MDLZ) is building the best snack company in the world, with 2016 net revenues of approximately US $26 billion. Creating more moments of joy in approximately 165 countries, Mondelēz International is a world leader in biscuits, chocolate, gum, candy and cheese, featuring global brands such as Oreo and Prince Biscuits; Milka and Suchard chocolate; and Trident gum. Mondelēz International is a proud member of the Standard and Poor's 500, NASDAQ 100 and Dow Jones Sustainability Index.

We talk to Jesús Gómez, Sales Director for the Spanish market, about his experience dealing with the largest national and global retailers operating in the country.

Q. Jesús, how do you define key accounts within Mondelēz International?

We continuously prioritize our resources on projects and initiatives that will benefit our customers, driving category growth and supported by the Mondelēz brands. Key accounts are the partners that want to develop these projects with Mondelēz. We use the potential growth and profitability as the main drivers, and also consider other operational factors that are relevant for the business; for instance, the degree of integration of logistics, their interest in our product portfolio, the degree of co-operation at the point of sale (POS), and their support of the relationship. Based on these aspects, the classification of key accounts is produced.

Normally, there are not many changes from year to year, but sometimes we see shifts in our classification. For us, the segmentation of key accounts must be dynamic and up to date, as this informs our priorities and the allocation of resources.

In addition, we define key segments or channels that provide the foundations of our commercial strategy, allowing us to concentrate the focus of our efforts and investments where we may see the largest opportunities for future growth.

I would say that key accounts are, overall, those who value our strategic relationships, show commitment to our brands and willingness to innovate, and establish a two-way proactive and regular communication.

Q. How do you identify ways of adding value to your key customers?

Before talking about 'adding value', you have to cover something as basic as the agreed level of service. It is a challenge to maintain service level agreements when you are going through cultural changes within your organization. To keep and maintain key indicators for delivery and demand fulfilment is crucial. We aspire to be within the top five businesses in the Advantage Report™ Ranking, an established benchmark of consumer goods companies where the retailers value the manufacturers, with customer service being a very important driver.

Beyond that, we aim to develop tailored propositions for our most strategic clients such as customer-specific merchandise, branding materials for the point of sale, specific campaigns, etc. Everyone wants to offer differentiation to their shoppers, and that is something that we need to keep in mind, in order to be the category leaders for them.

Q. To what extent do these customers engage in joint planning and value creation?

The food retail market is very consolidated and established, and so are the relationships between manufacturers and customers. We work on joint business plans on a regular basis, though within a framework. Generally speaking, our key customers expect investments and leadership in some food categories. As leaders in some of these consumer categories and brands we are proactive in building the joint business plans through high levels of engagement.

In the out-of-home channel (ie professional food service or impulse), you could argue that customers expect an even higher level of commitment to joint business planning from the manufacturer. They seek support from established brands and the development of relationships that allow sustainable growth by helping them in their outlets and in engaging their consumers.

For instance, Mondelēz sales teams are much valued. Our retail customers recognize their expertise in the point of sale, their skill in placing and organizing the product, and their ability to demonstrate and sample our brands. This approach will generate growth for both sides.

Q. And you said that all this has to be negotiated; does the customer ever adopt a 'tough' approach?

Yes, I just said the joint business plans are developed in the context of negotiation. Sometimes there is a temptation to take a distributive negotiation approach when agreeing some of the details of joint business plans. However, a genuine commitment to collaborating with the customer and maintaining leadership positions in your categories will always lead to a successful outcome for both retailers and manufacturers.

Q. Building on the topic of value creation, what are the practices that add value beyond the product?

Technology, new formats, brands, recipes and formulas are essential. Retailers also value efforts to adapt certain brands to shopper preferences. We are working to offer a different point of view to our customers, trying to balance the relevance of our brands with the strategic priorities of the retailers.

It is critical for us to be listening to consumers; only by doing this can we truly respond to their needs. We invest in innovation and talk to thousands of consumers across Europe to gather key insights that inform new products and improvements on existing ones.

We also work to ensure the sustainability of all aspects of our supply chain, with a focus on those areas where we can have the greatest impact: sustainable agriculture and reducing the environmental footprint of our own operations. We also believe we have a responsibility to make a positive impact on all our stakeholders.

Q. How do you overcome the inherent tensions of adding value and maintaining margins?

We come from a period over the last few years of placing much emphasis on trading margins. The financial crisis had a big impact, and this, coupled with the steady increase in the price of raw materials, has had a negative impact on margins across the entire food value chain.

Now it appears that the economic recovery is enabling the development of innovation, an increase in the consumer average spend, and the return to buying branded and premium products... all of which contributes to a better environment.

It also helps manufacturers and distributors to focus on creating value, category development and innovation, which is where we are at the moment. Nevertheless, price increases are needed to ensure the sustainability of your business. When talking with senior executives in our team, we know they value our approach to innovation; they recognize we understand and lead our categories, and they trust in Mondelēz.

Q. Just to finish, what is your view of the future of Key Account Management?

To conclude, I would say we need to move the needle towards a more advisory kind of selling, taking into account digital transformation. We're operating in a constantly changing ecosystem, from shifting consumer habits and the rapidly evolving retail environment to the advent of Big Data and new technology. The only way to succeed is to rapidly test and learn, while embedding new capabilities.

The 'old' model of KAM solely focused on products is no longer relevant. In the coming years, key account managers will play a consultant role in understanding customer needs and delivering value through the products being commercialized. The interaction with the customer will be wider than just seller-buyer; in this sense we have cross-functional teams working for the more strategic customers. Technology will become a key facilitator. Thus, it will be important that key account management is up to date from a digital standpoint.

Thank you so much Jesús

Questions for managers

- When engaging with key customers in value co-creation, what are the prerequisites for this to work effectively?
- Which practices associated with value co-creation are harder to develop and why?
- If you were to assess the current state of your organization across the practices of co-diagnosis, co-ideation, co-design, co-testing, co-launching and embedding, how would you rate your current capabilities?

References

[1] Ballantyne, D and Varey, R J (2006) Creating value-in-use through marketing interaction: the exchange logic of relating, communicating and knowing, *Marketing Theory*, 6 (3), pp. 335–48.

[2] Payne, A F, Storbacka, K and Frow, P (2008) Managing the co-creation of value, *Journal of the Academy of Marketing Science*, **36** (1), pp. 83–96.

[3] Heinonen, K, et al (2010) A customer-dominant logic of service, *International Journal of Service Industry Management*, **21** (4), pp. 531–48.

[4] Frow, P and Payne, A (2007) Towards the 'perfect' customer experience, *Journal of Brand Management*, **15** (2), pp. 89–101.

[5] Helkkula, A, Kelleher, C and Pihlström, M (2012) Characterizing value as an experience: implications for service researchers and managers, *Journal of Service Research*, **15** (1), pp. 59–75.

[6] Macdonald, E K, Kleinaltenkamp, M and Wilson, H N (2016) How business customers judge solutions: solution quality and value in use, **80** (3) May, pp. 96–120.

[7] Vargo, S L, Maglio, P and Akaka, M A (2008) On value and value co-creation: a service systems and service logic perspective, *European Management Journal*, **26** (3), pp. 145–52.

[8] Grönroos, C (2008) Service logic revisited: who creates value? And who co-creates? *European Business Review*, **20** (4), pp. 298–314.

[9] UFS (2012) Unilever Food Solutions Corporate Website [online] www.unileverfoodsolutions.com

[10] UFS (2012) British Roast Dinner Week [online] www.unileverfoodsolutions.co.uk

[11] UFS (2012) Helping your brew a better business [online] http://prod.ufs.teatips.co.uk

[12] Benjamin, K (2012) Unilever tops 2012 Marketing Society Awards nominations [online] http://www.marketingmagazine.co.uk/news/1129581/

[13] Unilever (2014) Product innovations [online] http://www.unilever.co.uk/innovation/productinnovations/

[14] Unilever (2011) Annual report and accounts [online] http://www.unilever.com /images/Unilever_AR11_tcm13-282960.pdf

[15] UFS (2011) World Menu Report [Online] http://www.ufs.com/company/media-center/world-menu-report.

[16] Occhiocupo, N (2011) Innovation in foodservice: the case of a world leading Italian company, *Marketing Review*, **11** (2), pp. 189–201.

[17] Grönroos, C and Voima, C (2013) Critical service logic: making sense of value creation and co-creation, *Journal of the Academy of Marketing Science*, **41** (2), pp. 133–50.

[18] Nätti, S, et al (2014) The intermediator role in value co-creation within a triadic business service relationship, *Industrial Marketing Management*, **43** (6), pp. 211–57.

[19] Reckwitz, A (2002) Toward a theory of social practices: a development in culturalist theorizing, *European Journal of Social Theory*, **5** (2), pp. 243–63.

[20] Cohen, M D and Bacdayan, P (1994) Organizational routines are stored as procedural memory: evidence from a laboratory study, *Organizational Science*, **5** (4), pp. 554–68.

[21] Cohen, M D (2007) Reading Dewey: reflections on the study of routine, *Organization Studies*, **28** (5), pp. 773–86.

[22] Harmsen, H and Jensen, B (2004) Identifying the determinants of value creation in the market: a competence-based approach, *Journal of Business Research*, **57** (5), pp. 533–47.

[23] Barney, J (1991) Firm resources and sustained competitive advantage, *Journal of Management*, **17** (1), p. 99.

[24] Prahalad, C K and Hamel, G (1990) The core competence of the corporation, *Harvard Business Review*, **68** (3), pp. 79–91.

[25] Teece, D J, Pisano, G and Shuen, A (1997) Dynamic capabilities and strategic management, *Strategic Management Journal*, **18** (7), pp. 509–33.

[26] Karpen, I O, Bove, L L and Lukas, B A (2011) Linking service-dominant logic and strategic business practice: a conceptual model of a service-dominant orientation, *Journal of Service Research*, **15** (1), pp. 21–38.

[27] Terho, A et al (2012) 'It's almost like taking the sales out of selling': towards a conceptualization of value-based selling in business markets, *Industrial Marketing Management*, **41** (1), pp. 174–85.

[28] Wieseke, J, Geigenmüller, A and Kraus, F (2012) On the role of empathy in customer-employee interactions, *Journal of Service Research*, **15** (3), pp. 316–31.

[29] AstraZeneca (2016) Can drag and drop cancer simulation speed up drug discovery? [online] https://www.astrazeneca.com/media-centre/articles/2016/can-drag-and-drop-cancer-simulation-speed-up-drug-discovery.html [accessed 31 October 2017]

[30] Russo-Spena, T and Mele, C (2012) 'Five Co-s' in innovating: a practice-based view, *Journal of Service Management*, **23** (4), pp. 527–53.

[31] McColl-Kennedy, J R et al (2012) Health care customer value cocreation practice styles, *Journal of Service Research*, **15** (4), pp. 370–89.

[32] Aarikka-Stenroos, L and Jaakkola, E (2012) Value co-creation in knowledge intensive business services: a dyadic perspective on the joint problem-solving process, *Industrial Marketing Management*, **41** (1), pp. 15–26.

[33] Grönroos, C (2011) A service perspective on business relationships: the value creation, interaction and marketing interface, *Industrial Marketing Management*, **40** (2), pp. 240–47.

[34] Sampson, S E and Spring, M (2012) Customer roles in service supply chains and opportunities for innovation, *Journal of Supply Chain Management*, **48** (4), pp. 30–50.

[35] Dong, B, Evans, K R and Zou, S (2008) The effects of customer participation in co-created service recovery, *Journal of Academic Marketing Science*, **36** (1), pp. 123–37.

[36] Meuter, M L et al (2005) Choosing among alternative service delivery modes: an investigation of customer trial of self-service technologies, *Journal of Marketing*, **69** (2), pp. 61–83.

[37] Edvardsson, B et al (2014) Negative critical waves in business relationships: an extension of the critical incident perspective, *Journal of Business and Industrial Marketing*, **29** (4), pp. 284–94.

[38] Rolls-Royce (2014) Rolls-Royce Corporate Website [online] www.rolls-royce.com

[39] Frank, N (2014) Powering the future – Rolls Royce total care business success [online] http://productserviceinnovation.com/home/2014/08/20/powering-the-future-rolls-royce-total-care-business-success/

[40] Ryals, L (2010) Rolls-Royce Totalcare: meeting the needs of key customers, KAM Club Executive Briefing, Cranfield School of Management, Bedford, UK, 2010.

[41] Pugh, P (2002) *The Magic of a Name: The Rolls-Royce story. Part 3, a family of engines*, Icon Books, Cambridge, UK.

[42] Lazonick, W and Prencipe, A (2005) Dynamic capabilities and sustained innovation: strategic control and financial commitment at Rolls-Royce plc, *Industrial and Corporate Change*, **14** (3), pp. 501–42.

[43] Foden, J and Berends, H (2010) Technology management at Rolls-Royce, *Research Technology Management*, **53** (2), pp. 33–42.

[44] Marcos-Cuevas, J et al (2016) Value co-creation practices and capabilities: sustained purposeful engagement across B2B systems, *Industrial Marketing Management*, **56**, pp. 97–107.

[45] Edvardsson, B et al (2014) Institutional logics matter when coordinating resource integration, *Marketing Theory*, **14** (3), pp. 291–09.

[46] Xerox (2017) Co-innovation at Xerox [online] https://strategicaccounts.wistia.com/medias/0ahtcdwchd [accessed: 31 October 2017].

[47] Gebauer, H, Paiola, M and Saccani, N (2013) Characterizing service networks for moving from products to solutions, *Industrial Marketing Management*, **42** (1), pp. 31–46.

[48] Ng, I C L, Ding, D X and Yip, N (2013) Outcome-based contracts as new business model: the role of partnership and value-driven relational assets, *Industrial Marketing Management*, **42** (5) pp. 730–43.

[49] Sharma, A, Iyer, G R and Evanschitzky, H (2008) Personal selling of high-technology products: the solution-selling imperative, *Journal of Relationship Marketing* (2008) **7** (3), pp. 287–308.

[50] Storbacka, K Polsa, P and Sääkjärvi, M (2001) Management practices in solution sales- a multilevel and cross-functional framework, *Journal of Personal Selling and Sales Management*, **31** (1), pp. 35–54.

[51] Macdonald, E K et al (2011) Assessing value-in-use: a conceptual framework and exploratory study, *Industrial Marketing Management*, **40** (5), pp. 671–82.

[52] Lemmens, R, Donaldson, B and Marcos, J (2014) *From selling to Co-creating: New trends, practices and tools to upgrade your sales force*, BIS Publishers, Amsterdam.

[53] Peñaloza, L and Mish, J (2011) The nature and processes of market co-creation in triple bottom line firms: leveraging insights from consumer culture theory and service dominant logic, *Marketing Theory*, **11** (1), pp. 9–34.

PART THREE
Designing customer-centric approaches and processes

The role of the key 07 account manager and the KAM team

'Abandon the urge to simplify everything, to look for formulas and easy answers, and begin to think multidimensionally, to glory in the mystery and paradoxes of life, not to be dismayed by the multitude of causes and consequences that are inherent in each experience – to appreciate the fact that life is complex.'

M SCOTT PECK

How can your organization ensure that your key account managers have the right skills and competences to manage today's increasingly strategic and complex customer relationships?

Overview

This chapter focuses on the role and competences of key account managers (KAMgrs) and on the importance of the KAM team in effective KAM. It is nearly 40 years since David Ford [1] first argued that in managing long-term business-to-business relationships there is a clear role for a *relationship manager* who is the major contact person for the customer and who takes responsibility for the successful development of the relationship with the customer. It should be 'someone of sufficient status to coordinate all aspects of the company's relationships with major clients at the operational level' [1]. The idea of the *relationship manager* promulgated by Ford further evolved during the 1980s, 1990s and 2000s. Early authors referred to national account managers [2] then major account managers [3] and more latterly, key account managers [4], [5] and global account managers [6], [7]. Finally, the term strategic account manager is also used to describe this role [8]. For the purposes of this book we will use the term *key account manager (KAMgr)*.

In this chapter we argue that the role of the KAMgr has evolved to become complex and multifaceted and is a very different role to that of traditional sales, often requiring the ability to reconcile tensions that are inherent in the function across boundaries and time, and developing competences to strategically plan key customer activities, mobilizing resources to deliver seamless execution. World-class key account management calls for a widely shared understanding of performance measures and what achieving them entails. Sustaining this performance involves the creation of environments where people can thrive despite experiencing complexity, pressure and paradoxes. Sustained top performance needs to be underpinned by the adoption of new leadership approaches abandoning 'safe' models that are still so prevalent in businesses today. As well as focusing on the key roles of KAMgrs and the role of the KAM team we will also look at how KAMgrs should be recruited, developed and managed in order that they can thrive and be successful.

The role of the key account manager

In this section we look at some key aspects of the complex and multifaceted role of the KAMgr.

A fundamentally different role from sales?

As the role of the KAMgr has developed, some researchers have argued that the role of the KAMgr is a very different job to that of traditional sales [7], [8]. All these authors came to the same conclusion that the role of the KAMgr was both a multi-faceted one and complex. This held true for many occupying the role of account manager, whether it is called key, global or strategic. It is also evident that the role is still evolving and will 'continue to evolve as companies move away from traditional buyer–seller relationships to those involving multiple supply chain relationships and networks, where all parties are seeking value and are more focused on the co-creation of value and more collaborative ways of working' [8]. The competences and skills required in this type of role are fundamentally different to those of a traditional salesperson, even a senior salesperson, and this also has implications for the levels of authority and scope that are given to KAMgrs. The role stretches far beyond the sales function where it has traditionally been seen as residing and encompasses the whole organization, which in turn needs to become customer-centric.

Indeed, in recognizing KAM as a management process and not a sales process we were warned [6] that many KAMgrs were ill-prepared for the wider and more demanding roles that take them into areas of business development, industry/market analysis, benchmarking, relationship management and so on. In fact, very early on in the literature, some argued that the role 'should be regarded as an activity carrying responsibilities and requiring competences closer to the *general management function* or senior marketing function, in preference to its current location in sales' [9]. More recently this has been challenged further [8], with the term *general manager* believed to now be inadequate because general managers are charged with managing people and resources that are allocated to them. They have clear reporting structures and delineated responsibilities, which does not seem to be the case with KAMgrs:

> They must manage people and resources over which they have no direct authority in conditions often redolent with ambiguity and are charged with the realization of entrepreneurial value not often demanded of general managers. This we believe suggests the emergence of a new managerial role embodied in the concept of the boundary-spanning KAMgr [8].

Voice of the practitioner

It is not just academic researchers that think this is a fundamentally different role. Here are some practitioner views.

From the supplier organization

'These are business managers. They are not senior salespersons. If you give the senior salesperson the title of Global Account Manager and send them off to the customer, they can see right through them from day one.' (Sales Director, global consultancy company.)

'The people you need in these sorts of positions are light years away from traditional salespeople. All the competences are the sort of skills framework we expect for rising CEOs and managing directors.' (Senior Manager, engineering company.)

From the customer organization

'The superficial role of the salesperson with fancy presentations and all that is not what we look for in the supplier's global account manager. What we're really looking for is a global account manager who really sees themselves as part of us, really understands us and sees themselves as wearing two hats, and they're not easy to find.' (Customer of a global components company.)

'We were specifically looking for somebody who had supply chain management understanding and not just a salesperson who had a good story to tell and didn't really understand what they were talking about in relation to our organization and what mattered to us. We find it really frustrating that the calibre of some of our suppliers' key account managers is so poor. We would like to work more strategically with them but it just isn't possible. This really isn't any good for us as a business, you know.' (Customer working for a technology company.)

The key account manager as boundary spanner

The role of the KAMgr and strategic sales professional has evolved to become a *boundary-spanning* one of *knowledge broker*, designing and delivering networks and interfaces for value-creating supplier–customer relationships [8]. In contrast to the traditional sales role, the KAMgr faces multifaceted and complex challenges, suggesting that both external (customer focused) and internal (process driven) orientations are required. In fact, some account managers are seen as *business managers* given the business risk involved in their areas of responsibility. Some define a KAMgr as a *political entrepreneur* [7] as the individual performs a boundary-spanning role across both the external interface with the customer and the internal interface with their own organization [6]. In most industries, the role will continue to evolve as companies move away from traditional buyer–seller relationships to those involving multiple supply chain relationships and networks, where parties emphasize the co-creation of value and collaborative ways of working.

The real internal role of the KAMgr

A major part of the KAMgr's role is managing the internal organization. Customers often demand from the KAMgr the ability to mobilize and to motivate in their organization those individuals responsible for delivery to the customer. This is a major challenge for organizations implementing KAM and possibly the main challenge for KAMgrs, as we will see later in this chapter. Historically, sales roles have been represented in terms of the relationship to the customer. The salesperson role has

Figure 7.1   The boundary-spanning role of the key account manager

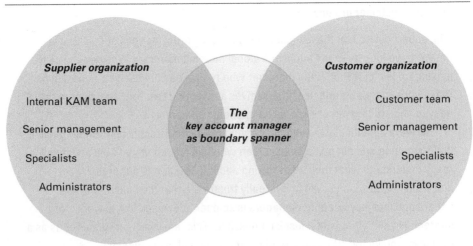

been seen as a customer-focused one, with the old adage ringing true: 'Why are you sitting at your desk? You should be out on the road selling to customers.' But why is this seen as an important issue? Well, if people in customer-focused, boundary-spanning-type roles are performing internal tasks, they are often described in terms of having to 'firefight', because the assumption is that the organization is not sufficiently aligned to the customer. For many practitioners there is simply no recognition that these roles may have some legitimate internal focus. Generally, salespeople and KAMgrs are rewarded for what they achieve with the customer, not for what they achieve internally.

Our research [6] has shown that there is a legitimate internal role for KAMgrs that often comes as a complete surprise to senior managers who still see the role as largely customer-focused. We didn't just interview KAMgrs; we also interviewed their senior management, their internal KAM team members and, most importantly, their customers. The customer group is particularly important here, in that they identified a range of activities that they expected the KAMgr would carry out on their behalf when back in the supplying organization.

The customers described the role as *championing* their requirements back in the KAMgr's organization, as *representing* their interests or *fighting our corner for us* with the KAMgr's senior management. They also expected the KAMgr to present the customer's strategies to senior management and to articulate the customer's requirements at that level. This might also involve *making specific business cases* on the customer's behalf.

Voice of the practitioner

The following are four quotes from KAMgrs about the internal nature of their role:

- 'This job is more about the internal facing stuff than it is about the external facing stuff. I have to manage a large team of people internally who are all involved with the client but who don't report directly to me.' (KAMgr, IT company.)

- 'It is about managing the organization to manage the customer.' (KAMgr, engineering consultancy.)

- 'Most of my challenges in my role are not so much with managing the customer but are about managing the internal interfaces.' (KAMgr, insurance company.)

- 'Communication and implementation of the customer strategy internally is one of my biggest challenges. That takes about 60–70 per cent of my time.' (KAMgr, financial services.)

Figure 7.2   Typical time spent by the key account manager as a boundary spanner

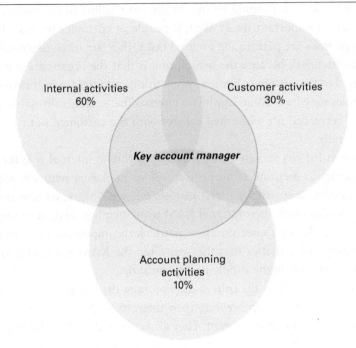

The time spent by KAMgrs on the internal part of their role is significant and if we look at the challenges of the role in Figure 7.3, it becomes evident why. The average time spent by KAMgrs on customer-facing activities, internal activities and account-planning activities is shown in Figure 7.2. As you can see, the time spent internally is, on average, twice the amount of time spent with the customer. Key account planning is also a time-consuming activity if done properly and the 10 per cent of the KAMgr's time includes not just developing the plan but also bringing the team together to work on the plan, as well as the subsequent dissemination and monitoring including, if possible, involving the customer.

The eight key challenges of the KAMgr role

The ultimate aim of the KAMgr is to deliver long-term value for both their customer and their own organization. In this value-driven context KAMgrs face a number of unique challenges, identified by one researcher [10]. Figure 7.3 shows these eight challenges faced by KAMgrs as they look to develop and manage their customer.

1 Value ambassador

KAMgrs need to be value ambassadors and customer advocates. As value ambassadors they understand what their customers value and how to respond to these needs.

Figure 7.3   Eight key challenges of key account managers

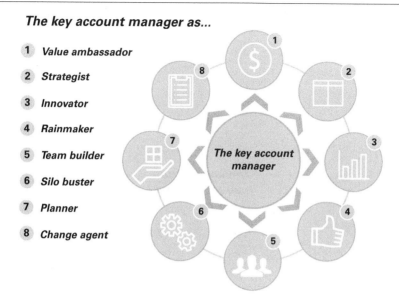

The key account manager as...

1 *Value ambassador*

2 *Strategist*

3 *Innovator*

4 *Rainmaker*

5 *Team builder*

6 *Silo buster*

7 *Planner*

8 *Change agent*

As customer advocates they are the *focal point of contact* for the customer. Research with KAMgrs [11] shows how important it is for customers to feel they have one person who has overall responsibility for their relationship with the supplier. Indeed, they identify four different facets of the KAMgr being the focal point of contact, as shown in Figure 7.4.

a *Single point of contact*: customers expressed that they wanted a main or focal point of contact and this was particularly important in a complex or pan-geographic context.

b *Strategic point of contact*: while it is recognized as essential to have a focal point of contact for the relationship, in a global relationship it is not usually physically possible for the KAMgr to be everywhere at once. Therefore, what they need to be is the strategic point of contact, while recognizing that there will also be other key contacts at local or regional levels.

c *Similar point of contact*: this was an interesting point that emerged in terms of customers looking for a similar point of contact that they felt comfortable with. Where the relationship is a major strategic one for both parties, it is important that there is also strategic fit between the individuals involved in managing the relationship.

d *Escalatory point of contact*: there is a clear role for the KAMgr as an escalation vehicle for problem solving as and when necessary.

Figure 7.4   The key account manager as the focal point of contact

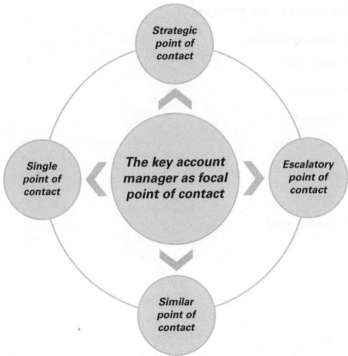

2 Strategist

A major difference between selling and key account management is the requirement to develop a strategy that is focused around one key customer. This should identify ways of building sustainable value creation for both parties. The difference with key accounts is that these strategies often involve bigger investments and bespoke offerings. With very large key customers, this challenge is like managing a *business within a business*. KAMgrs may also have to make business cases internally, as the director of corporate accounts at a global bank pointed out:

> If the KAMgr identifies a project with the customer and that is going to need, say, some specific investment, then they will have to present me, and perhaps the board if it is significant, with a good case for doing it. This is the sort of thing that they have not traditionally had to do as KAMgrs.

The role of the KAMgr as strategist is also concerned with building strategic relationships, which again is a multifaceted role as, shown in Figure 7.5.

a   *Building multi-level relationships*: this is about the KAMgr building and facilitating relationships with different levels of people both in the customer's organization and their own.

Figure 7.5 The key account manager as the relationship-building strategist

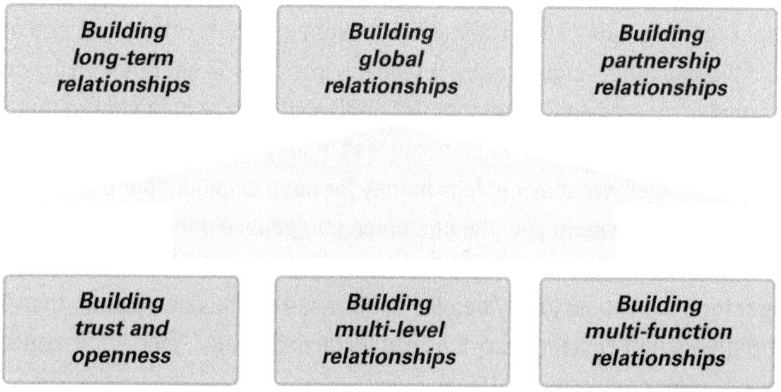

b *Building multi-functional relationships*: this is about the KAMgr building multi-functional relationships between both organizations, allowing the KAMgr to delegate and empower the local teams.

c *Building global relationships*: as customer relationships becomes more complex and pan-geographic the KAMgrs need to be able to build the customer/supplier relationships at the global level.

d *Building long-term relationships*: this is a critical aspect of the KAMgr as strategist. In more developed relationships building the longer-term strategy with the customer and taking the longer-term view of the relationship is paramount to success.

e *Building trust and openness*: being able to build an environment where trust and openness can flourish is another key requirement for the role. These are also aspects of the relationship that take time to build.

f *Building a co-creating relationship*: with the increasing importance of co-creating value in these types of strategic relationship, KAMgrs need to look for opportunities to build relationships around the co-creation of value for all parties involved.

The top three facets in Figure 7.5 are reliant, in part, on the bottom three facets.

Mini case: the KAMgr as strategist

Sometimes it pays off to take the long-term view, as described in this case.

'In the relationship, the truly global relationship that we have here, we suddenly questioned the way the customer was packing their product. This came about because for one or two reporting periods some of the boxes were getting wet in Asia and they had complained to us about it. We asked why they used that packaging, and it eventually transpired that nobody had really looked at the packaging for probably 10 years or so. So, I instigated a study and introduced the customer to a global packaging company. The first kick-off meeting was very interesting because of the packaging samples sent. I said that I thought we could reduce the size and weight of the packaging significantly, which the customer liked. But then my contact turned round to me and said, "You [courier company] are not going to like that very much are you, because you're going to get less money for each shipment." And my response was, "Well, we may get less money for each shipment but because of this project we're going to keep you, the customer, competitive and therefore you should be able to take more market share, and we should get more shipments. Therefore, in the longer term we should jointly be able to increase our business rather than lose market share with the current way they are being delivered."' (Global Account Manager, courier company.)

3 Innovator

Ensuring that key customers keep viewing you as a key supplier requires constant regeneration of value-adding offerings. Being creative and innovative can 'fly in the face' of delivering profits today, but the need to look to the future is critical if a long-term partnership is to be maintained. Customers are constantly looking for innovation from their suppliers, even where there is little room for innovation, for example in a commodity market. Figure 7.6 shows some key components of the KAMgr innovator role, taken from research with customers.

As you can see, the customers expect the KAMgr to be a *visionary, innovator* and *consultant* as they are looking for them first to *develop new and common business opportunities*, second to *develop bespoke and tailored solutions*, and finally

Figure 7.6   The key account manager as innovator

to look for ways to *develop existing capability in new ways* in both organizations. Ultimately, the customers see this as the development of joint strategic value.

Voice of the practitioner: customers want innovation

'We're looking into opportunities where we can create business or, let us say, where we see a chance that [the supplier] could do something that will help us. Or where they suggest something like a new opportunity we can explore together. So, between the KAMgrs and I, we're looking for common business opportunities for both organizations. They need to be constantly innovating... it is about looking at immediate opportunities and then at longer-term potential.' (Customer of a logistics company.)

'I saw an opportunity for us jointly, with the KAMgrs, to take a broader view of the capabilities of the supplier and understand what opportunities there might be for our two companies to partner in certain areas where we identified we had, in particular, complementary assets. You know, how we best fit together in terms of the relationship in a way that was different to the traditional relationships we had with our suppliers. The KAMgrs and I were trying to look at joint business opportunities and the landscape for both organizations was constantly shifting. It was difficult, but ultimately we both reaped rewards from our joint innovation.' (Customer of a multinational IT solutions company.)

---

4 Rainmaker

It is often said that salespeople do not make good KAMgrs. This is because they lack some of the skills (described here) such as project management, strategy and leadership. A skill they do possess, however, is that they can sell. They are good with customers, can handle rejection and have the energy and motivation to make a sale. This ability to 'make rain' and win business is a highly valuable skill, and can be hugely underestimated. The view should be taken that salespeople can absolutely make excellent KAMgrs, but they will need to develop some additional skills. Never underestimate the value of good rainmakers. Without sales, there is no top line. And with no top line, there is no business. Equally, and more prevalent in highly technical industries, many KAMgrs have come from a technical background and often need to be given the commercial skills to be great rainmakers.

5 Team builder

The ability to manage a cross-functional (and sometimes cross-geographical) team of people virtually is a necessary skill. Managing teams when you have no direct reporting line is possibly one of the most difficult leadership challenges. Great KAMgrs have team-building skills; they gain alignment from people who follow their energy, passion and vision. We will look at some of the issues for KAM teams in more detail later.

The KAMgr needs to develop top performance leadership skills [12] to manage their team effectively; this is often a challenge because unless they have been sales managers or in a functional management position, they are often leading for the first time in their careers when they move into this role. As the teams are usually virtual in nature they are also having to develop great influencing and persuasion skills as they are in the position of having to *influence without authority*.

6 Silo buster

KAMgrs have to work horizontally across their organization and, therefore, across business *silos* whose goals and objectives are often operationally focused rather than customer focused. Any large organization achieves great things by having smaller divisions and operating units that have financial, functional and operational focus. Organizations have marketing, supply chain, R&D, finance, HR, regional and country leadership along with other business units. Great things are achieved by allowing organizations to operate in these carefully controlled *cells*. Getting things done for the customer often requires connecting with these cells and seeking support. *Silo busting* may sound like an aggressive approach to business, but this internal selling, by gaining resources and support from leadership groups who may well not be focused on the customer, is a vital skill. KAMgrs bust their own silos (they often have to bust customer silos as well).

Successful KAMgrs are generally very good networkers and can also use their informal networks to bust silos. Informal networks can be flexible and adaptable to change, responsive, creative, innovative, efficient and individually rewarding. Practitioners report a number of benefits that can be gained from utilizing informal networks such as re-energizing stalled projects, customizing client solutions, facilitating inter-functional coordination, encouraging effective collaboration and enhancing business performance. So, informal networks can be very useful for KAMgrs to build both inside their own organization and when managing relationships with a key customer or client.

7 Planner

This aspect of the role is so important that we have dedicated a whole chapter of this book (Chapter 3) to the importance of understanding the customer in depth; it also highlights the critical importance of having great key account plans for effective KAM. Any strategy is only as good as the detailed planning that turns *strategy* into *action*. Being able to produce detailed plans that get innovative concepts both developed and implemented requires great project management and planning skills.

8 Change agent

Dealing with new strategies and getting your own organization to *do something different* requires an ability to sell the new idea and to get things done differently. This could be new products, services, data systems, financial reporting or people. All these things are *different ways of doing business* and, therefore, they all require change management.

Key account manager competences and skills

We can link the competences and skills of the KAMgr back to the Value Planning Framework introduced in Chapter 3. Figure 7.7 below starts to describe the competences that are required by the KAMgr, as each stage of the KAM Value Planning Cycle is executed. There are 28 competences listed in the five sections of Figure 7.7, and these can be grouped as follows:

- researching and investigating;

- innovating and developing new ideas;

- strategizing and planning;

Figure 7.7   Linking the key account manager competences to the Value Planning Framework

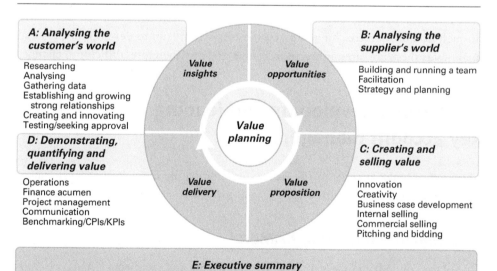

- selling and negotiating;
- communicating and coordinating;
- driving operational standards.

No single person will be exceptionally talented at all of these, but these activities need to be exceptionally executed to enable effective key account strategy. The secret is that KAMgrs are generally very good at networking and aligning their own organization to get these things done and, therefore, harnessing the wider capability of the organization. If the KAMgr doesn't have the competency then hopefully they will know and connect with someone in their KAM team or their organization who does. This is a starting point, as the list could go on and on. What is evident here is the issue that KAMgrs have to be proficient in several competences, or at least to have an ability to make these things happen effectively.

While we are often asked by companies, it is difficult to come up with a definitive list of competences and skills as these will differ according to, for example:

- different industry requirements;
- the type and level of key account, eg a local account vs a global account;
- the complexity of the customer's organization and requirements;
- the complexity of the product, service or solution the supplier is providing;
- the maturity of the customer and/or supplier in KAM.

As well as identifying the competences and skills for KAMgrs, there are also some personal qualities that have been identified as shown in Figure 7.8.

It is worth pointing out that many competences and skills can be developed through training and coaching. However, it is more difficult to develop the personal qualities as these are often inherent in people and are, therefore, difficult to change.

Recruiting, developing and leading key account managers

This section looks at some of the issues surrounding the recruitment, development and management of KAMgrs.

Selecting and recruiting KAMgrs

One of the conundrums for managers when selecting and recruiting KAMgrs is finding the best fit for the role. Obviously potential KAMgrs need to demonstrate they have a good understanding of the core roles and competences as outlined above; however, there are a number of decision areas that may need to be addressed.

Figure 7.8   The personal qualities of successful key account managers

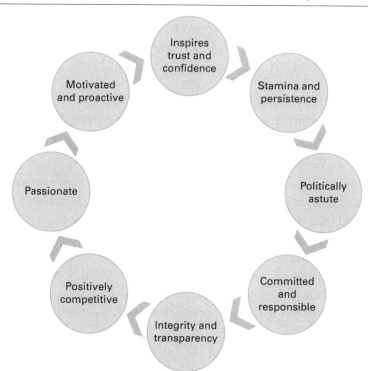

Experienced salespeople vs technical knowledge

This is often a major headache for managers, particularly in highly technical and complex industries. Should they look to select (internally) or recruit (externally) from those with experience in sales/KAM who will hit the ground running with this expertise, but who may lack the technical knowledge to be credible in front of the customer? Or do they select or recruit people with the technical knowledge who may lack the commercial skills, but who may be more credible with customers? Some companies have decided to go down the route of having a mixture of KAMgrs who can help and support each other with their different expertise. This needs to be carefully managed to avoid factions, but with the utilization of workshops, exchange of best practice opportunities, and careful coaching and mentoring it can work to the advantage of all.

Internal vs external hires

This is another consideration that companies juggle with. Should they home-grow their KAMgrs or recruit them externally? Again, there is no simple answer to this. One piece of advice is to look for potential KAMgrs from across the organization and not just in the sales function. Often people in other functions really understand the capabilities of their own organization and are, therefore, unlikely to overpromise to customers on what can be achieved and delivered. Equally, getting an injection of new blood from experienced external KAMgrs can also bring benefits, especially if they are from the same industry. However, KAMgrs from other industries can also prove to be very effective if inducted properly. Again, it is probably effective to have KAMgrs that are a mixture of internal and external hires.

Selecting or recruiting high-performing salespeople

Many companies are tempted to move their most high-performing salespeople into a KAMgr role or to recruit salespeople with an impressive track record in winning new business. However, the competences and personal qualities of high-performing sales-people do not always sit well in a KAMgr role. Often these individuals are driven by the excitement and buzz of winning new customers; their compensation is usually linked to this and they enjoy high levels of income. Put them in a long-term KAMgr relationship management role and they can become bored and dysfunctional. Indeed, as reported by Jones et al [12], individuals often get promoted to leadership and senior management positions in sales because they are good at selling. However, leading people, as we have established is essential for KAMgrs, requires different skill sets and expertise.

Developing KAMgrs

Developing KAMgrs is often neglected by many organizations but it is an important topic that needs to be addressed.

Professionalization of the KAMgr role

One of the frustrations for many organizations is the complete lack of professional sales qualifications available for sales professionals, sales managers/directors and KAMgrs. Many KAMgrs report they have either had no development, or that their development has been confined to short courses. Organizations like the Association for Professional Sales (APS) in the UK and the Strategic Account Management Association (SAMA) globally, are constantly working towards the professionaliza-tion of sales, but there is still a lack of the type of career path qualifications available for marketing, finance, HR and procurement/supply chain functions, for example. Yet anecdotal evidence suggests that there are 10 people working in sales to every one person in marketing!

However, things are gradually changing as both graduate and post-graduate programmes for sales professionals are beginning to emerge. But what to do in the mean-time? As already mentioned, mentoring and coaching are important, dependent on the history and expertise of the KAMgr. There are programmes available to help KAMgrs with their key account planning, strategic negotiation and conflict management. Where KAMgrs are managing large, complex, strategic accounts with high levels of senior management engagement on both sides then many organizations are sponsoring their KAMgrs on executive Master's in Business Administration (MBA) programmes.

Creating internal opportunities, for example for exchanging best practice and successes, keeping up with developments in KAM, utilizing experienced KAMgrs to mentor those less experienced, and utilizing information systems are all ways to develop KAMgr expertise in the organization. But too few companies do this in a planned and systematic way.

KAMgr longevity and succession planning

Another issue for managers is how long a KAMgr should be in their role with a particular key customer. Customers report that a KAMgr is not wholly effective until they have generally spent two years in the role, as it takes them this long to really understand the customer's business environment and to build trust. Organizations therefore need to consider that a KAMgr needs to be in their role with a particular customer for four to five years. This can represent a challenge where KAMgrs are keen to move on with their careers, so organizations need to develop attractive retention and reward mechanisms (see Chapter 9). Succession planning is also important here as customers do not like sudden changes of KAMgrs. Often organizations can involve the expected successor in the customer relationship and actively manage the expectations of the customer so they don't get a complete and unwelcome surprise.

Leading KAMgrs in a performance environment

It is not the intention here to look at how to motivate and incentivize KAMgrs, as this is covered in Chapter 9. However, if KAMgrs are to succeed in their strategic role then it is important to create a *performance environment* [12]. Engaging great leaders alone rarely guarantees success in organizations; the creation of a performance environment is also required, where nurturing enabling factors such as appropriate incentives, values, mindsets and behaviours is paramount. These are part of the *fabric* of people who deliver sustainable top performance [13]. We need to create thriving environments which are characterized by delegation and empowerment, by good working relationships, a feedback culture, accountability and ownership, and clearly defined goals [13]. So KAMgrs need to be given the freedom and authority to thrive. Indeed, a major frustration that customers report is the lack of authority given to many KAMgrs by the supplier organization, which then leads to slower decision making and responsiveness by the supplier.

In managing KAMgrs, their success is also tied up with how good their management is. Those in sales management or key account director positions need to be *real* and not *safe* leaders [12]. *Safe* leaders are driven by their need for rewards and the status and power that come with being *the boss*. This makes them unwilling to put themselves on the line because of the threat of losing their position if they get it wrong. *Safe* leaders keep their heads out of the firing line, they are risk-averse and there is little or no innovation or challenging of status quo during their tenure. This approach is often manifested in over-emphasis on delivering short-term financial outcomes. Safe leaders are also likely to allow the star sales performers to get away with behaviours that may be detrimental to the team, tolerating a sole focus on their own targets, possibly at the expense of achieving those of the team.

What KAM and KAMgrs need is *real* leadership. *Real* leaders, as opposed to *safe* leaders, are driven much more by the challenge and opportunity to take calculated risks that can make a difference; this is what leadership is about for them. *Real* leaders are highly visible and strive to make things happen, employing practices that are sensitive to the organizational context and culture. They encourage challenge, innovation and risk taking, as well as tackling hard issues as soon as they arise; they are not afraid of confronting the egos and behaviours of those that threaten the unity, performance and ethos of their teams. This is the leadership style that provides a successful environment for high-performing KAMgrs.

CASE STUDY   Wipro's approach to the role of the KAMgr

Wipro is a global information technology services company that is headquartered in India. Wipro have long taken a very sophisticated and strategic view of senior sales leadership roles, including those of what they call Global Client Partners (GCPs). For senior sales roles Wipro promote *Leading the way to excellence.*

Leading the way to excellence.

Wipro is on a journey to instil excellence in our Go-To-Market organization with the objective of bending the growth curve to significantly higher revenue and margin. Our existing Go-To-Market function comprises a large and diverse team of men and women, working across more than 30 countries in sales, pre-sales, large deal and alliance roles.

Wipro actively seek sales professionals including experienced KAMgrs.

Are you the right fit?

At Wipro Sales we seek enthusiastic individuals who are committed to excellence. The career opportunities within Sales provide a breadth of experience for sales employees in each business unit and service line, including Account Management (existing clients), Hunting (new business/clients) and Practice and Geography-specific roles. Within each of these tracks, we offer roles at the Individual Contributor/Specialist level as well as at Manager and Leader levels.

Wipro invests heavily in developing the competency profiles of the different sales leadership roles. As Robert Racine, UK Vice President says:

At Wipro we recognize the important strategic role that our GCPs have in managing our most strategic clients. The competences they need to do this are more akin to leadership and service delivery competences but we still need them to be excellent at strategic selling and relationship building.

Helena Stoy, Director of Sales Management Practice at Wipro, believes strongly that the strategic sales leadership roles, including the GCPs, are the most important occupation in the business world for the following reasons:

- 1 per cent sustained improvement in the operating margin equates to a 6 per cent increase in the market capitalization value of the organization;
- 1 per cent sustained improvement in growth rate equates to a 27 per cent increase in the market capitalization value of the organization;
- therefore, sustained growth is 4.5 times more valuable than sustained cost efficiencies.

Some specific aspects of the Wipro GCP role include:

- Understanding strategic account management and planning for large and global accounts with large cross-sectional team members across various geographies or countries.
- Understanding how to sell and deliver in complex environments, to large stakeholder groups, across different projects, across multiple continents/countries, with a diversity of cultures, multiple customer lines of business, revenue size of over £30 million, a large number of products and service lines, strategic business solutioning, selling to c-suite, outcome-based operation models, business transformation, customer engagement and satisfaction.

Wipro also make sure that the GCPs have support and ongoing development from their managers and the organization including:

- account planning;
- account growth coaching;
- account plan reviews;
- quarterly account reviews;
- strategic opportunity management;
- encounter planning;
- three-level relationship building and conversations.

The first four of the above are all to do with developing the emergent account strategy, which is about the concept of 'living account plans'. Based on the experiences of Wipro, the most successful of the GCPs provide their customers with thought leadership and contextualized solutions that are pragmatic and relevant to the client's business. To achieve this level of engagement typically requires a mindset of what Robert Racine refers to as 'outcaring' for your customer versus the competition.

Key account teams

Our final topic in this chapter is the importance of the supplier's KAM team in managing strategic KAM relationships. This is about aligning the whole organization around key customers and is the major challenge reported by companies when implementing KAM. However, to date, little research has focused on this very important topic. We have already discussed earlier the very real internal role of the KAMgr and the time spent on the internal part of their role. A large chunk of this internal time is spent leading and motivating their KAM team. We have also looked at the *silo busting* and *team leader* roles of the KAMgr, which are fundamental when aligning the organization around customers.

Why is it important to focus on KAM teams?

Anecdotal evidence from practitioners attending the Cranfield Key Account Management Best Practice programme identified the following three important aspects of why organizations need to focus on KAM teams:

1 they are a key critical success factor for successful KAM for suppliers and customers;

2 internal alignment of the organization on the customer is the biggest challenge for best practice KAM;

3 managing the internal interface is the biggest challenge for KAMgrs.

Types of KAM team

There are two distinct teams that a KAMgr may have to lead. The first is what is generally termed a cross-functional delivery team made up of all the key functions involved in delivering for the customer. A typical cross-functional KAM team is shown in Figure 7.9. As can be seen, the KAM team has members from both key frontline delivery functions such as operations or product/research development and what are traditionally seen as support functions such as finance and marketing. Generally, this team of people should be involved and engaged in the key account plan for the customer or client, as well as in its execution and monitoring.

Another KAM team that a KAMgr might need to lead is what is generally referred to as the pan-organization or pan-geographic customer-focused team. These occur either when the customer is highly complex with lots of touchpoints, or the customer

Figure 7.9   A typical cross-functional team

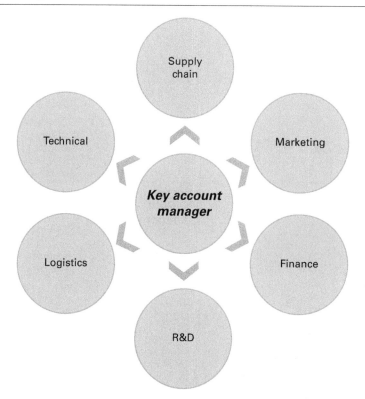

is being managed on a pan-geographic basis. A typical pan-organization or pan-geographic team is shown in Figure 7.10. Generally, the team is made up of those in customer front-line roles such as local KAMgrs, salespeople and customer services people. More on pan-geographic teams can be found in Chapter 11.

Some KAMgrs will need to lead both types of team and as stated earlier they are likely to be leading *virtual teams* in the sense that members of both types of team do not generally report directly to the KAMgr but have a *dotted line* relationship instead. However, the virtual nature of the team does have some advantages, such as being a flexible engagement model, with cross-functional needs with a mix of skills sustained by reporting in function, and cross-boundary needs with a mix of locations sustained by reporting in geography.

Some key considerations for KAM teams

There are a number of considerations and issues that you might want to think about if you are implementing a KAM team approach.

Figure 7.10   A typical pan-organization or pan-geographic customer front-line team

Formal vs informal?

Some companies may feel that an informal approach is the simplest way for the KAMgr to build the team, eg to use their networking and silo-busting skills to persuade people to work with them. In smaller companies this may work but in larger, more complex organizations there needs to be some sort of formality around KAM teams where the organization recognizes this approach, including having team charters (see below) and team measures and KPIs.

Team charters

One of the ways of supporting KAM teams is for each team to develop a team charter or *modus operandi* for the team. This can include:

- the roles and responsibilities of the team members;
- the overall goals and KPIs for the customer;
- the overall goals and KPIs for the KAM team;
- frequency of meetings;
- conduct of meetings.

Core team and wider team

Generally there will be a core team, as illustrated in Figures 7.9 and 7.10. However, there will be occasions when the team has to draw on expertise that is not found within the team, usually for specific customer projects, research and development or solutions.

What a KAM team is not

A KAM team is not a selling team, business development or bid team which comes together to address and win a specific opportunity, although the KAM teams will get involved with opportunities with existing customers. A KAM team is also not a project team that has a time-bound project and then disperses. KAM team members will get involved in customer-specific projects as they arise but on completion of the project the core KAM team will still be there.

Success factors for KAM teams

Research [11], [14] found that there were eight key success factors for KAM teams. This research has been updated in the light of more recent developments in KAM and Figure 7.11 shows the current success factors for KAM teams. Some of the factors would apply to any successful team but others are specific to KAM teams led by a KAMgr.

Figure 7.11   Key success factors for KAM teams

What do KAM team members say they need from the KAMgr?

Finally, what do KAM team members say they need from the KAMgr in order for them to be engaged and successful in their role? They want a KAMgr who:

- builds the customer relationship at strategic level;
- is the strategic/global link with the customer;
- develops contacts I can use at local level;
- is the information channel about the customer;
- has the big picture of the customer;
- knows what is happening with the customer in other areas, regions, countries;
- identifies projects and opportunities I can use to penetrate the customer at local level;
- gives direction and leadership when needed;
- gives support and back-up for resources;
- facilitates exchanging good ideas with other parts of the organization.

Conclusions

The chapter has looked at the role of the KAMgr and KAM teams. How will the role of the KAMgr change in the future? We have seen it develop over the last 20 years from that of the key account salesperson to the complex strategic role that it is today in many organizations. As we have demonstrated this is a very different role to that of the traditional salesperson and one which requires very different competences and skills. It is likely to continue to evolve over time and we are likely to see a decline in the more traditional sales approaches in business-to-business markets, as customers become more demanding, discerning and value driven. We are seeing a trend where the more strategic-minded customers are looking to form close relationships with suppliers within a context of collaboration and co-creation of value as they recognize they get more value from the relationship than through a transactional focus. We have also seen that the management of the internal interfaces and the KAM team is a big challenge both operationally and for KAMgrs. Again, companies who have been the most successful in implementing KAM have recognized the importance of getting the internal alignment right.

Questions for managers

- Do I really understand the difference between a traditional sales role and that of a KAMgr?
- What competences and skills do my KAMgrs need in my context?

- Do my KAMgrs have the right personal qualities?
- What decisions do I need to make about the recruitment and selection of KAMgrs, eg salespeople vs technical and internal vs external?
- What current or future development needs do my KAMgrs have?
- Have I got succession plans in place for my KAMgrs?
- Do I have the right reward and motivation systems in place that reward a strategic and long-term focus as well as necessary short-term goals?
- Do we have effective KAM teams aligned to the customer?
- Is there a formal structure for KAM teams and are the right support systems in place?
- Do we have a high-performance leadership approach to leading KAMgrs, eg real leadership rather than safe leadership?

References

[1] Ford, D (1980) The development of buyer-seller relationships in industrial markets, *European Journal of Marketing*, **14** (5/6), pp. 339–53.

[2] Shapiro, B P and Moriarty, R T (1980) National Account Management, *Report 80–104*, Marketing Science Institute.

[3] Barrett, J (1986) Why major account selling works, *Industrial Marketing Management*, **15** (1), pp. 63–73.

[4] Millman, T and Wilson, K (1995) From key account selling to key account management, *Journal of Marketing Practice: Applied Marketing Science*, **1** (1), pp. 9–21.

[5] McDonald, M, Millman, T and Rogers, B (1997) Key account management: theory, practice and challenges, *Journal of Marketing Management*, **13**, pp. 737–57.

[6] Holt, S and McDonald, M (2001) A boundary role theory perspective of the global account manager, *Journal of Selling and Major Account Management*, **3** (4) pp. 9–31.

[7] Wilson, K and Millman, T (2003) The global account manager as political entrepreneur, *Industrial Marketing Management*, **32** (2) February, pp. 151–58.

[8] Wilson, K and Holt, S (2014) The Strategic KAMgrs, in *Handbook of Strategic Account Management: A Comprehensive Resource*, ed D Woodburn and K Wilson, Wiley, UK.

[9] Millman T, and Wilson, K (1996) Developing key account management competencies, *Journal of Marketing Practice Applied Marketing Science*, **2** (2), pp. 7–22.

[10] Davies, M (2017) *Infinite Value*, Bloomsbury Business, London.

[11] Holt, S (2003) *Global Account Managers: Just what do they do?* Cranfield KAM Club Report, Cranfield School of Management, Cranfield University, Bedford.

[12] Jones, G et al (2015) *Leading Top Performance in Key Account Management*, Cranfield KAM Club Report, Cranfield School of Management, Cranfield University, Bedford.

[13] Jones, G, Gittins, M and Hardy, L (2009) Creating an environment where high performance is inevitable and sustainable: The High-Performance Environment Model, *Annual Review of High Performance Consulting*, pp. 139–49.

[14] Woodburn, D and McDonald, M (2011) *Key Account Management: The definitive guide*, Wiley, UK.

Measuring KAM performance 08

'It is no use saying "we are doing our best". You have to succeed in doing what is necessary.'

WINSTON CHURCHILL

How do we know whether or not we are succeeding in key account management?

Overview

The implementation of key account management (KAM) requires the investment of resources that are specific to a customer relationship and, often, more costly than those allocated to customers that do not get the 'key account' status. There is evidence that one of the major risks of KAM implementation for a supplier is not being able to capture the value of the relationship [1]. For example, a supplier may invest in a KAM programme with a specific customer but fail in being able to charge a premium price to obtain higher profits. Therefore, measuring performance is a critical step in the KAM implementation journey.

A major challenge is to select the right measures of KAM performance, as they need to be SMART: specific, measurable, achievable, relevant, and time-bound [2]. In addition, because of the strategic and relational nature of KAM, the performance metrics need to connect with the long-term perspective of building and nurturing customer relationships.

Supplier companies should answer the following questions:

WHAT aspects of performance should be assessed?

HOW should the selected aspects of performance be measured?

WHO should be involved in providing the inputs for the measurements?

WHEN and how frequently should each performance metric be assessed?

This chapter proposes a framework for measuring KAM performance that should be useful to suppliers that are interested in checking whether they are capturing the right value from their KAM initiatives or not. This framework should also help executives to better understand the critical success factors for KAM implementation and the requirements for measuring and managing performance metrics. It must be noted that the framework is not intended to be totally comprehensive or directly applicable to any supplier; it is evident that each industry and each company has its own particularities that will suggest some adaptations to the framework in order to fit the specific industry and market contexts. Supplier companies should be ready to adjust the way they measure KAM performance in order to obtain profound insights about the customer.

The complexity of KAM performance

Measuring KAM performance can be difficult given the complexity of the practice of KAM. First, it is about planning, developing, managing, and evaluating customer relationships; therefore, a number of factors at different stages influence how good or bad the implementation of a KAM programme can be. Second, KAM requires the right balance between short-term accomplishments and long-term goals; consequently, performance measurement needs to take into account this dual objective, which often seems contradictory. In addition, the unit of analysis for performance management must be threefold: the supplier, the customer, and the interaction between these two; hence, a variety of perspectives is needed to truly assess KAM performance.

A number of KAM performance metrics have been suggested by experts in the field. For example, *growth* and *profitability* have been highlighted as critical indicators of KAM success, which relate to financial performance and a long-term view of the business [3]. Similarly, *customer lifetime value* has been proposed as a relevant forward-looking financial measure of KAM performance [1]; in simple terms, customer lifetime value estimates the future revenues and costs associated with a customer relationship and converts the resulting amount into 'today's money'. Another metric that has been suggested for assessing KAM financial performance is *shareholder value* [4] to stress the importance of the owners of the supplier firm as key stakeholders.

In addition to financial metrics, some non-financial metrics have been proposed as being important to assess KAM performance. For example, *relationship quality* combines elements of satisfaction, conflict, trust, and commitment with the other party [5]. Similarly, *relationship continuity* has been studied as a relevant outcome of KAM initiatives to signal the long-term goal of developing and growing the relationship as true partners [6]. In the same vein, measures of *customer loyalty* have also been suggested, such as customer retention and advocacy [7]. The main idea here is to recognize that KAM performance needs to be measured in terms of both financial and non-financial outcomes, the latter being linked to relational aspects of performance.

The definition of outcome metrics of KAM performance – the ones just mentioned above – is a must for most companies, because these indicators usually reflect the 'end result' of a KAM initiative. Often, board members of supplier companies will look closely at these metrics to assess how well or poorly KAM has been implemented. However, together with these results-driven measures of performance, KAM should have some metrics that speak to the quality of the processes being developed, the inputs that are needed for success, which normally precede the outcome measures; we refer to them as process-driven measures of performance. For example, previous research has looked at *processes' efficiency* (in terms of production, functional integration, and performance evaluation), *know-how development* (with respect to learning about technological advancements, improving operations, and generating ideas for products and services), and *information sharing* (in terms of content type and frequency) as critical performance metrics in KAM [8]. Likewise, *synergistic solutions* (the development of innovative solutions for both supplier and customer) and *role performance* (the capability to solve problems and develop strategic plans that benefit both parties) have also been studied as relevant input-type performance measures in KAM [9].

As we can see, measuring KAM performance can be very complex due to the many angles from which it can be assessed. One approach that has been used to consider the different perspectives on performance measurement is the balanced scorecard [10], which posits that an adequate assessment of performance requires four perspectives: financial, customer, internal business, and innovation and learning. Still, if it is too complex, it may prevent people from being able to implement it successfully. In the next section, we present a framework that tries to find the right balance between comprehensiveness and practicality for measuring KAM performance.

A proposed framework for measuring KAM performance

In this section we propose a framework to measure KAM performance at the account level (see Figure 8.1). First, we distinguish between results-driven metrics and processes-driven metrics. In the first group, we have two types of metrics: *financial performance* (including revenue growth, profitability, and customer lifetime

Figure 8.1   Measuring KAM performance

Process-driven metrics	Results-driven metrics
Delivery to customer • Product/service mix • Solution development • Cost to serve **Co-development with customer** • Co-creation of value • Information sharing • Shared investment **Customer experience** • Pre-purchase • Purchase • Post-purchase	**Financial performance** • Revenue growth • Profitability • Lifetime value **Relational performance** • Customer satisfaction • Customer loyalty • Relationship quality

value) and *relational performance* (comprising customer satisfaction, customer loyalty, and relationship quality). In the second group, we consider three types of processes-driven metrics: *delivery to customer* (including product/service mix, solution development, and cost to serve), *co-development with customer* (comprising co-creation of value, information sharing, and shared investment), and *customer experience* (in the three key stages of the customer journey: pre-purchase, purchase, and post-purchase).

Financial performance

The first type of results-driven metrics refers to the financial performance that the supplier can obtain by having a business relationship with a key account. *Revenue growth* is an important metric given that a major goal for any KAM programme is to grow the supplier's business. *Profitability* is also needed as evidence shows that KAM relationships can be very costly due to the unique investments involved and, therefore, profits may be elusive. *Lifetime value* of a customer is suggested to explicitly account for the long-lasting and strategic nature of KAM.

Revenue growth

Revenue growth is the rate of growth that the supplier achieves in terms of the revenues (sales in value) from the business with a key account, in a certain period of time. To many companies this is a 'must have' performance metric. The following quote, from a senior executive involved in KAM at a mechanical and industrial engineering company, illustrates the importance of growth:

The importance of *growth* in KAM

'We'd define key account management as those customers we can have a sustainable long-term growth relationship with… we maintain business relationships and grow our business across multiple platforms (we call it) over time. So it's pretty simple stuff and it's pretty much how we evaluate key account management within our organization.' (Senior executive in KAM, mechanical and industrial engineering industry.)

Revenues should be measured with data on sales in value (£, $, etc) coming from the information systems in the supplier company. It is recommended that, in addition to 'total revenues', suppliers report how revenues are divided among relevant units of analysis: product/service categories, channels, business units, etc. The rate of growth is simply calculated as the percentage of increase/decrease in total revenues and within the different units of analysis.

Profitability

Profitability is defined as the level of profits/losses that the supplier obtains from the business with a key customer, in a certain period of time.

All the revenues and expenses attributable to a key account relationship should be included, and this information should come from the information systems in the supplier company. Revenues normally include gross sales income, but could include other sources (eg fees, commissions). Expenses should include all costs associated with the products and services sold to a customer, supply chain and distribution, pre-sale activities, and post-sale activities. It is important to be precise with these calculations; if a supplier does not have detailed information about all cost components for a key account, they can either use only the data that is reliable, or use some management accounting method to support the process, such as activity-based costing [11].

The two critical questions are:

- Which sources of revenues and expenses are clearly linked to the specific customer relationship?

- How accurately can we calculate those revenues and expenses?

Revenues are typically easier to calculate as they come mostly from directly selling products and services to the customer. The price, the payment terms, the volume sold, the duration and conditions of the service provision, as well as fees, commissions, refunds and rebates, and extra consultancy services are usually known or easy to obtain.

The real challenge for accurately measuring customer profitability comes from the costs (expenses). It is often difficult to obtain all the relevant costs associated with a customer relationship during a certain period of time (eg one year), and these may vary significantly from one customer to another. For example, the production costs associated with customer 'A' can be significantly higher than those of customer 'B' if the former receives special conditions in terms of product specifications and packaging. Likewise, the pre-sale costs of a supplier (eg the expenses involved in presenting the products/services to customers and pursuing them to buy) could be much higher with customer 'B' in our example, if the purchasing process of this account requires several rounds of interaction with different people and units within the company and a lengthy approval process. Table 8.1 describes the main types of costs associated with dealing with a key account, together with the identification of some elements that produce variations in the costs among different customers.

Table 8.1 Costs involved in KAM

Cost type and description	Possible sources of variation among customers
Pre-sale Costs associated with understanding customer needs, analysing the market/industry, designing a solution, presenting it, and following up until a sale is achieved.	• Geographical location and dispersion of an account's business unit affects the cost of customer visits • A customer's requirement of having a top manager from the supplier firm in the negotiation process increases the costs in terms of the time of senior executives • Some customers have a very complex and lengthy buying process, which requires that the supplier company mobilizes a whole team of people to accommodate the interests of different stakeholders within the key account
Sale Costs of production, storage, packing, order processing, distribution, delivery, etc., linked to the products and services being sold.	• Some key accounts require tailor-made products and services, with unique specifications (eg size, packaging) which increases production costs • A customer may get special conditions in the timing and size of products' delivery, which translates into higher storage and financial costs • Some customers may require that suppliers undertake some extra quality controls and services (eg inventory management) during the distribution of products
Post-sale Costs linked to technical support, training, solution implementation, other services, adjustments to the initial offering, etc.	• A customer may command the close supervision and consulting services of the supplier during the implementation of a solution • A key account may not have the required skills in their personnel to use a product adequately, and so the supplier may need to provide some training to the customer • A global customer may need to adjust a specific solution to the context of different countries where it operates, which may need extra support from the supplier

Therefore, to accurately calculate the profitability of a key account, the supplier must identify and describe in great detail the specific conditions and characteristics of the business with each key account relationship, in each of the three stages (pre-sale, sale, and post-sale) and analyse the cost implications and values. To support this process, the supplier needs a reliable information system and an appropriate method for costs allocation.

In addition to having the measures of customer profitability, to evaluate performance with a key account, suppliers need to understand *how* that level of profitability is being obtained, ie the qualitative drivers behind the metric. To exemplify, Table 8.2 shows the profitability of two customers, M and Z. Both accounts give the supplier company a profitability of 500; therefore, they have the same performance. However, a closer look at *how* this level of profitability is obtained for each customer tells us that the *nature* of Customer M's profitability is totally different from that of Customer Z. With Customer M, profitability comes mainly from selling high volumes of products (with a contribution margin of 28 per cent), with a significant effort in the pre-sale stage of the selling process. In contrast, the profitability from Customer Z derives from the sale of half the volume of products (relative to Customer M) but with a higher contribution margin (41 per cent), plus the provision of services, which requires more effort in the post-sale stage of the selling process. Evidently, a thorough performance assessment of these two customers should look beyond the bottom line, and ask questions such as: 'How can we increase the profitability of these two customers?', 'Can we increase the contribution margin of Customer M, or perhaps be more efficient in terms of the pre-sale costs?', and 'Can we increase the provision of services to Customer Z, whilst being more efficient in the post-sale service we currently provide?'

Table 8.2   Example of profitability analysis for two customers

Profitability analysis	Customer M	Customer Z
Volume sold	600	300
Average unit price	25	34
Revenues (products)	15,000	10,200
Revenues (services)	0	1,000
Product unit cost	18	20
Cost of services delivery	0	750
Gross margin	4,200	4,450
Pre-sale expenditures	2,300	1,450
Post-sale expenditures	1,400	2,500
Profitability (£, $)	**500**	**500**

Lifetime value

Customer lifetime value is a quantitative estimation of the present value of a customer relationship, based on the expected future revenues and expenses that a supplier would obtain for a certain period of time, and a discount rate that converts money in the future to money in the present. The formula for the lifetime value of one key account is:

$$CLV = \sum_{t=1}^{n} \frac{r_t - e_t}{(1+i)^t}$$

Where:

   r_t: revenues (expected) from the key account relationship in t

   e_t: expenses (expected) from the key account relationship in t

   i: rate of discount (usually interest rate)

   t: time period (t = 1, 2, ..., n)

   n: number of relevant periods (lifetime)

Similarly to customer profitability, all the revenues and expenses attributable to a key account relationship should be included. The main difference is that, for customer lifetime value, it is not the historical data but forecasts of future revenues and expenses that need to be analysed. Therefore, the current existing data from the information systems in the supplier company is only one source of information, which can provide the inputs to try several forecasting methods (eg time series analysis, multiple regression analysis). In addition to that, supplier companies should bring in new information that comes from the key customer (eg purchases forecast, growth plans, future investments, etc) and from industry and market sources to anticipate future trends.

The following case study illustrates the use of customer lifetime value analysis of a supplier with three of its key customers.

CASE STUDY   Customer lifetime value of three key accounts

The commercial director of Construmart (pseudonym), a large supplier of construction materials, decided to calculate the profitability brought by three of their most important distributors (named as customers A, B, and C) to the company in the past year, to justify their *key account* status when presenting the financial results of the business unit to the company's president. He recognized that, so far, they have not computed such profitability. After several weeks of gathering data on revenues and costs associated with these three customers, the commercial director was able to come up with the profitability calculations, as shown in Table 8.3a. The results were irrefutable! Customer B was by far the most profitable customer among the three accounts. Should Construmart, then, invest more resources in growing the relationship with Customer B? Well, not necessarily. Here is where the notion of customer lifetime value comes into place. It would make sense to invest in Customer B if its lifetime value looks promising, relative to that of the other two key accounts.

The second task for Construmart was, consequently, to forecast the lifetime value of customers A, B and C, looking forward rather than using the 'rear-view mirror'. To that end, the commercial director organized a series of activities to gather information about industry and market trends and, in particular, to analyse the business model, current situation, and future plans of the three customers. After a few weeks of inquiry and discussions with these customers and internally, the commercial team of Construmart prepared a customer lifetime value analysis for distributors A, B and C, considering a 'lifetime' of eight years (see Table 8.3b). The results were surprising! Customer B, which had the highest profitability in year 2017, was in fact the account with the lowest lifetime value. Conversely, customer A was found to have the highest lifetime value, which seems odd in light of the relatively low profitability it generated in 2017. The commercial director organized a meeting with his team to discuss and try to understand the rationale behind these unexpected results. What could be a sound explanation?

Table 8.3a   Construmart: Profitability analysis for customers A, B and C

Financial results 2017	Customer A	Customer B	Customer C
Volume sold	500	300	100
Average unit price	26	32	37
Revenues (products)	13,000	9,600	3,700
Revenues (services)	0	0	0
Product unit cost	15	11	11
Cost of services delivery	0	0	0
Gross margin	5,500	6,300	2,600
Pre-sale expenditures	3,000	1,225	400
Post-sale expenditures	2,000	2,275	600
Profitability (£, $)	**500**	**2,800**	**1,600**

Table 8.3b Construmart: Lifetime value analysis for customers A, B and C

Customer A	2017	2018	2019	2020	2021	2022	2023	2024	2025
Volume sold	500	540	600	620	590	630	670	670	680
Average unit price	26	26	27	27	28	28	28	29	29
Revenues (products)	13,000	14,040	16,200	16,740	16,520	17,640	18,760	19,430	19,720
Revenues (services)	0	500	800	800	800	1,500	1,500	1,500	1,500
Product unit cost	15	15	15	15	15	14	14	14	14
Cost of services delivery	0	350	560	560	560	900	900	900	900
Gross margin	5,500	6,090	7,440	7,680	7,910	9,420	9,980	10,650	10,800
Pre-sale expenditures	3,000	3,000	2,700	2,475	2,750	2,700	2,700	2,650	2,496
Post-sale expenditures	2,000	2,000	1,800	2,025	2,250	2,700	2,700	2,650	2,704
Profitability (operational)	500	1,090	2,940	3,180	2,910	4,020	4,580	5,350	5,600
Interest rate	10%	10%	10%	10%	10%	10%	10%	10%	10%
Net Present Value (NPV)	500	991	2,430	2,389	1,988	2,496	2,585	2,745	2,612
Cumulative NPV	**500**	**1,491**	**3,921**	**6,310**	**8,297**	**10,794**	**13,379**	**16,124**	**18,737**

Customer B	2017	2018	2019	2020	2021	2022	2023	2024	2025
Volume sold	300	290	270	260	250	240	240	230	230
Average unit price	32	32	31	31	31	31	31	30	30
Revenues (products)	9,600	9,280	8,370	8,060	7,750	7,440	7,440	6,900	6,900
Revenues (services)	0	0	0	0	0	0	0	0	0
Product unit cost	11	11	11	11	11	11	11	11	11
Cost of services delivery	0	0	0	0	0	0	0	0	0

	2017	2018	2019	2020	2021	2022	2023	2024	2025
Gross margin	6,300	6,090	5,400	5,200	5,000	4,800	4,800	4,370	4,370
Pre-sale expenditures	1,225	1,225	1,225	800	800	1,000	2,520	2,520	2,730
Post-sale expenditures	2,275	2,275	2,275	3,200	3,200	3,000	1,680	1,680	1,470
Profitability (operational)	2,800	2,590	1,900	1,200	1,000	800	600	170	170
Interest rate	10%	10%	10%	10%	10%	10%	10%	10%	10%
Net Present Value (NPV)	2,800	2,355	1,570	902	683	497	339	87	79
Cumulative NPV	**2,800**	**5,155**	**6,725**	**7,626**	**8,309**	**8,806**	**9,145**	**9,232**	**9,311**

Customer C	2017	2018	2019	2020	2021	2022	2023	2024	2025
Volume sold	100	100	110	110	110	115	100	110	120
Average unit price	37	37	38	38	38	40	40	41	42
Revenues (products)	3,700	3,700	4,180	4,180	4,180	4,600	4,000	4,510	5,040
Revenues (services)	0	700	700	900	900	1,000	1,000	1,000	1,200
Product unit cost	11	11	12	12	12	13	13	13	14
Cost of services delivery	0	420	420	540	513	570	570	550	660
Gross margin	2,600	2,880	3,140	3,220	3,247	3,535	3,130	3,530	3,900
Pre-sale expenditures	400	480	520	520	546	546	616	616	616
Post-sale expenditures	600	720	780	780	754	754	784	784	784
Profitability (operational)	1,600	1,680	1,840	1,920	1,947	2,235	1,730	2,130	2,500
Interest rate	10%	10%	10%	10%	10%	10%	10%	10%	10%
Net Present Value (NPV)	1,600	1,527	1,521	1,443	1,330	1,388	977	1,093	1,166
Cumulative NPV	**1,600**	**3,127**	**4,648**	**6,090**	**7,420**	**8,808**	**9,785**	**10,878**	**12,044**

The Construmart case study tells us that suppliers should not only analyse the past or current profitability of their customers, but also forecast their expected future profitability and translate those estimates into financial value in the present, to assess customer lifetime value. This forward-looking exercise can give a better indication of which customer relationships should receive more attention and resources to achieve long-term profitable growth. Construmart realized that Customer B (a family-owned, medium-sized local distributor) was not willing to invest in updating or upgrading their business model (eg by incorporating new technologies in their operations or by expanding into new markets). On the other hand, Customer A was planning to evolve from a regional player into a national one, by acquiring SMEs, hiring highly qualified professionals, and developing a more efficient, technology-based distribution system. Finally, Customer C planned to focus on a specific niche in the market, which would make them a very profitable customer for Construmart, and a natural candidate to develop joint added-value activities.

Relational performance

A second type of results-driven metrics is the relational performance that the supplier firm can achieve with a key account. *Customer satisfaction* is considered a very relevant metric because it affects customer loyalty and financial performance; it can also provide useful information about the aspects of the offering to the customer that may need some extra attention. *Customer loyalty* is also an important indicator of relational performance, as it is closely linked to revenues and profitability, and can act as a buffer when environmental conditions are unfavourable for the supplier. Loyal customers are more likely to engage in cooperative behaviour and seek mutual long-term benefits. Furthermore, *relationship quality* assesses the health of the relationship with the customer, which constitutes a platform to develop it further.

Customer satisfaction

Customer satisfaction is a customer's appraisal of all aspects of the working relationship with a supplier. It includes an overall evaluation of the satisfaction with the relationship, plus the assessment of specific aspects, such as products/services, delivery and logistics, communication, personnel, day-to-day interaction, etc. Figure 8.2 illustrates an example of possible dimensions for customer satisfaction.

Customer satisfaction is usually assessed with a customer survey administered by a third party (eg independent consultant or research firm). The respondent(s) needs to be knowledgeable about the aspects under inquiry and, therefore, it is common to use several people to complete a questionnaire (eg purchasing manager, finance director, supply chain executive and chief executive officer). Several questions are used to

Figure 8.2   The dimensions of customer satisfaction

measure each dimension of customer satisfaction, to make sure that the information is valid and reliable. The following sample statements provide an illustration of how customer satisfaction could be measured.

Survey to customer: customer satisfaction

With respect to *SN* (name of supplier), please indicate the degree to which you agree or disagree with these statements, on a scale from 1 to 7, where 1 means 'strongly disagree' and 7 means 'strongly agree'.

Quality and variety of products:

- We are very pleased with the average quality of the products we buy from *SN*.
- The quality of *SN* products is consistent over time.
- The variety of *SN* products is very appropriate.
- The packaging of *SN* products is optimal.

Delivery of products and invoicing:

- *SN* normally delivers the products in the right quantities and varieties.
- The timing of delivery of *SN* products is adequate.
- *SN* documentation is easy to read and interpret.
- *SN* usually sends the documentation on time.

Post-sale services:

- We are happy with the post-sale service *SN* provides.
- *SN* is ready to offer us assistance in the use of its products when needed.
- The quality of the training *SN* provides to our personnel is very good.
- *SN* keeps us up to date with information that supports the use of its products.

Claims management and inquiries:

- *SN* is very receptive to our complaints and inquiries.
- When we have a serious problem with *SN*, they explain to us exactly what happened.
- The solutions that *SN* provides to our claims are very good.
- *SN* compensates us when we incur financial losses due to problems originated by them.

Day-to-day interaction:

- We are happy with the frequency of interaction with *SN* sales representatives.
- We have enough contact with *SN* top managers from headquarters.
- The day-to-day interaction with *SN* is very pleasant.
- We have very good communication with people at *SN*.

Access to information and people:

- It is easy to contact the people we need at *SN*.
- We always get the right information from *SN*.
- *SN* is very responsive to our inquiries.
- *SN* is very active in providing us with information that supports our business.

Quality and attitudes of the personnel:

- People at *SN* have good expertise with their products and services.
- *SN* personnel care about us and are always willing to help.
- People at *SN* have the required skills to help us run the business.
- *SN* employees are very professional.

Financial value captured:

- The prices that *SN* charges are fair relative to the quality they provide.
- Compared to other suppliers, we are happy with the profitability we get from *SN* products.
- The cost of doing business with *SN* is low, relative to other suppliers.
- The *SN* brand adds value to our business.

Overall satisfaction:

- We feel good about our relationship with *SN*.
- Our relationship with *SN* has more than fulfilled our expectations.

Customer loyalty

Customer loyalty refers to a customer's inclination to prefer and promote the offerings of one specific supplier or brand over those of competing firms. It has both an attitudinal component and a behavioural one. The former is the willingness to purchase more quantity more frequently from a supplier and promote its brand relative to that of competing firms. The latter is the act of buying more quantity and variety of a supplier's products and services relative to competitors, whilst recommending that supplier to other people or companies.

A customer survey (administered by a third party) can be used to assess attitudinal loyalty, while internal data on sales can be used to evaluate behavioural loyalty. Figure 8.3 shows some commonly used measures of customer loyalty, both from an attitudinal and a behavioural perspective.

Figure 8.3 The two types of customer loyalty

Relationship quality

Relationship quality is an assessment of the present state of the relationship between a supplier and a key account, as well as a judgement of the expectations of how this relationship will progress into the future. It involves the level of conflict in the relationship, the extent to which there is mutual trust, and the degree of commitment to an ongoing relationship (see Figure 8.4).

Ideally, this metric would be assessed from the customer's perspective, but it is also possible to measure it from the supplier's point of view. In fact, a good option is to get both perspectives to identify possible gaps in the perceptions of both companies. Relationship quality can be captured through a survey, and the following sample statements can be used:

Survey to customer: relationship quality

With respect to *SN* (name of supplier), please indicate the degree to which you agree or disagree with these statements, on a scale from 1 to 7, where 1 means 'strongly disagree' and 7 means 'strongly agree'.

Conflict:

- We have a tense relationship with *SN*.
- We have significant disagreements with *SN* when working together.
- We frequently dissent with *SN* on how the two companies should do business.

Trust:

- *SN* is very concerned about our wellbeing.
- We trust *SN*'s capabilities to perform effectively.
- *SN* cares a lot about our needs.
- *SN* is highly knowledgeable about our company and business.

Commitment:

- *SN* is willing to make a long-term investment to support us.
- *SN* is very committed to us.
- *SN* sees our relationship as a long-term alliance.
- *SN* has a strong sense of loyalty to us.

Figure 8.4   The dimensions of relationship quality

Delivery to customer

A first type of processes-driven metrics relates to the delivery of the supplier's offering to the key account. *Product/service mix* is an indicator of the quality of the sales to the customer in terms of the portfolio of products and services. Generally speaking, suppliers will consider it a success to sell a broad mix of products and services to a key customer. *Solution development* goes beyond the mix of products and services to measure the extent to which tailor-made solutions have been developed for the customer; the rationale is that effective solution selling should foster customer loyalty and profitability. Finally, *cost to serve* is a metric of efficiency, which should lead to greater profitability and lifetime value due to the learning that happens in how to deal with the customer and the reduced need for controlling mechanisms between the two parties.

Product/service mix

The product/service mix refers to the composition of the sales to a key account in a certain period of time. Suppliers must determine the desired portfolio to be sold to each key account, and then check the extent to which they achieve that portfolio.

The measurement of this performance indicator must come from internal data on sales by product/service type, and a simple gap analysis may be used to evaluate how close the current sales portfolio is to the target one. The supplier could establish certain percentages to represent the desired allocation of products and services to a customer, based on the profitability goals and other strategic criteria (eg penetrate a new market or create a higher dependency from the customer). Table 8.4 presents an example of how this process might work.

Solution development

This metric is the extent to which tailor-made solutions have been developed for the customer. As illustrated in the following quote from the Global Head of KAM

Table 8.4 Example of a product/service mix analysis

Products and services portfolio assessment	Customer XYZ	Customer MNP	Customer DEF
Sales target (revenues)	£300,000	£500,000	£420,000
Target distribution of sales by product and service for each key account			
Product A:	15%	30%	
Product B:	20%		40%
Product C:	30%		25%
Product D:	10%	15%	
Service A:	10%	10%	10%
Service B:	15%	20%	
Service C:		10%	
Service D:		15%	25%
Average score:	**100%**	**100%**	**100%**

Excellence at a pharma company, nowadays customers expect solutions that not only solve a specific problem directly related to the supplier's main area of expertise, but also connect more broadly with the whole customer journey.

Solutions in today's KAM

'With the emergence of these increasingly governed payer accounts, they are asking for solutions that "go beyond the pill", as we call them. Just because you've got a medicine – "Great, it works in the clinical trial programme, but how well is it going to work in my healthcare system? Can you tell me? And are you willing to help me with other aspects of the patient journey? Can you help me with prevention, disease management?" They are looking for pharmaceutical companies in the payer community to move away from just selling product, transacting and agreeing price, and moving into more being disease area partners.' (Global Head of KAM Excellence, pharma industry.)

We adopt Storbacka's definition of customer solutions [12]:

Longitudinal relational processes, during which a solution provider integrates goods, service and knowledge components into unique combinations that solve strategically important customer-specific problems, and is compensated on the basis of the customer's value in use.

Figure 8.5 The process to develop customer solutions

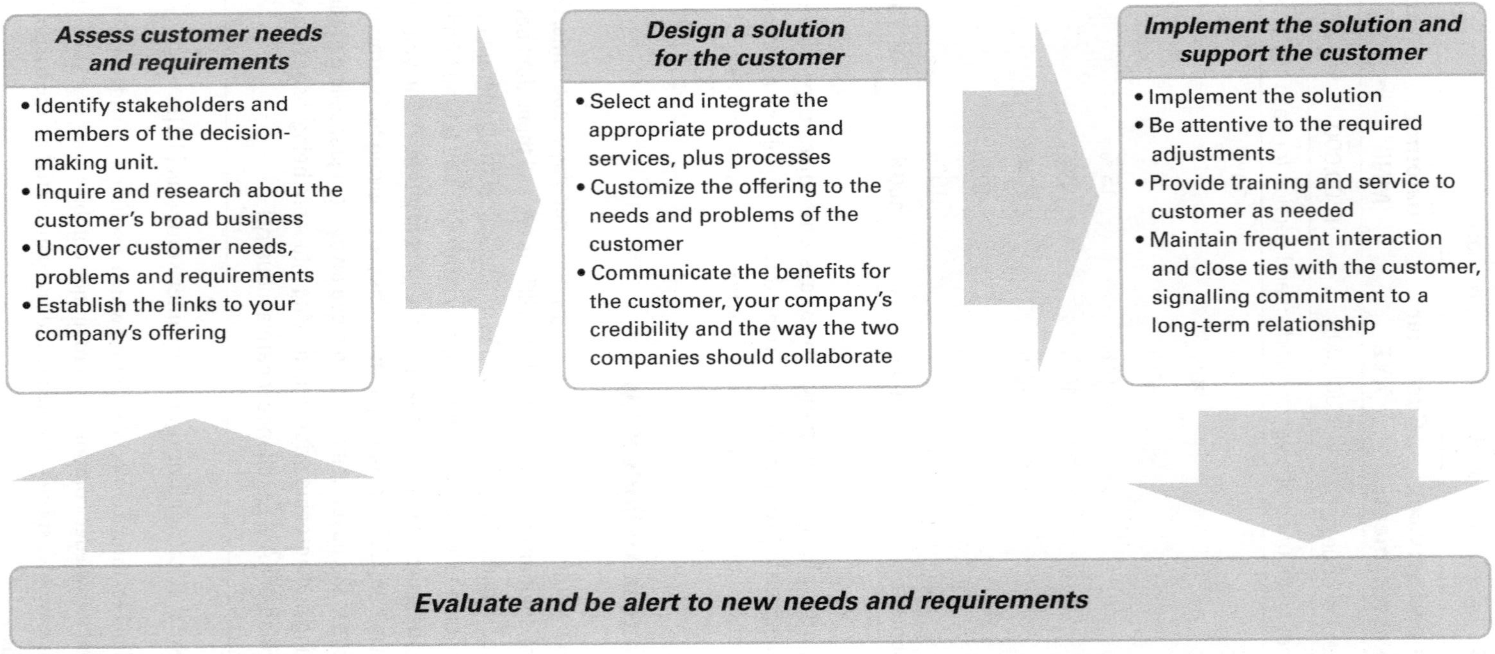

Assess customer needs and requirements

- Identify stakeholders and members of the decision-making unit.
- Inquire and research about the customer's broad business
- Uncover customer needs, problems and requirements
- Establish the links to your company's offering

Design a solution for the customer

- Select and integrate the appropriate products and services, plus processes
- Customize the offering to the needs and problems of the customer
- Communicate the benefits for the customer, your company's credibility and the way the two companies should collaborate

Implement the solution and support the customer

- Implement the solution
- Be attentive to the required adjustments
- Provide training and service to customer as needed
- Maintain frequent interaction and close ties with the customer, signalling commitment to a long-term relationship

Evaluate and be alert to new needs and requirements

This definition highlights the notion that a solution is not simply a bundling of products and services, but relational processes [13] which start with a clear identification of the customer's needs and requirements. Then, a combination of products and services is developed in a way that is customized to the client's needs and integrated with the internal resources of the supplier. Next, the solution is implemented, which often requires as much attention as the previous stages; this is when new requirements may emerge. Figure 8.5 depicts and explains the process to develop customer solutions.

One way to measure solution development is to assess the degree to which each of the three stages has reached the desired level. It is recommended that this evaluation be made by both the supplier and the customer. For example, a self-assessment made by the key account manager may look like this:

KA manager self-assessment: solution development

With respect to (name of the key account), please rate the level of development in the following aspects of solution development on a scale from 1 to 7, where 1 means 'not accomplished' and 7 means 'totally accomplished'.

Assess customer needs and requirements:

- We understand the customer's broad business.
- We have identified the members of the decision-making unit
- We have actively explored with the customer their needs with respect to our business.
- We have clearly identified a problem that the customer has.
- We are certain about how our offering could solve the customer's problem.

Design a solution for the customer:

- We have selected and integrated the appropriate products, services and processes.
- We have customized the offering to the needs and problems of the customer.
- We have communicated to the customer the potential benefits of our solution.
- We have established our credibility with the customer through previous experiences, expertise and storytelling.
- We have proposed to the customer how we expect the two companies to work together on the solution.

Implement the solution and support the customer:

- We have implemented the solution for the customer.
- We have been attentive to any required adjustments to the solution.

- We have provided post-sale service to this customer to support the solution implementation.
- We have provided training to people for this customer, as needed.
- We have maintained frequent interaction and close ties with the customer during the solution implementation.
- We have provided the customer with clear signals about our interest in building a long-term relationship with them.

Cost to serve

This performance indicator is the quantification of the costs associated with serving or managing the customer relationship on a daily basis. Some examples of the activities included are visiting the customer, preparing communication material, attending customer inquiries and managing complaints, bringing in senior managers to meet with the customer, etc.

The measurement of the cost to serve is very straightforward once the supplier has determined exactly which activities should be considered. An activity-based costing method can be a useful tool for this purpose.

The following quote from a senior manager and expert at an important sales consulting company highlights that effective KAM can significantly reduce the cost to serve by virtue of learning how the customer's business really works.

Cost to serve: an important metric and a consequence of good KAM

'The key thing for us is that first of all this enables us to get a much deeper understanding of the customer, which makes what we have to offer more valuable straightaway. But also it reduces the effective cost of sales, because you're in the same place, you're selling to the same stakeholders and it's the depth of the issue that sells it. Whereas if you're running around from one account to another, you dilute your ability to genuinely understand what's happening there. So for us that's one very critical driver.' (Senior manager at a sales consulting company.)

The cost to serve can also be analysed together with the average price being charged to the key account over a period of time and for specific products and services. The rationale for doing this is that such an approach may help to uncover a situation

Figure 8.6   The cost to serve vs average price analysis

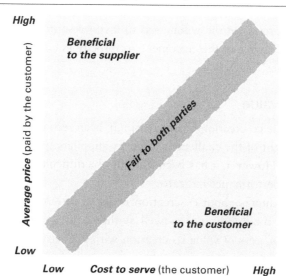

of power imbalance between the supplier and the customer, which will then inform actions to move towards a fair distribution of financial costs and benefits between the two parties.

Figure 8.6 shows a two-dimensional space, where suppliers can locate their key account relationships based on the cost to serve and average price. Thus, they can identify customers with a high cost to serve relative to others, given the financial benefits received. The upper-left zone represents locations that are beneficial to the supplier, whereas the lower-right zone characterizes locations that are beneficial for the customer. The diagonal zone diagonal is the *fair* zone, beneficial to both parties. The underlying assumption of this analysis is that key account relationships are more likely to last and grow when both parties benefit from them in a fair way.

Co-development with customer

A second type of processes-driven metrics relates to the extent to which the supplier and the customer engage in co-development of various kinds. *Co-creation of value* is a critical indicator of KAM success, as it involves the joint development of products, services, solutions, promotional activities, supply chain processes and the like. It is increasingly difficult for companies (both suppliers and buyers) to differentiate themselves from their competitors, and one way to face this struggle is to partner with other companies within the value chain. *Information sharing* has been a key driver of successful business-to-business relationships, particularly between suppliers and buyers. In KAM, it is expected that this exchange be predominantly of strategic information, in order to create competitive advantages based on unique market knowledge. Finally, *shared investment* is a metric that reflects the level of commitment to the relationship in terms of the willingness to invest resources jointly. In a way, this metric assesses the degree of the customer's reciprocity in considering the supplier as a 'preferred provider'.

Co-creation of value

The notion of value co-creation has increasingly been recognized as 'the way to go' in KAM, in the light of the challenges faced by suppliers when trying to differentiate their offering. However, it has been found to be difficult to implement, and it is seldom used as a performance indicator.

The following quotes about co-creation of value in KAM from two experts in the field illustrate the importance as well as the challenges of pursuing this path. Interestingly, the process of value co-creation with key customers requires that key account managers and other team members move out of their comfort zone.

Co-creation of value in KAM

'... when we look at key account management, co-creation is probably the cornerstone of what we want to do... I think the opportunities for success through co-creation are far higher than through conventional product/market innovation.' (Max Walker, Commercial Leader of Strategic Accounts at 3M.)

'...the co-creation of value is vitally important and I think this is where I see our stakeholders becoming part of the solution in terms of identifying value and what we can do... I believe it is the one thing that people just are not very good at, because it comes from the uncomfortable conversation that people don't want to have... In order to co-create a proposition with a key customer you have to be honest, you have to put your cards on the table, you have to actually say what it is that you want and you are calling out that you have a commercial objective.' (Louise Collins, Managing Director at Louise Collins Associates Limited.)

Information sharing

This KAM performance metric is the perceived quality of the information-sharing process between the supplier and the key account. As discussed earlier in this book, information sharing and communication are important drivers of the quality of the relationship between a supplier and a buyer. The following aspects are usually considered to assess information sharing:

- *Quantity*: the extent to which a significant amount of information is shared, in breadth and depth.

- *Frequency:* the extent to which the exchange of information between the customer and the supplier happens regularly.

- *Timing*: the extent to which the sharing of information occurs in a timely way, quickly when needed, on time, with respect to the other party's requirements, and with opportune release of strategic information that supports the joint business.

- *Reliability*: the extent to which the information is credible and accurate.

- *Relevance:* the extent to which the information exchanged has a strategic impact on the business and is valuable for the operation of the activities that are core to the joint business.

- *Exclusiveness*: the extent to which the two companies engage in sharing information that is not shared with all or other suppliers/customers that do not have the 'key partner' status.

Ideally, information sharing should be evaluated by both the supplier and the customer, given the *joint* nature of the metric.

Shared investment

This performance metric is the extent to which idiosyncratic investments in the buyer–supplier relationship are shared between the two companies. A successful KAM relationship should evolve towards a fair distribution of the benefits and investments/costs in the exchange between the two parties. Some examples of items that are typically considered as shared investment are:

- financial budget to promote products and services;

- organizational structure that is unique to the relationship (eg from the supplier's side, hiring a dedicated key account manager and other team members);

- training in knowledge and skills that are required specifically to grow the business, which comes from the relationship between the two companies;

- senior management involvement, in the form of established dedicated time to the relationship and a formal role (usually called 'executive sponsorship');

- information systems and data analysis capability to develop a business intelligence system to support the dyadic relationship between the supplier and the key account.

Customer experience

Customer experience is 'the customer's cognitive and affective assessment of all direct and indirect encounters with the firm relating to their purchasing behaviour' [14].

It recognizes a customer as more than just a rational being, seeking fulfilment of his hedonic, emotional and sensory aspirations. In other words, it emphasizes that customers look for more than competent services and products; they need engaging, compelling and memorable experiences.

Customer experience should be assessed in all relevant touchpoints within the customer journey, that is, the instances of direct or indirect contact between the supplier and the customer. The customer journey has three main stages:

1 *Pre-purchase*: includes the recognition of needs, as well as the search, consideration, and evaluation of alternatives.

2 *Purchase*: involves the decision making on a specific choice, the ordering and payment, as well as other considerations for the purchasing process itself.

3 *Post-purchase*: contains the usage/consumption of products, services or solutions, the request of additional information or services, and the engagement with the supplier's offering through a variety of possible actions or behaviours (eg recommending the supplier, sharing the usage experience with other companies, etc).

To measure customer experience as a KAM performance metric, the supplier company needs to follow a few steps. First, they need to identify the relevant touchpoints in each stage of the customer journey. Then, recognize the critical experience factors – those that determine whether the customer's experience in that touchpoint is good or bad. Next, measure each experience factor adequately. Finally, the supplier should assess their performance in terms of achieving a good customer experience.

Linking performance to insights

As argued in previous sections of this chapter, measuring the performance of each key account provides the supplier with relevant information about the current status of each account, and this should inform decisions on resource allocation to different customers.

The performance measurement process can have some variations or *add-ins* to obtain relevant information from key customers. One recommendation is to obtain qualitative insights that explain, in depth, the results of a quantitative performance assessment. The second suggestion is to be open to the possibility that some specific key accounts have their own performance measurement instrument.

Even if a supplier uses a questionnaire to measure KAM performance, it is still important to obtain qualitative insights to understand the *why* of those performance metrics. One option is to include some open questions to uncover reasons that support the score given to the different dimensions of performance. Another alternative is to first analyse the survey results, and then request a meeting with the customer to discuss the findings in detail, to obtain insights on the *why*. This process should be conducted by establishing inter-company conversations across the different functional areas; for example, the supplier's engineers with the customer's engineers, the legal team in one company with the legal team in the other company, etc. By doing this, the supplier company not only obtains a better understanding of how to perform well with the customer, but also establishes social ties and interpersonal bonds with people from the key account, which could then be instrumental in gaining advocates within the buying company.

In addition to obtaining the qualitative insights associated with a performance assessment, it is also possible that some specific key accounts require their *own* assessment of performance, to account for the particularities of those relationships and to signal commitment to those key accounts. By doing this, it is expected that the supplier will obtain relevant and up-to-date insights from the customer. The following quote from a senior executive in KAM explains the logic of this approach.

Getting insights from measuring performance

'The customer is measuring us. We don't force a questionnaire on this customer; instead, we get them to tell us which are the things that are important to them. And we encourage this account to review this regularly. By doing that, we lose the ability to make comparisons with other customers, but we get much deeper insights into what is really important to them today.' (Richard Vincent, OEM Strategic Operations Manager, Hewlett Packard Enterprise.)

Conclusion

This chapter proposes a framework to measure KAM performance at the account level. A first step is to recognize that performance should be assessed from different angles; in particular, both results-related and processes-related metrics are important. Within each of these groups, various aspects need to be considered to account for financial and non-financial indicators, as well as supplier-driven, customer-driven, and joint-driven metrics. The proposed framework should allow suppliers to compare the performance of different key accounts on the mentioned dimensions.

Questions for managers

- Do we have a balanced approach to measure KAM performance, with both results-driven and processes-driven metrics?

- Which are the key results-driven performance metrics in our business? Which are the relevant processes-driven metrics?
- Do we assess relational performance (customer satisfaction, loyalty, and relationship quality) in addition to financial performance?
- Can we estimate the lifetime value of our key accounts?
- How are we doing in terms of developing solutions for customers?
- Are we currently co-creating value with key accounts? What are the challenges in this space?
- How should we measure customer experience?
- What can we do to obtain qualitative insights from the customer when measuring KAM performance?

References

[1] Lemmens, R and Vanderbiesen, T (2014) Using customer profitability and customer lifetime value to manage strategic accounts, in *Handbook of Strategic Account Management: A comprehensive resource*, ed D Woodburn and K Wilson, pp. 267–86.

[2] Doran, G T (1981) There's a S.M.A.R.T. way to write management's goals and objectives, *Management Review*, 70 (11), pp. 35–36.

[3] McDonald, M and Rogers, B (2017) *Malcolm McDonald on Key Account Management*, Kogan Page, London.

[4] Woodburn, D and McDonald, M (2011) *Key Account Management: The definitive guide*, John Wiley & Sons, London.

[5] Guesalaga, R (2014) Top management involvement with key accounts: the concept, its dimensions, and strategic outcomes, *Industrial Marketing Management*, 43 (7), pp. 1146–56.

[6] Shi, L H et al (2010) Global account management strategies: drivers and outcomes, *Journal of International Business Studies*, 41 (4), pp. 620–38.

[7] Davies, I A and Ryals, L J (2014) The effectiveness of key account management practices, *Industrial Marketing Management*, 43 (7), pp. 1182–94.

[8] Gounaris, S and Tzempelikos, N (2014) Relational key account management: building key account management effectiveness through structural reformations and relationship management skills, *Industrial Marketing Management*, 43 (7), pp. 1110–23.

[9] Guenzi, P, Georges, L and Pardo, C (2009) The impact of strategic account managers' behaviors on relational outcomes: an empirical study, *Industrial Marketing Management*, 38 (3), pp. 300–11.

[10] Kaplan, R S and Norton, D P (2005) *The Balanced Scorecard: Measures that drive performance*, Harvard Business School Publishing.

[11] Kaplan, R S and Anderson, S R (2007) *Time-Driven Activity-Based Costing: A simpler and more powerful path to higher profits*, Harvard Business Press.

[12] Storbacka, K (2011) A solution business model: capabilities and management practices for integrated solutions, *Industrial Marketing Management*, **40** (5), pp. 699–711.

[13] Tuli, K R, Kohli, A K and Bharadwaj, S G (2007) Rethinking customer solutions: from product bundles to relational processes. *Journal of Marketing*, **71** (3), pp. 1–17.

[14] Klaus, P and Maklan, S (2013) Towards a better measure of customer experience, *International Journal of Market Research*, **55** (2), pp. 227–46.

Motivating, incentivizing and rewarding for KAM

09

'If you want to live a happy life, tie it to a goal, not to people or objects.'

ALBERT EINSTEIN

How can your organization design rewards and incentive systems to enable the effective implementation of KAM programmes?

Overview

Throughout the book so far, we have conceptualized and presented the implementation of KAM as a complex, multifaceted and interconnected endeavour. Furthermore, we have argued that KAM is long-term-oriented and customer-focused in nature. KAM, as a strategy distinct from sales, requires designing incentive systems in sync with these characteristics. This chapter focuses on how to use rewards and incentives in enabling effective KAM implementation. It outlines the motivation frameworks that best apply to KAM and exposes some of the potential shortcomings of applying compensation schemes that are well-established in sales to KAM functions. The chapter finishes with a set of guidelines for designing and implementing incentive systems that best work for KAM.

The need for revisiting compensation systems in KAM

Sales organizations today often promote professionals to key account or sales management roles who have a track record in sales, often in transactional or product-based contexts. This approach has a number of shortcomings [1]. First, the role of a salesperson is often linked to obtaining individual results but a sales manager is tasked with promoting team-based outcomes, often resulting from intensive coaching and motivation of the sales team. Second, it can be hard for them to resist the temptation to 'close the sale' for the representative, potentially undermining her/his motivation. Third, they may neglect managerial and control-oriented tasks that are seen as 'bureaucracy'. Sales management and selling are two different functions in an organization, requiring different role descriptions and associated skills sets.

More fundamentally, businesses in a number of industries still motivate and reward KAM roles using the approaches developed for sales organizations, despite the fact that selling is increasingly evolving from product-based to value-based business models [2]. In this evolution a number of tensions manifest, first a longer-term outlook to customer relations and business growth.

Whereas sales organizations typically focus on short-term, often quarterly and yearly results, KAM organizations extend the planning horizon, being mindful that the cycle for creating value with strategic customers can extend well beyond one year. Another key tension to be balanced is the interplay between supplier- and customer-centric processes and practices. Traditional sales organizations are

Figure 9.1   Differences across sales and KAM business models

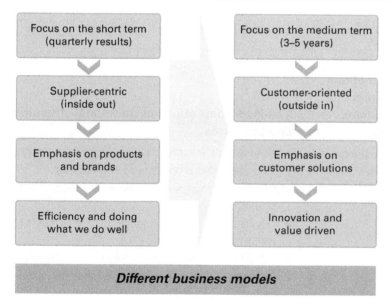

Adapted from Davies [2]

often product-focused as opposed to KAM structures that feature customer-centric cultures and structures. Innovation and new forms of value creation in customer solutions often underpin the core strategies in KAM, in contrast with the stress on efficiencies and short-term returns inherent in sales.

Sales has evolved to become more consultative and complex [3], resulting in adaptations of policies, systems and processes across a number of dimensions, rendering established compensation schemes potentially outdated.

As one of our recent studies suggests, a number of high-level transformations in sales have occurred, including:

- integrated offerings comprising products, services and experiences;
- enhanced customer business knowledge;
- wider and deeper relationships across boundaries;
- accountability across extended end-to-end processes;
- skills and competences in customer management roles;
- transparency and accountability.

These high-level transformations in a wide range of organizations have resulted in mid-level adaptations (see Table 9.1). These adaptations call for reward systems and motivation practices that support the KAM function, assisting customer operations characterized by complexity, interconnectedness and long-term orientation.

Table 9.1   Transformations in customer management organizations

High-level transformations in customer management functions	Mid-level adaptations of traditional structures and processes
Integrated offerings comprising products, services and experiences	• Changes in the approach to sell to (key) customers • Extended value propositions become expected • New contractual arrangements are needed (eg revenue-sharing schemes) • Development of better understanding of risk transfer and risk ownership • Sales forces needed before solutions are created • Business models need to be revisited to account for the complexity of the supplier/customer interfaces

(continued)

Table 9.1   (*Continued*)

High-level transformations in customer management functions	Mid-level adaptations of traditional structures and processes
Enhanced customer business knowledge	• Higher level of involvement and understanding of the customer organization • Longer time frames to understand the customer requirements and expectations and particularly subtle value drivers • Increased focus on both present and future needs • Organization of highly interactive workshops and other means to create new insights • Encouragement of knowledge sharing • Potential need to create 'parallel' account management organizations, one relationship-oriented and another product-focused
Wider and deeper relationships across boundaries	• Need to avoid overserving some customers and underserving others • Appointment of multifunctional account teams • Creation of new ways of developing relationships when access to customers is not granted or regulated • Definition of enabling mechanisms for the account teams to engage internally with their own organization
Accountability across extended end-to-end processes	• The scope of the KAM function extends, encompassing end-to-end business processes, not just business and customer development • Emergence of two types of sales organizations – transactional and strategic
Skills and competences in customer management roles	• Conventional skills that emphasize persuasion become increasingly questioned, giving way to an integrated set of managerial competences (functional, relational, managerial and cognitive)
Transparency and accountability	• Work policies, corporate codes of conduct and ethical guidelines are necessary but not sufficient to create trusted relationships. • Personal integrity and ability to make ethical decisions are key in customer management roles

Traditional rewards and their limitations for KAM roles

Reward and compensation systems in sales use a number of instruments to enhance motivation and performance; in general, these can be classified as financial and non-financial [4].

Financial rewards

The most commonly used types of financial rewards in sales are salary, commission, bonus, and other incentives [5]:

A *Salary*. The base salary is a fixed sum paid on a regular interval to the job holder. A number of factors affect the amount awarded including, experience, competence, and the level of responsibility and risk attached to the position.

The role of the base salary is to reward effort put into activities whose results are not directly measurable but that need to be undertaken, such as market research, client needs analysis, etc. Management normally sets salary levels that are sufficient to attract, retain and stimulate the required sales professionals.

Fundamentally, basic salary is aimed at providing security for the salesperson and encouraging loyalty and commitment towards the role and the organization. Basic salaries need to be calibrated to avoid low performers being overpaid and high performers underpaid.

B *Commission* is a payment given for achieving a certain level of performance whereby salespeople are paid for the short-term results achieved. Commission is usually remunerated based on volume, revenue or profit, thereby directly linking salespeople's efforts to outcomes. Commission payment has the disadvantage of directing the sales force towards short-term sales revenues, sometimes at the expense of long-term profit and customer satisfaction. Furthermore, reward schemes with a strong commission component can result in declining levels of loyalty, commitment and time dedicated to other non-sales activities.

C *Bonuses* are widely used in sales for achieving or surpassing a certain level of performance, often in the form of a particular quota or target. Arguably, commissions and bonuses have a strong effect on motivating staff to improve their performance, since payment is related to results for both the individual and the company.

D *Sales contests* are also used as short-term initiatives to encourage additional effort. The winners of the contest could receive additional monetary payments or non-financial rewards. Sales contests, in addition to other programmes such as incentives and recognition programmes can, when used appropriately, improve morale and team effort [6].

Non-financial rewards

Companies also use a range of non-financial instruments to enhance motivation and increase employee satisfaction and commitment. These include:

A *Benefits*, such as health insurance, pension funds or a company car. Other benefits can also include shares or stock options.

B *Opportunities* for career development, through setting career paths and the reimbursement of tuition fees for university, seminars, workshops and training. Career and professional development opportunities could be powerful sources of motivation to younger professionals.

C *Recognition*, which can be provided both informally and formally. Informal forms of recognition often occur in manager–employee feedback conversations. Formal recognition is provided in the form of awards and honours.

Most companies structure their reward schemes, combining various instruments in order to help capture the diversity of contexts in which they operate and the range of corporate objectives they pursue.

Motivation to achieve short-term targets, a widely desired outcome in sales organizations, can paradoxically trigger a number of unintended consequences [7]. In the next part of this chapter, we present some of these, before analysing the motivational paradigms associated with compensation in sales and KAM and outlining some guidelines for designing and implementing KAM-oriented incentive schemes.

Unintended consequences of performance-related incentives

Sales targets are extensively used by sales organizations. Performance goals define a 'desired', 'promised', or 'aspirational' level of performance and it is reported that about 95 per cent of Fortune 500 companies use performance goals in their sales compensation schemes, making sales compensation payments as much as $800 billion in the US economy [8].

Compensation schemes linked to performance targets have received criticism after reports that they drive deviant behaviour. For instance, in September 2016, it was reported in the United States that 5,300 Wells Fargo employees had been dismissed after the discovery that they had created over 2 million fake accounts. The Consumer Financial Protection Bureau revealed that the Wells Fargo staff had secretly opened these unauthorized accounts to hit sales targets and receive bonuses [9].

In the UK, the Financial Conduct Authority claimed that aggressive sales goals with bonuses linked to them underpinned a number of high-profile cases of mis-selling in the financial sector. According to some estimates, 20 of the world's biggest banks have paid more than US $235 billion in fines and compensation for misdeeds [10], ranging from fines for manipulation of currency and interest rate markets, to compensation to customers during the period 2008–2015.

Targets and incentives are mainly used for motivating specific behaviours, establishing expectations, and evaluating and rewarding performance. At present, despite the ubiquitous use of performance targets linked to financial incentives, there is growing criticism of the potentially dysfunctional behaviours associated with their use [11], [12]. Some of the most prominent unintended consequences of reward and incentive schemes are *narrowing views, short-termism, misrepresentation, misinterpretation* and *ossification* [13] (see Table 9.2).

Sales organizations are thought to develop narrow views when managerial effort is devoted to the aspects of performance that are measured at the expense of those aspects that are not measured or are less measurable. Measurability and importance are two very different dimensions and thus, whilst some phenomena such as customer value creation, relationship transparency or trust are not readily measurable, these are the foundations of successful supplier–key account relationships.

Short-termism, or managerial myopia [14], [15], refers to the focus on short-term financial achievement at the expense of the accomplishment of longer-term objectives. Internal pressures (eg from shareholders) or from the market (eg customers) force organizations to deliver against short-term budgets and expectations, allocating resources and making decisions that address short-term indicators and measures but do not take into consideration the required investments in capability that will strengthen the development of the business over the long term.

Misrepresentation refers to manipulation of information in a way that results in reported performance differing from actual performance. The most common case is the misrepresentation of financial statements, and it is argued that the structure of management incentives, as well as the application of the Generally Accepted Accounting Principles underpin this crucial issue in corporations and businesses, as

Table 9.2 Summary of unintended consequences of measures and rewards

Unintended consequences of metrics and rewards	Observations
Information manipulation	Misrepresentation, misinterpretation, reclassification or making up of information in order to give the impression that the organization is meeting the expectations of the measurement system. Example: misrepresentation of financial statements
Gaming	Individuals behave in opportunistic ways, just to fulfil the performance expectations, or even engage in unethical or questionable conduct. Examples: mis-selling of products customers do not need; distorting information about markets and customers so performance targets are lowered in the next period
Selective attention	Individuals and organizations focus on 'what gets measured', not necessarily on the tasks that best align to stakeholders' interests. Other less measurable goals such as trust and collaboration tend to be overlooked. Examples: excessive focus on profitability; over-emphasis on new customers
Illusion of control	When using measurement frameworks, managers can develop the belief that what the system captures accurately reflects the 'real' performance of the system and the behaviours of the actors involved in it [13]. This can lead to short-termism and blindness to cause–effect mechanisms. Example: quality problems in competitor's products result in an increase in demand for the supplier; the performance system does not capture this phenomenon and managers attribute this growth to the sales team's efforts

recent cases such as Enron, WorldCom, Tyco International, Lehman Brothers and General Motors have shown.

Misinterpretation refers to the lack of proper analysis and synthesis of performance data and information. Cognitive biases and limitations in information processing can lead to the wrong decisions being taken, with detrimental effects for both the key account managers (KAMgrs) and the company. Misinterpretation of information can manifest itself in the flawed analysis of causal links between the driver and the outcome of a measure [13].

Ossification refers to the emergence of rigidities or organizational paralysis [16] resulting from inflexible performance evaluation systems. The measures and performance indicators that are used, particularly when linked to rewards, promote behaviours and practices that may have become irrelevant. For instance, 'new customers' is a widely used performance indicator in sales organizations. The practices and processes necessary to achieve this measure may limit the organization's ability to develop existing customer relationships, generating upselling and cross-selling opportunities. Likewise, excessive focus on customer profitability may discourage the account manager from exploring new and innovative offerings that may add value over the long term.

In sales organizations, another important unintended consequence of using rewards linked to short-term goals is the emergence of *problematic behaviours* [7] that could include attributing sales generated in one period to another, reducing cooperation, over-claiming or overemphasizing the benefits of certain products, and accepting transactions with customers with high credit risk.

Lastly, a subtle but fundamental unintended consequence of rewards and measurement systems is the erosion of trust-based, high-quality relationships. Performance management systems have the potential to change how social relationships operate in organizations. Evidence shows that systems designed to monitor through performance measures, targets and incentives (ie agency theory-related) can promote transactional relationships that diminish trust and generate disparity [17], [18].

Conversely, organizations that operate high-control systems can evolve towards becoming trust- and commitment-based organizations [19]. In these, the nature of social relationships experienced amongst key actors can move from suspicion and alienation to confidence and interdependence.

The question that emerges is, given the potentially dysfunctional effects of reward systems, why do so many organizations design and implement such systems? We argue that control-based systems are effective in contexts where (1) the link between effort and performance is clear, and (2) individuals are primarily motivated by extrinsic factors. These conditions largely exist in transactional and product-based selling. However, in complex selling and long-term customer relationships, there are multiple circumstances affecting outcome performance and individuals may be motivated by factors of an intrinsic nature. We will now briefly describe core motivation theories before outlining the principles and guidelines for the design of effective reward systems in KAM.

Motivation theories that underpin traditional reward schemes

Motivation theories aim to understand people's attitudes towards work and the behaviours they display when putting effort into accomplishing tasks. Influential theories that have been applied to the context of sales include Herzberg's motivation–hygiene theory [20], Vroom's expectancy theory [21], and goal-setting theories [22], [23].

Herzberg's motivation–hygiene theory distinguishes between factors that cause dissatisfaction, known as 'hygiene factors' (for instance, working conditions, salary, company policies and supervision), and factors creating job satisfaction, known as 'motivators' (for example, achievement, recognition, responsibility and opportunity for growth and advancement). The underlying idea of this theory is that hygiene factors do not motivate and do not improve performance, but they can lead to a decrease in performance when they are absent. Sales managers must keep hygiene factors in place whilst providing additional motivators to improve performance. The implication of this theory is that aspects such as recognition, sense of achievement and job interest, in terms of providing new challenges and enhanced responsibility, may be crucial for motivating sales workforces.

Vroom's expectancy theory makes a more explicit link between behaviour, performance and rewards, and forms the basis of much work in sales-related motivation. According to this theory, people's behaviour and motivation are dependent on their expectations about the extent to which their efforts will be rewarded, as well as the value they attach to the rewards received in exchange for their efforts. Hence, it is important that sales organizations clarify the behaviour and performance that will be rewarded and understand the motivational preferences of their people (for instance, the extent to which they value money, time, job fulfilment or any other element used to reward their performance).

Proponents of *goal-setting theories* argue that people perform better when they are assigned specific and difficult targets than they do when they are assigned easy targets or 'do your best'-type targets. Thus, the effects of setting targets for performance are influenced by target difficulty, that is, the extent to which the assigned goals are perceived to be achievable; target specificity, which can be defined as the extent to which the targets are clearly defined; and target controllability, in other words, the degree to which individuals have control over the tasks required to achieve the set goal [24].

Traditionally, reward systems in sales are characterized by a number of assumptions that derive from motivational theories, including but not limited to:

- *Extrinsic drivers*: individuals expect their organizations to meet their hygiene factors, eg salary, and thus monetary rewards will trigger satisfaction with the role and the organization.

- *Clear link between effort and results*: individuals can identify an unequivocal link between their efforts and the results that are rewarded.

- *Achievability of targets*: targets set by the organizations, and how they can be largely achieved.

- *Self-interest and agency*: the assumption is that individuals are self-interested and focused on maximizing their own utility. Agency theory paradigms [25] also assume risk-averse individuals who are reluctant to engage in new ways of working if these practices are associated with perceived risk.

Reward systems in sales (and to some extent in business in general) are largely designed based on paradigms of agency theories. Whilst agency principles fit a number of contexts, eg short-term relations, discrete transactions, and exchanges of commodity products, they are not suitable in key customer relationships, which are often characterized by blurred relationships, long-term orientation and complexity of integrated offerings of products and services.

The fulfilment of extrinsic factors is an important consideration, since these move individuals to work 'harder'. However, working 'smarter' [26] is required in contexts that demand customer-centricity, innovativeness and joint problem solving. Moreover, in situations where there is no direct and unique link between individual behaviour and precise outcomes, traditional theories of motivation become largely invalid. Major breakthroughs in customer value propositions and committed long-term relationships are underpinned by a wide range of team-based efforts. Sustained growth and value creation in supplier–key customer relationships are not the outcome of single actions but the result of integrated practices and processes.

Lastly, the definition of 'stretch but achievable' targets derives from accurate and sound forecasts. In volatile market contexts, it becomes very difficult to accurately predict revenue growth. Furthermore, a number of organizational factors influence sales forecasting [27], including climate, capabilities and organizational learning. In contexts where the supplier is developing new propositions for customers, or where there is no track record or precedent, plausible forecasts are rare, and therefore associating compensation to imperfect targets can be demotivating and potentially dysfunctional.

Motivational and organizational theories that support KAM approaches

As indicated above, there are few traditional theories of motivation that can explain and inform how to enhance commitment and engagement in KAM roles. Self-determination and stewardship theories can likely better explain how to drive individuals towards long-term key account relationships.

Self-determination theory [28] distinguishes between extrinsic motivation (doing an activity for an instrumental reason such as getting a bonus) and intrinsic motivation (doing an activity because it is interesting and satisfying). The theory associates the performance of complex tasks with the need for intrinsic motivation, as intrinsic motivation has been found to generate active information seeking, perseverance and resilience, which are critical factors for succeeding in this type of task. The theory predicts that intrinsic motivation is enhanced in environments where people perceive a sense of autonomy, development, meaningfulness and community; it is reduced or 'crowded out' in environments that focus on high stretch performance targets and monetary incentives. Thus, this theory implies that, for example, for the development of complex or relational sales involving multiple and complex tasks, sales organizations need to create environments that are more favourable to intrinsic motivation. This insight is of crucial importance as it suggests that, in the long term, the use of quotas and monetary incentives in these complex contexts may reduce motivation and performance rather than enhance them.

In contrast to agency paradigms, *stewardship theory* [29], [30] which draws from sociology and psychology, assumes that employees are not necessarily opportunistic. Employees can be stewards who work hard and whose behaviour and interests are in line with the long-term interests of their organization. With these principles in mind, stewardship theory proposes that commitment and motivation can be sustained by having a clear and well-understood mission (or cause) that helps individuals to direct their decisions and actions towards it. The alignment of the customer management organization can be achieved by relying on intrinsic rather than on extrinsic rewards (ie using mechanisms that enable a sense of meaningfulness, autonomy and progress), or at least balancing extrinsic and intrinsic factors in new ways.

Promoters of *stewardship theory* emphasize the recruitment of those individuals who are intrinsically motivated to achieve the goals of the business and aligned to the mission of the organization. Stewardship-based management approaches have been found effective in enabling performance in contexts where its assumptions are valid and where the mission and goals of the organization have low measurability and are oriented to the long term.

As we have argued, the contexts in which the key account function operates are increasingly characterized by protracted time frames, complexity, and relationship intensity. The KAM strategies that lead to success are rarely linear, measurable and predictable. In these circumstances KAM leaders need to consider motivation and reward approaches that embrace in a more fundamental way the nature of the contexts in which they operate. We argue that management approaches and practices informed by stewardship theories may better contribute to the effective implementation of KAM.

Guidelines for implementing KAM-oriented rewards

The design of compensation schemes in customer management roles is typically informed by a number of factors [31] such as sales processes and roles, the extent to which results are measurable, the situation and organizational culture of the company and its philosophy, and industry norms and practices.

Design reward systems that reflect the nature of KAM

When looking at incentive schemes to support the implementation of KAM, five key factors need to be considered.

- *Eligibility: make eligible all individuals involved in key customer relations.* This factor refers to who in the key account team is entitled to receive incentive pay and how much influence each person has on the overall performance of the relationship with the key customer. In order to better align each member of the account team towards working for the customer's best interest, those whose role can significantly contribute to the development of the relationship with the customer and its growth should be entitled to receive incentive pay.

- *Incentive size: modest relative to total pay.* The incentive size should be internally and externally equitable. This means that it should take into account internal equity levels and should be in line with the incentive size typically used by peer companies. The size of the incentive should also consider how much direct influence KAMgrs have over customer growth and profitability. The higher the influence the larger the potential size of the incentive, because it will reward achievements derived from individual effort and not from other indirect sources. Success in strategic relationships with key customers typically results from the involvement of several functions, including new product development, operations, technical specialists, etc. Myriad factors, including relational, financial and technical, influence the choice of a strategic supplier and the development of key account relationships over time. Therefore, the size of incentives should be small in comparison to total pay.

- *Payout frequency: longer periods linked to value creation.* The payout frequency refers to how often incentives are paid to key account teams. In sales organizations it is customary to offer quarterly and yearly incentives. In key account relations, the frequency of payout should be in line with the customer processes, the company's strategic planning horizon, and in sync with the value creation lifecycle. This motivates longer-term focus and behaviours more aligned to the customer's strategic agenda.

- *Focus: enhancing strategic relationships.* The focus of incentives in KAM needs to be in line with the way in which KAMGrs work and the way in which customer development processes unfold. Relationships are the cornerstone of KAM and thus incentives should support the establishment, development and consolidation of long-term, strategic key customer relationships.

- *Performance–payout relationship: use multiple approaches.* The performance–payout relationship refers to how incentive payments are calculated and how differences in performance will impact and affect the amount of incentive pay awarded to individuals. In compensation schemes, different methods are used to define the performance–payout relationship: linear, regressive or progressive; the use of caps versus no caps; payments starting at 100 per cent of target or at a fraction of a target, etc. Each design aspect needs to be aligned with the context in which the organization operates as it will have different effects on behaviour and thus performance. For the context of KAM, the following would be advisable:

  - Discretionary vs formulaic calculation of incentive pay: adopting some degree of discretion rather than strict formulae to allow managers to decide the allocation of incentive pay in specific circumstances.

  - Single vs multiple raters/evaluators: given that performance in a KAMgr role is highly subjective, input from various informants (including the customer) would be advisable.

  - Single vs multiple measures: various measures including leading indicators (behaviours) and lagging indicators (outcomes) will form the basis of a better reward system for KAM.

It is difficult to design a perfect pay-for-performance scheme. A number of organizations still find that transition difficult, as the following quote from a sales director at a manufacturer of industrial products illustrates.

> 'I believe at the moment we are doing two different roles (traditional sales and account management) and we are only being measured in one.' (Sales director, industrial manufacturing.)

One of the keys to designing effective reward systems in KAM and other management functions is the link between incentives, sales targets and the performance measures used in the organization

There is growing evidence about difficulties in setting targets in sales that do not derive from dysfunctional behaviour [11], [12]. But targets are rarely the source of dissatisfaction on their own. When looking at the effects of performance targets on behaviour it is important to focus on the way in which incentive pay is associated with targets and on the characteristics of the performance measures for which targets are being set. Research shows that performance targets, incentive plans and performance measures cannot be considered in isolation. They are highly interrelated and thus need to be designed and managed using an integrated approach, informed by the following guidelines [32].

Clarity

Ensure that everybody in the KAM organization understands the performance measures and targets used to assess and reward their performance. KAMgrs first need to precisely articulate how certain actions will lead to the results that the organization expects, and second, must understand how their performance measures are calculated and what they mean for better behavioural results.

Research in sales targets, incentives and performance measures [11] reveals that incentive schemes are often poorly understood, as the following statement from a key account executive from a media company illustrates: 'We've got a bonus structure that is very complex. It's not actually, but I don't understand it.'

Review

Conduct periodic reviews of the targets set for the short term as well as for the long term in order to ensure their validity and achievability. Concurrently, also review the performance accomplished against targets, communicating and feeding back key observations and recommendations. Positive feedback on outputs has a significant positive effect on the performance of salespeople [33].

'The salespeople have special product sales targets. These are constantly not met by most salespeople. Nothing is talked about when we meet to improve these figures. These measures should be used not only as a measurement tool but also to identify weaknesses in our teams.' (Sales executive, construction products company.)

Fairness

Strive to set targets and measures in ways that are perceived as fair. KAMgrs must perceive their targets to be impartial and equitable, ie that they do not favour any particular customer manager, team or (if applicable) territory person.

'Overall there seems to be little interest, leading to a lack of motivation to achieve the targets and sometimes resentment based on the opinion that another part of the team has an "easier" target set' [11].

Communication

Ensure the timeliness (and clarity) of the communication of performance targets and results, and their associated compensation schemes. Salespeople need to know what the target is, how it has been calculated, who will contribute to its achievement, and the extent to which the expectations of behaviours and results are being met. Performance targets must be communicated well before the target period starts. Timeliness and transparency in communicating performance measurement information have a direct effect on sales behaviour.

'We are not informed about how measures and targets are performing until the period is over; this has a negative effect.' 'By the time we are told what the target is, half the year has gone' [11].

Completeness

As discussed in Chapter 8, the processes involved in KAM are inherently complex. Thus, the performance measurement and reward systems need to capture key performance dimensions (eg financial, relational, operational). If the number of key dimensions is high, consider prioritization and conducting some correlation analysis to understand how the different dimensions of performance interact and whether some dimensions can be excluded from the incentive system as they are highly correlated with others. For instance, if two performance measures are highly correlated we can collect data on both measures but just use one of them for pay purposes.

Agreement

Involve KAMgrs in identifying and agreeing the performance measures that are going to be used for assessing and rewarding their performance. Conduct focus groups and structured discussions to select, prioritize and implement those measures that matter for KAMgrs in your organization (see Chapter 1, Table 1.2).

> 'Targets are imposed by the company without any discussion or involvement of the salesperson.'

Seamlessly combine extrinsic and intrinsic elements

KAMgrs are motivated by extrinsic ambitions, but also by intrinsic drivers. Effort and energy are compelled by extrinsic motivators. Innovative behaviour and sustained long-term commitment are enhanced by intrinsic sources.

Thus, in addition to designing performance targets and financial incentive schemes, put in place practices that foster intrinsic motivators, which, as suggested by self-determination theories, relate to:

- sense of autonomy, allowing freedom to pursue customer development strategies in flexible ways;
- sense of meaningfulness, revitalizing the significance of customer-centricity and long-term value creation;
- sense of development, offering all-encompassing (eg product, technical and managerial) knowledge development and defined career paths for the KAM function; and
- sense of community, creating a culture that fosters support and security, particularly in contexts where KAMgrs need to take calculated risks and engage in new ways of working with key clients. Foster intimacy within the community by celebrating not just 'numbers' but also the accomplishment of the highest behavioural standards.

Conclusion

In this chapter we have focused on addressing how to motivate KAMgrs and how to design rewards and performance measures that enable the effective implementation of KAM.

The key takeaway from the chapter is the need to rethink sales-oriented targets, performance measures and incentives and to adapt them to the context of managing key customers. These adaptations often require evolution from short- to long(er)-term incentives, and flexibility to consider subjective measures that could reflect the complexities of managing key customers better than objective and quantitative indicators.

We have argued that stronger emphasis on the fixed component of incentive schemes and rebalancing variable pay will, in a number of situations, allow intrinsic motives to drive behaviour, and enable the promotion of the customer's best interests.

Some believe that the necessary control of key customer processes requires 'hard and measurable' indicators. However, other mechanisms such as collegiality, trust and an organizational culture that values performance will, in the long run, stimulate the behaviours that drive customer value and generate competitive advantage.

Questions for managers

- If you asked your high-performing KAMgrs about the factors that motivate them, what would they say? Furthermore, to what extent is the current incentive scheme in line with these motivators?

- How do you define who becomes eligible for the incentive schemes?

- What is the size of incentives relative to total pay for KAMgrs?

- If you award variable pay in your organization, what is the frequency of the payments? How do these periods correspond with the processes of establishing, developing and monetizing business with key customers?

- How do you define the 'right' pay for KAMgrs? How do you know whether you are paying them too much or too little?

References

[1] Zoltners, A A, Sinha, P and Lorimer, S E (2012) Think twice before promoting your best salesperson, *Harvard Business Review* [online] https://hbr.org/2012/07/think-twice-before-promoting-your-best [accessed 26 December 2017].

[2] Davies, M (2017) *Infinite Value: Accelerating profitable growth through value-based selling*, Bloomsbury, London.

[3] Marcos Cuevas, J (2018) The transformation of professional selling: implications for leading the modern sales organization, *Industrial Marketing Management*, **69**, pp. 198–208.

[4] Johnston, M W and Marshall, G W (2013) *Sales Force Management*, 11th edn, Routledge, Abingdon.

[5] Marcos Cuevas, J, Donaldson, B and Lemmens, R (2016) *Sales Management: Strategy, process and practice*, Palgrave Macmillan, London.

[6] Zoltners, A, Sinha, P and Lorimer, S E (2006) Increasing sales force motivation through sales contests, SPIFFs, and recognition programs, in *Complete Guide to Sales Force Incentive Compensation*, pp. 377–408.

[7] Murphy, W H (2004) In pursuit of short-term goals: anticipating the unintended consequences of using special incentives to motivate the sales force, *Journal of Business Research*, **57** (11), pp. 1265–75.

[8] Zoltners, A, Sinha, P and Lorimer, S E (2012) Breaking the sales force incentive addiction: a balanced approach to sales force effectiveness, *Journal of Personal Selling and Sales Management*, **32** (2), pp. 171–86.

[9] Egan, M (2016) 5,300 Wells Fargo employees fired over 2 million phony accounts, *CNN Money* [online] http://money.cnn.com/2016/09/08/investing/wells-fargo-created-phony-accounts-bank-fees/index.html [accessed 02 January 2018].

[10] Reuters (2015) Banking misconduct bill [online] http://graphics.thomsonreuters.com/15/bankfines/index.html?utm_source=twitter [accessed 12 July 2016].

[11] Franco-Santos, M (2009) The impact of performance targets on behaviour: a close look at sales force contexts, Cranfield School of Management – CIMA Report, Bedford, UK.

[12] Ordóñez, L D et al (2009) Goals gone wild: the systematic side effects of overprescribing goal setting, *Academy of Management Perspectives*, **44** (1), pp. 6–16.

[13] Gómez-Mejía, L R, Berrone, P and Franco-Santos, M (2010) *Compensation and Organizational Performance: Theory, research, and practice*, ME Sharpe Incorporated.

[14] Laverty, K J (1996) Economic 'short-termism': the debate, the unresolved issues, and the implications for management practice and research, *Academy of Management Review*, **21** (3), pp. 825–60.

[15] Merchant, K A (1990) The effects of financial controls on data manipulation and management myopia, *Accounting, Organizations and Society*, **15** (4), pp. 297–313.

[16] Smith, P (1995) On the unintended consequences of publishing performance data in the public sector, *International Journal of Public Administration*, **18**, pp. 277–310.

[17] Chwastiak, M (2006) Rationality, performance measures and representations of reality: planning, programming and budgeting and the Vietnam war, *Critical Perspectives on Accounting*, **17** (1), pp. 29–55.

[18] Conrad, L and P G, Uslu (2012) UK health sector performance management: conflict, crisis and unintended consequences, *Accounting Forum*, **36** (4), pp. 231–50.

[19] Segal, L and Lehrer, M (2012) The institutionalization of stewardship: theory, propositions, and insights from change in the Edmonton public schools, *Organization Studies*, **33** (2).

[20] Herzberg, F (2005) Motivation-hygiene theory, in *Organizational Behaviour I: Essential theories of motivation and leaderhip*, ed J Miner, Routledge pp. 61–74.

[21] Vroom, V H (1964) *Work and motivation*, Wiley, New York.

[22] Latham, G P (2004) The motivational effects of goal-setting, *Academy of Management Excellence*, **18** (4), pp. 126–29.

[23] Locke, E A (2004) Linking goals to monetary incentives, *Academy of Management Excellence*, **18** (4), pp. 130–33.

[24] Latham, G P and Locke, E A (1979) Goal setting – a motivational technique that works, *Organizational Dynamics*, **8** (2), p. 68.

[25] Eisenhardt, K M (1989) Agency theory: an assessment and review, *Academy of Management Review*, **14** (1), pp. 57–74.

[26] Sujan, H, Weitz, B A and Sujan, M (1988) Increasing sales productivity by getting salespeople to work smarter, *Journal of Personal Selling and Sales Management*, **8** (2), pp. 9–20.

[27] Davis, D F and Mentzer, J T (2007) Organizational factors in sales forecasting management, *International Journal of Forecasting*, **23** (3), pp. 475–95.

[28] Gagné, M and Forest, J (2008) The study of compensation systems through the lens of self-determination theory: reconciling 35 years of debate, *Cananadian Psychology*, **49** (3), pp. 225–32.

[29] Davis, J H, Schoorman, F D and Donaldson, L (1997) Toward a stewardship theory of management, *Academy of Management Review*, **22** (1), pp. 20–47.

[30] Silva, T (2012) Toward an understanding of the psychology of stewardship, *Academy of Management Review*, **37** (2), pp. 172–93.

[31] Zoltners, A, Shina, P and Lorimer, S E (2006) *The Complete Guide to Sales Force Incentive Compensation* AMACOM, New York.

[32] Franco-Santos, M, Marcos, J and Bourne, M (2010) The art and science of target setting, *IESE Insight*, **7**, pp. 34–41.

[33] Chakrabarty, S, Oubre, D T and Brown, G (2008) The impact of supervisory adaptive selling and supervisory feedback on salesperson performance, *Industrial Marketing Management*, **37** (4), pp. 447–54.

KAM and procurement

10

The buyer's perspective and value-based negotiation

'The most important thing in a negotiation is to get inside your opponent's head and figure out what he really wants.'

JACOB LEW

Question: How should key account managers ensure that they establish the best deal and price when dealing with customer buying functions?

Sales, negotiation and KAM: what's the difference?

Key account management can often draw from and focus on the strategic and process-fuelled aspects of business. Analysing the strategic needs and market position of the key customer is, of course, important but at some stage the resulting customer value proposition has to be packaged and presented to the customer. This conversation usually takes place with some type of buyer and, whilst the supplier may have carried out an A+ job, if this 'value presentation' is not carefully planned and executed with the right people, value will evaporate and, potentially, a lower price or fee secured than would have been possible.

This chapter considers the very real stage of key account management that can almost undo the hard graft and investment undertaken by suppliers as they look to grow business with more strategic customers. The reality is harsh: if you do not understand or have a good relationship with the buying function of the customer business, you may well end up fighting on their terms (usually price) and not your own (this should definitely be the value that you will generate for the customer over a sustained period). Yet these aspects are often under-estimated and left to chance. There may be several reasons for this, but here we discuss some of the more troubling examples we have seen in our work consulting with and supporting organizations looking to transition to a KAM model.

First, there is sometimes a lack of consideration for the difference (and connection) between selling and KAM. Of course, there is a step-change when a supplier shifts from 'selling' to a large portfolio of smaller, less complex customers to focusing greater resources on a smaller portfolio of larger key customers. With the sales model, large numbers of salespeople can rely on the products and brands that are being provided to convey the 'value message' to the customer. Relationship building and trust between supplier and customer are vital, but the depth of strategic understanding and the extent of customizing a value proposition for each customer are limited. KAM, however, is a far more bespoke activity. The emphasis is on standing back and deeply understanding the customer's business. Once this deeper view is captured, a new and bespoke customer value proposition can be developed. This process is discussed throughout this book and is vital to successfully developing a compelling reason for the customer to buy your advanced offerings. What should not be forgotten is that relationship building is still a vital skill in KAM. If selling is executed correctly, the customer should see significant value from the salesperson as an advisor and expert. Of course, the depth and strategic impact increase with KAM; however, it is a mistake to think that because a KAM team is now in place, the relationship aspect of selling can stop. Selling does not stop when you adopt a KAM approach; it evolves and becomes more advanced through discussions, but selling still needs to take place.

The other skill that needs consideration is negotiation. There can be an assumption that, with sales teams skilled in consultative, value-based relationship management, SPIN selling or 'customer challenging', all your problems are gone. These are all valid and essential sales approaches in their own different ways, but they are incomplete in one area. The negotiation process determines the final strength of a supply deal. Of course, a strong (value-based) sales approach will put the supplier in a better position to negotiate, but if one fails to negotiate effectively a good buyer will 'squeeze the juice' out of a potential price.

The voice of the practitioner

'We spent about $500,000 on a global solution-selling training programme. It was great and is now the way that we do business. Unfortunately, we were just not able to convert our new ideas into profit! After observing the sales cycle, it became apparent that aggressive buyers were better at negotiation than our salespeople.

> So, we did some fairly simple negotiation development that has complemented our new approach to selling. For us, it seems that selling and negotiation work together, but separately they are less effective.' (Vice President Marketing, global automotive components manufacturer.)

Strong supplier organizations have a clear understanding of strategic selling and KAM. They invest in both of these activities, and carefully consider the connections and overlaps between selling and developing bespoke offerings and strategies for those few, carefully selected higher-value customers. A strong organizational understanding is vital, along with solid capability in sales, KAM and negotiation, since they ultimately lead to an organization that is focused on value co-creation and achieving the best commercial deal.

Interview with Steve Fry

Steve is Global Head of Onshore Consulting at eClerx Financial Markets, based in New York. He has been a consultant, sales director, and business start-up entrepreneur in the FinTech industry, working and selling to key enterprise clients all over the world. Steve is a businessman who describes himself as a salesman first.

Q. You have been a managing director and founding partner of two successful businesses... and yet it always strikes me that you have retained 'selling' at the core of what you do. Why is that?

At the core of any business is the need to generate revenue. The route to revenue generation largely depends on the business model and the business plan. While many firms make use of marketing, I've learned through experience never to confuse the roles of marketing and selling. Marketing can be useful in getting a product to market and plays a role in what I see as indirect selling. People do business with people and this direct approach to revenue generation has proven most effective in my career. Building relationships that drive repeatable revenue is at the core of a successful business. These relationships tend to have the effect of blocking out competitive forces so long as the buyer remains satisfied with the products and services of the seller. That's why a direct sales approach has always been core to my business activities.

Q. How do you deal with buyers/procurement? What advice do you have for making the buyer an advocate of the value your firm can deliver and not just focused on fee/price?

I've always believed that it is important to understand the motivation and priorities of your client's procurement group. An effective way to achieve this is to embrace their agenda and demonstrate how you and your company can help them achieve their goals. Ideally a procurement department is focused on providing value for money to its firm. This isn't or shouldn't simply be price focused. If you are close to your client's procurement group, you should be able to show how value for money sometimes means spending more. The answer to this question goes to the core of relation-based selling. Establishing a relationship is so much more than just a presentation and a follow-up call.

Q. What do you think is the connection between selling and negotiation?

I've always seen negotiating as an integral part of selling. If the sale is based on a relationship then the buyer can very often guide the seller to the buying firm's buying parameters. This can be helpful in reducing the risk of any negative connotations that one party is seen to have won over the other – an important aspect if the salesperson wants to do more business with that buyer.

How do buyers look at you?

Building a KAM strategy, when carried out properly, provides a much broader and deeper perspective on the customer's business. Consider what they are looking to achieve; the macro and competitive external forces they face; internal organizational strengths and weaknesses; and the strategies and actions they are following to achieve these goals. All these things provide an exceptionally strong canvas that the supplier can analyse in order to develop growth strategies.

Investing time and resources to build these strategies sits at the core of KAM; in fact it is part of the definition for a key customer: 'A customer that has so much potential it warrants additional investment and effort.'

Walking in the customer's shoes and thinking as if you are the customer's CEO are both techniques to help establish a more strategic viewpoint. There is, however, a problem with this approach. Customers deal with suppliers via their procurement function and their view of you, as a supplier, may be very different from your view of them. This is a significant challenge for the key account manager (KAMgr). As one commercial director once reflected:

> We have excellent relationships with our customers but they require us to deal with their buyers. These guys have incredible power. They are capable and bright people, but to get them away from a price conversation is very difficult. We really struggle to understand what they want.

Figure 10.1   The Kraljic Purchasing Classification Matrix

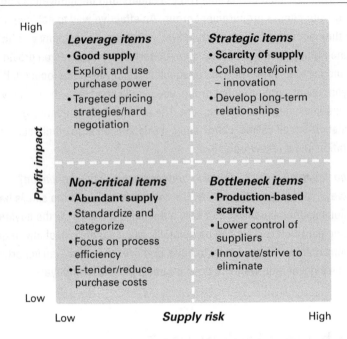

One way to start understanding the buyer is to consider how they look at the supplier portfolio. In the same way that suppliers should segment the customer portfolio, they too have techniques to assess and classify relationships. Figure 10.1 shows an adaption of The Kraljic Purchasing Classification Matrix. It was first introduced in a *Harvard Business Review* article published in 1983 [1]. Today, the model is one of the dominant strategic tools guiding purchasing activities in organizations.

Kraljic looked at suppliers on two axes:

Supply risk: what would be the impact on the business if these purchased goods and services were disrupted?

Profit impact: what do these purchased goods and services do to help us make profit and generate cash?

Four bucket positions emerge from the grid:

Strategic items: suppliers of strategic items are in a good position. The buyer recognizes them as high value and high risk. They will collaborate and invest time and energy working with these organizations. This aligns very nicely with everything we are trying to achieve in KAM!

Leverage items: given that there is a high potential profit impact for these suppliers, the word 'leverage' seems a bit harsh! However, if you are in this bucket you need to play to these strengths. Your customer sees you as having high potential for their profit, but they do not see you as unique. Your response should be to emphasize your value proposition and strengthen how they see you as a potential source of profit.

Bottleneck items: these are potentially items that can irritate the supplier. They do not generate significant profit but they could cause problems. If you are a supplier in this category, emphasise your intent to avoid supply shortages and seek out ways to shift the profit you can generate – work hard to become strategic!

Non-critical items: oh dear. As a supplier, if you are in this category, you neither generate profit nor offer anything unique. This is a rich hunting ground for buyers. If you are here, there is probably only one currency and that is price. Your strategy might be to fight on price. If not, use KAM techniques to dig yourself out of this hole and start supplying something that is more valuable to the buyer.

The Kraljic model provides great insights into how buyers think about suppliers. The model should sit in any KAM plan. Even though you may have an aspiration of 'what is' and 'what might be', remember that all relationships work two ways. Speak to your buyer and ask him to plot you on the Kraljic matrix. (Be prepared for a potentially harsh assessment of your business!)

Realistic relationships

Figure 10.2 shows the classic model that is used by suppliers to capture the relationship that they have with key customers. In the early stage, the KAMgr and the buyer typically have a relationship and a *'point to point'* bow tie relationship emerges (the rest of their corresponding organizations sit behind them). As things develop, more people across both organizations develop relationships. There is less reliance on the KAM and buyer functions – they shift to the back of the organization and 'orchestrate' the relationships between the two companies. This is a diamond structure. There are other models that sit between these two but, essentially, this is the established model to describe supplier and customer relationships in KAM.

The model does a good job: it is simple, clear and captures the intent and challenges faced by KAMgrs. However, it can sometimes be a little misleading. Looking at the two triangles (representing supplier and customer organizations) and considering the scale to which these are drawn, an imbalance can sometimes occur. Typical imbalances might be:

Figure 10.2   Diamonds and bow ties

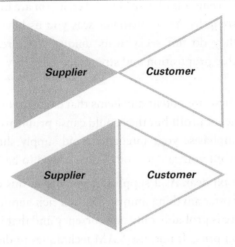

Figure 10.3   Diamonds and bow ties (scaled by value)

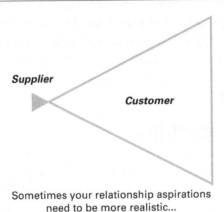

Sometimes your relationship aspirations
need to be more realistic...

- the customer organization dwarfs the supplier (financially, geographically, headcount);
- the buyer sees the supplier as an insignificant provider of products and services;
- the buyer sees the supplier as an insignificant provider of value.

Figure 10.3 attempts to re-draw the model. The concept and idea of the bow tie and diamond approach are very valid, but a realistic sprinkling of realism needs to be applied.

If your relationship is out of scale (you are dwarfed by the customer) do not be disheartened. Always focus on the value that you can produce. Try to re-draw the model with the triangle sizes based on your ability to generate profit and value (the

Kraljic model suggests that buyers prefer suppliers with higher profit impact). Of course, finding and delivering a strong customer value proposition is hard work and requires investment. This is key account management: leveraging and focusing your resources on customer 'segments of one' is the secret to your success.

Another way to consider the relationship you have with a customer is to look at the complexity that exists in the way both organizations are structured and organized. Modelling your supply organization against the customer organization is not linear and neatly aligned; it is messy, confusing and often changes on a regular basis! Value resides in the various departments and functions of your customer's business, such as operations, supply chain, finance, HR, marketing, etc. As a KAMgr, you need to understand their needs and try to create a compelling offer that helps them to achieve the corporate objectives for which they are responsible.

Figure 10.4 shows how this might look. Rather than a series of straight lines, with an aligned KAMgr–buyer relationship, activities are far more organic and messy.

Although it is complex, these messy organizations are where value opportunities (for supplier and customer) can be found. The engagement, connection and collaboration between both parties are critical skills for a KAMgr. Given all the noise and complexity, it is easy to see why buyers plot their suppliers into the Kraljic matrix; they simply do not have the time to look at every supplier and establish the value that they could generate.

High-performing KAMgrs understand this as well as the challenges that buyers face and how they think. They do the hard work of striving to understand the customer business and aligning their own organization to generate potential solutions. Buyers need to be aware and endorse the KAMgr to have these conversations, but realistically they are not the people who have the insights.

Figure 10.4   A far more complex reality

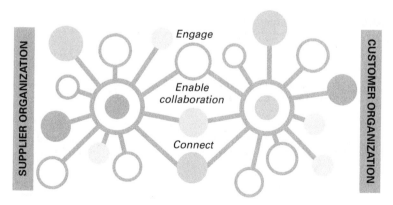

Key account managers need to be expert at
aligning 'messy' organizations

The voice of the practitioner

'I often get suppliers asking me to help them understand my organization. Sometimes they represent less than 1 per cent of my total annual spend. They are not on my radar, actually... (and honestly, I am incentivized to just get their price down). What they should be doing is bringing me reasonably developed, credible ideas that will save my company more money, then I might start to help them. Understanding my own company is very complicated... those conversations and that effort need to give me a return.' (Senior buyer, global telecom company.)

Buying and procurement (strategic and operational tensions)

There may be a problem in the way that key account teams think about the buyer. A little effort to understand the way that customers structure themselves in order to purchase and work with suppliers may be worthwhile.

Figure 10.5 is a simple way to approach this challenge. Many larger organizations structure their purchasing functions as a hierarchy, where procurement sits at the top of the organization. It sets strategy, determines parameters to position suppliers (critically selecting strategic and key suppliers) and organizes the rest of the purchasing operations.

Figure 10.5   Procurement hierarchy

The voice of the practitioner

'I'm sorry, I refuse to come and speak at an event called "The buyer perspective"; it would be beneath me. I am far more strategic in the work that I do here – my role is strategic and I am in the procurement function. You might want to change the title of your event and position it correctly, and then I might be interested.' (Global Head of Indirect Procurement, branded CPG non-alcoholic beverage company.)

[This was a conversation the author had when trying to secure a speaker for a Cranfield KAM Best Practice Club event in 2015. And yes, we did change the title and emphasis of the event.]

Procurement is the strategic heart of the organization. Depending on the size of the company, there will be quite a small number of decision makers at this level. Operating at c-suite level, they are often on the board of the organization, setting not just the buying strategy but also contributing to the overall strategy and commercial decisions of the wider business.

If procurement sits at the top of this pyramid, and is located at headquarters or a global location, then there are two other possible levels for executing the strategies that they set. Global organizations may have regional and/or divisional purchasing groups. These are large teams and will be setting localized strategies to purchase, but their emphasis leans towards execution. Then, at local or country level (if the countries warrant separate purchasing), there will be teams that execute on a local basis.

The model presented in Figure 10.5 is obviously too simple and prescriptive. Every organization develops and structures its purchasing function differently. However, there is nearly always a strategic centre (procurement) as well as attached or localized centres (purchasing or buying) teams that execute these strategies.

Figure 10.6 illustrates the relationship between procurement and buying or purchasing a little further. As a KAMgr, relationships are essential on both sides of this spectrum; however, a greater focus on the strategic procurement or c-suite level

Figure 10.6 Procurement vs buying activities

Buying	Procurement
• Operational	• Strategic
• (Middle-lower) management	• C-level
• Execution	• Visionary
• Focus on cost	• Focus on value
• Risk averse	• Open to innovation

should be an ambition. For a more strategic relationship with a customer, you must be recognized, by the senior leadership that sets policy with the most important suppliers, as a high-value or strategic supplier. Again, this is an aspect that differentiates those organizations that thrive through KAM from those that struggle.

Thoughts from leading experts: Interview with Professor Carlos Mena

Carlos is Assistant Professor at Michigan State University and a leading global expert specializing in supply chain strategy and procurement.

Q. What do you think are the main (2–5) themes that will become interesting to procurement teams over the next few years?

1) Geopolitical changes. Most companies rely extensively on global sourcing and there are geopolitical trends, like Brexit and the renegotiation of NAFTA, that might change the playing field completely. The problem is the degree of uncertainty, because things might not change at all, but companies have to be ready if they do. The role of China is also changing as they increase their global influence, particularly in Asia, Oceania and Africa. They are also investing heavily in innovation and that means they will move upstream in the supply chain, with fewer contract manufacturers and investing in R&D to compete directly with western brands. I think the role of China in shaping global supply chains will continue to increase over the next few years.

2) Technology. There is a big conversation currently taking place about things like block chains, real-time data, data analytics, and cyber-security. The sense is that leading companies are already taking advantage of some of these technologies, but most procurement teams don't have the right skills to address this issue, so they ignore it.

3) Talent. This point is related to the previous one, but is also a permanent problem for procurement. Procurement tends to pay less than other functions in the business so it struggles to attract or retain the best people. This issue has become more significant due to the need to address the technology issue mentioned above, because data scientists are scarce and don't come cheap, so it's difficult to bring the right talent. Perhaps outsourcing the analytics piece will be the solution.

Q. Are buyer and seller organizations collaborating more? What factors help or hinder this way of working?

Collaborative practices depend on many different factors, including culture, industry sector, company orientation, economic conditions, etc, so it's difficult to give a definitive answer. Some surveys in the automotive industry indicate that western companies have become more collaborative as they try to copy Japanese practices. However, they also show that some of the Japanese companies have become less collaborative over time, so the playing field is more levelled. It's difficult to get data in other industries, but my impression is that trends towards collaboration are in constant flow; if the industry sector is doing well, collaboration flourishes, but if the situation gets tighter, most companies revert to arm's-length approaches. I think the basic issue is that when companies believe they can make the pie grow, they collaborate, but when they think the size of the pie is fixed, then they fight over the size of the slices.

The supplier assessment framework

To enable suppliers to start understanding how procurement might be seeing and positioning them, a broader and more detailed model has been developed. Figure 10.7 is a simple 'tick' model that will help suppliers to expand their understanding of the procurement assessment process.

The framework is intended for use in two ways. First, KAMgrs and their teams can use it to simply consider, 'How might procurement be looking at us?' We suggest that this is always done as a first step as it makes you ask questions about your own supply position and will lead to better conversations when you do meet with procurement (as the process helps the team to identify and explain 'what might be' to the customer). The second way of using the framework is to sit down with the customer and get them to discuss and tick (categorize) each factor. You could send the framework to them, but it is strongly suggested that you sit down with procurement and get the context 'behind the ticked box'. This process always leads to a deeper understanding between the buyer and seller, especially if there is a wide discrepancy between where you see yourself as a supplier and where they see you. It is always critical to understand the perception of how procurement views you as a supplier in order to respond accordingly. Be warned though, reality is perception – how the customer perceives you can feel harsh at times.

There are five categories that structure the framework, which will now be explained and expanded further.

1 Supplier position

This is how procurement is 'broadly' categorizing and segmenting you as a supplier. Potentially crude and mechanical, the questions posed provide an understanding of where you sit as a supplier using several common factors. There are four sub-categories.

Figure 10.7 Supplier assessment framework

Supplier position	Value	Relationship	Contract structure	Supplier management approach
Supplier category • Direct • Indirect **Supplier rating** • Top 30 • Middle (31–100) • Bottom (>100) **Supplier (Kraljic) position** • Strategic (partnership) • Leverage • Bottleneck • Non-critical **Supplier spend (per annum)** • High spend • Medium spend • Low spend	**Documented value** • High • Medium • Low **Value proposition breadth** • Product • Services • Solutions **Quality** • 100% fail safe • Robust and predictable • Disposable **Potential value** • Significant potential • Medium potential • Keep buying if we have to...	**Relationship intent** • Value co-creation • Buying and selling • Transactional (no contact) **Geography** • Global • Regional • Local **Status** • Sole supplier • Preferred/listed • OBWN (only buy when needed) **Effort and time** • Invest time for future growth • Listen for good ideas • Who?	**Time frame** • Multi-year • Annual • As required/ad hoc **Structure** • Outcome/performance based • Value based • Cost based **Risk** • High risk (sole supply) • Medium risk (few suppliers) • Zero risk (play the market)	**Negotiation style** • Collaborative/relaxed • Win win • Win lose **Bidding and tendering** • Agreement (non-competitive) • Competitive tenders/bidding • E-bid/online price based **Collaboration** • C-level • Senior management • Web based (no contact)

Supplier category

Direct suppliers provide products and services that contribute to 'cost of goods sold'. They are essential parts of the customer's core offering, for example raw materials. Indirect suppliers are all the non-core products and services that are needed to maintain operations.

Supplier rating

Where are you in the overall supply portfolio? Are you regarded as a 'top 30 supplier'? Or perhaps you fall into the next band? In this model, bands such as top (30), middle (32–100) and bottom (100 and lower) are suggested. Of course, each procurement team has their own calibration for this, but they will have some form of crude positioning by number. Try to find out the system adopted by procurement and where you sit in this model.

Supplier (Kraljic) position

Kraljic is widely adopted by procurement professionals, so they should understand this model. We have lifted the four categories and placed them as tick boxes. If the customer has used a different model, ask them which one and adapt the feedback.

Supplier spend (per annum)

This customer may be a huge slice of your annual turnover, but to them you may represent an insignificant spend per annum. High, medium and low levels are presented here (you should try to get values, if possible). Understanding how large, small or insignificant you are within the pecking order of spend is valuable and enlightening.

2 *Value*

One of the conclusions and fundamental themes of this book is that KAM will only prosper if there is a dogged focus on value and value co-creation. Suppliers must always shift the conversation from price to value. This is not easy and requires additional investment, work and commitment. (Nobody said KAM was going to be easy!) This category looks at how procurement looks at you as a provider of value, and asks four questions.

Documented value

If you have been following KAM principles for a number of years, you should have been capturing the value you have delivered. (The customer will not do this, why should they?) If procurement is looking at you as a supplier, with no historical evidence that your organization has generated value for them, and it has been formally signed off as your work, you will receive zero credit. There are two key messages here: first, measure the value you deliver and second, make sure that procurement is fully aware of this value-adding work. Failure to do this will result in your hard work simply evaporating away.

Value proposition breadth

It is unlikely that you are supplying just products; most suppliers have a range of services that 'wrap around' the products they provide. This broadens the customer value proposition. Many suppliers provide these services without fully realizing the full commercial benefits, essentially providing them free of charge. Again, it is critical to gain a perspective on how procurement perceives your offering: is it a product, a service or a solution?

Quality

If you are making and supplying a 100 per cent fail-safe product (supported with highly robust service systems) but procurement is looking for a cheap and disposable offering, then you have a fundamental misalignment. It may be that the customer's wider operations need (and value) a high-quality offer, but if procurement does not accept this, there will be a tension in your supply position.

Potential value

This may be the 'acid test' of the value section: how does procurement perceive you as a supplier? To be a key supplier, there really has to be 'significant potential' value, since you want them to be investing in the relationship. At the other end of the spectrum, 'keep buying if we have to' suggests that they are looking at you as a commodity and something of an irritation.

3 *Relationship*

The saying goes that 'companies don't buy from companies, people buy from people'. The relationship is important when describing a supplier position with a customer, and how procurement sees this relationship is very important. Discussing these questions with your customer procurement teams will get both parties thinking about aspects of trading with each other.

Relationship intent

Value co-creation should be the way that both parties look to work together, but if procurement sees the relationship as transactional and having no value intent, then there will be no foundation on which to work together. In the middle ground, 'buying and selling' may be the way that procurement sees things. Whilst better than being beaten up on price, it is still a stepping stone as you move towards a co-creating relationship. This is a great question to discuss to bring relationship intent out into the open.

Geography

A very practical consideration (and often a neglected one) is aligning the relationship geographically. The customer organization may be global and behave in a central-ized manner, or it may be global and allow decisions to be made locally. This will change depending on what they are buying and how they classify the customer. If they see you as a transactional, low-value and small supplier you may be left to deal with local buying teams. Larger (more highly valued) suppliers may be handled by global head office. This sounds like a simple question to ask, but it is often ignored or misunderstood. You must ask the question, have the debate and gain a solid understanding.

Status

Status describes the way that the relationship works relative to other suppliers in your category (your competitors). If you are unique and exclusively selected, a posi-tion of 'sole supplier' can be attained. At the other end of the spectrum is 'only buy when needed' – forcing a more competitive position. Note that buyers will always seek to gain a spread of suppliers for one category; even if you are on the preferred or listed schedule, there will be an element of competition. Of course, this is healthy, but suppliers need to be as focused as possible on the unique aspects of their offer. KAM is an essential technique to develop these bespoke, high-impact offers that will shift you towards 'sole supplier' status (because nobody else can do what you do).

Effort and time

Just as you, as a supplier, decide to place more effort on key account customers, procurement places more effort and time on certain suppliers. These sub-categories are fairly obvious, but if procurement is asking 'Who?' when you call, maybe it is time to re-evaluate your position.

4 Contract structure

The way that procurement constructs and positions service-level agreements and the basics of legal documents describes a lot about your supply position. Time frame, structure and approach to risk are three elements that have been chosen to describe contracts.

Time frame

Contracts that span several years demonstrate an intention to collaborate with and trust a supplier. Multi-year contracts take time to set up, but assume that there will be a long-term return and that there is belief in the supplier. Conversely, 'as required' contracts tend to be issued with little intent to go beyond the period of the order. There is little investment or intent to collaborate.

Structure

The way that a contract is structured (linked to value and price) is covered later in this chapter. It is an area that is being chosen by many procurement teams to define and show the ethos of how a contract or relationship will work. With bigger, more complex supply positions there is a tendency to shift performance risk to the supplier (if you deliver results you will be rewarded on outcome). A more transactional approach is taken when procurement buys on cost (and makes no allowance for value add). Value-based structure is where most key account suppliers should be aiming, since it aligns with the intent of being rewarded for extra effort applied.

Risk

Procurement will view you as a high-risk supplier if you are the sole organization in the market offering what they need. This can be a good position for a supplier, but generally it puts you at risk since procurement will try to engineer a means to reduce your commercial and operational leverage. Conversely, do not try to be 'one of many' and become a gift for the bidding and price process. Analysing risk will help you to understand how the customer looks at you as a supplier.

5 Supplier management approach

This final section collates the preceding four categories and describes how procurement will try to manage you as a supplier. Of course, this is a very wide and complex set of activities (the procurement profession would be highly offended to be categorized into just three boxes) but this model focuses on three areas that mainly impact key account management when dealing with procurement teams.

Negotiation style

If you are supplying, there will always be a negotiation (regardless of how 'strategic' you think your offer is). There will be differing approaches adopted by procurement, depending on how they see the supplier. If you are not viewed as a key or important supplier, negotiation may be almost wholly based on price and focused entirely on the customer's needs (they win, you lose). If they want you to prosper for a longer-term relationship, this becomes win–win. For very strategic supply positions, negotiation may become extremely relaxed, and some consulting practices get into this style of negotiation. Quite often procurement is excluded from the negotiation and senior management just states: 'This is what we want – make it happen.'

Bidding and tendering

Procurement functions gain considerable leverage on suppliers from bidding and tendering. Again, these techniques can align with the way that procurement looks at and handles differing types of suppliers. Being asked to constantly tender online or via third parties might be a signal that you are not a valued supplier. Key suppliers usually enjoy a slightly more relaxed approach to tendering (since they are trusted and provide more value).

Collaboration

The last question that can be asked of procurement is how they see the level of collaboration between your two organizations. True collaboration exists at a very strategic leadership level. When suppliers are seen as highly strategic, this can be at c-suite level, with conversations with the board. Different levels, with equally important collaboration intent could be at a senior or middle-management/operational level. If there is no evidence of collaboration (this links with lower scores across the other questions in this framework) there could be reason to challenge the way that the relationship with procurement is working.

This framework is not intended to be fully prescriptive and unconditional. However, it will provide a useful structure and set of questions to start thinking about how your customer's procurement function sees you, as well as a useful way to get them to articulate ways of working. A realistic relationship works in two directions; if procurement talk about strategic intent (the upper tick boxes) but clearly treat you in a transactional manner (the lower tick boxes) then something is wrong. If things are wrong, you need to fix them or find another key account on which to focus your precious resources.

Cost, price, value, risk (price and contract options)

When discussing value and negotiating a supply position with procurement it is important to gain clarity regarding the language of what is being discussed. It is quite often the case that critical components are described but actually misunderstood.

Figure 10.8 shows these phrases and provides some definitions. Discussions should focus on the value that the supplier provides, not price. These conversations often break down, however, due to two main reasons.

Figure 10.8   Cost: price: value: risk

COST	PRICE	VALUE
The total cost that the supplier incurs supplying the product and service package.	The price that is offered to the customer by the supplier to obtain the products and service packages.	The benefits (hard and soft) that the customer receives as a result of buying the products and service packages.

RISK (for the supplier)
The real (and perceived) legal, commercial and reputational hazards of supplying these additional services to the customer.

RISK (for the customer)
The real (and perceived) legal, commercial and reputational hazards of relinquishing critical parts of their process to the supplier.

First, the buyer is the wrong person in the customer organization to have an appreciation of what value is potentially available. This perception could change if the supplier speaks with procurement professionals or other functions in the customer business. If that does not happen, and there is a conversation with an operational buyer, value will be stripped down to price (and possibly down to the cost of the supply).

The second reason is that the supplier has done an ineffective job of understanding the customer business and really quantifying what is important to them. When executed properly, KAM strategies and tactics will lead to the development of strong, aligned and impactful value propositions. When executed badly, poor value propositions result (usually describing the products that are on offer, thus making the proposition supplier-centric and not customer-centric).

Beyond cost, price and value, risk should always be discussed and defined between both parties. If the supplier is offering something unique and different it could be that the buyer is not able to rationalize the higher price for the additional effort, change and potential failure of supply to his business. Buyers strive for low prices but they equally want assurance that they are using suppliers that will not hinder efficient operations. KAMgrs should always quantify risk from the buyer perspective and for their own organization to be able to deliver new value propositions profitably.

Understanding cost, price, value and risk is one aspect of supplier and procurement, but marrying these critical concepts together is vital when constructing supply agreements. Figure 10.9 describes a construct for options to be considered, and captures several common pricing ideas.

Figure 10.9 Price and contract options

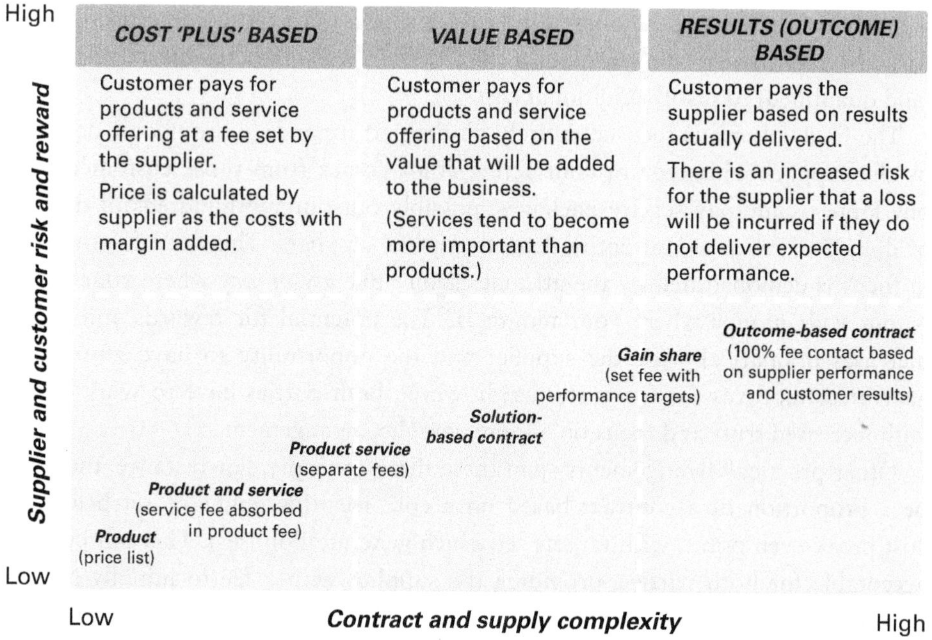

The table compares two axes: contract and supply complexity versus supplier and customer risk/reward. It is then split into three vertical sections, shifting from left to right to provide pricing and contract options that are more complex but focused on value co-creation principles.

The first column looks at 'cost plus based' options. The supplier looks at the cost of manufacturing and supplying the offer to the customer, adds a suitable margin and presents this value in the price. These are fairly straightforward agreements to establish and account for the vast majority of traditional sales and small account management activity. Supply organizations like this approach because it is straightforward to administrate, and procurement favours this approach because they know what they have to pay. Customers can also look to estimate the costs that the supplier will incur and negotiate on the profit margin they are making. Comparing prices against several suppliers is possible and stimulates competitive bidding. When services are provided they can be priced either as a separate fee or absorbed into the product fee. It is advisable to split the fee and keep it separate, so that the value delivered from these services can be tracked and monitored independently of the product performance.

The middle column shifts towards a value-based approach to business. Here, the focus of the price and contract structure shifts away from the 'cost basis' of the supplier towards 'value delivered' to the customer's operations and business. These numbers will be bigger, since the value of most supplier's products and services far outweighs the cost of delivery. Risk increases for the supplier, as they have to trust and rely on the customer collaborating to deliver an enhanced value proposition. Risk also increases for the customer, as they need to see commercial results delivered (and quantified) to justify additional cost.

The final column is focused entirely on the performance and outcome delivered by the supplier. This type of contracting ethos comes from those customers who buy large technology service packages, possibly outsourcing hundreds of millions of dollars of revenue and entire departments to suppliers. This need for this shift in focus is demonstrated by the attitude: 'Don't put *my money* where your mouth is, put *your money* where your mouth is.' The potential for rewards and profits increases dramatically for the supplier and the opportunity to have more value generated improves for the customer; however, both parties have to work harder with increased trust and focus on a more complex arrangement.

Other practical arrangements span these three concepts. For instance, there can be a proportion of a contract based on a core fee (this might be set below the cost break-even point, with targets set which generate bonuses). This can be more acceptable for both parties, providing the supplier with a fee to initially run the supply position and the customer with a clear contractual construct to make the programme work.

Interview with Nandini Basuthakur

Nandini is CEO and board member of Procurement Leaders, a rapidly growing membership community of over 27,000 senior procurement executives from 700 global corporations accessing in-depth insight, practical tools and an expert network. She is an experienced senior executive with over 20 years in public and private sector transformation internationally.

In her role Nandini speaks directly with CPOs to ensure that they are supported in accelerating their journey to superior performance, elevating all aspects of the existing business and product sets, and driving further global expansion of the membership base.

Q. What are the biggest challenges faced by your member organizations (or organizations that you work with) when managing their strategic suppliers?

At Procurement Leaders, we work with more than 700 member organizations around the globe and when it comes to managing their strategic suppliers, the challenges they face include:

- Identifying the most strategic suppliers, and then managing and building relationships with them, establishing far more sophisticated metrics, both internal and external, that are closely aligned with business goals and needs – be they driving innovation, co-creating customer experiences, reducing risks, combining profitability with social responsibility and sustainability, or just assuring continuity of supply.

- Once they have selected the strategic suppliers under management, the focus must shift to sustainable process execution. An effective supplier management framework and partnership appropriately aligns risk, effort and reward as key enablers of ongoing value creation. The approach needs to include segmentation (ie strategic, operational and tactical), performance management framework(s) and a clear articulation of organizational accountability, feedback mechanisms and responsibility. This can help with both looming challenges and promising opportunities, offering valuable customer insight, all while building mutually beneficial relationships with suppliers.

- Finally, this strategic and proactive approach must be resilient. As the economy changes, so too does the position of suppliers. Understanding their position in the market can provide the basis for identifying opportunities to mitigate risk and ensure that those areas in the supply chain that are exposed and might cause disruption can be effectively managed. Our members and their suppliers' strategic value can change if any party experiences a shift in direction or goals. Strategic supplier relationships and their management of the entire process – both today and tomorrow – have a critical part to play in that resilience.

Q. You have been involved in the research and practice of advanced buying and selling practice for many years. Do you think that the selling or buying communities are advancing more effectively today? Why is that?

The relationship between sales and procurement has always been a contentious one. The issue at the core of this tension is the concept of value recognition. Sales account managers accuse procurement of being purely price focused and not recognizing the components of value. Procurement executives on the other hand complain that sales account managers are always trying to 'work around them', and to make the commercial sale to R&D, operations, clinicians, or other senior business stakeholders. Salespeople complain that procurement 'does not recognize the value we bring to the business in terms of quality, service, and reducing the total cost of ownership!'

In terms of selling community advances, cross-functional stakeholders understand market share, functional impact, metrics, data and processes more readily than those pertaining to the buying community.

Q. Do you see any trend moving towards increased collaboration between suppliers and customer organizations?

We see advances in procurement transformation, digitization and artificial intelligence (AI) and supplier-enabled innovation (SEI) at our most progressive member companies.

Procurement transformation. With the procurement organization's influence expanding to cross-functional solutions and results, data, innovation, people, network movement, M&A, sustainability and risk, our research data shows that 82 per cent are currently engaged in transforming their procurement models. More than ever, procurement is driving the case for accelerated change of not just their function but the entire business.

Digitization and AI. Across virtually every industry we see business model disruption, caused by digital technologies, robotics, artificial intelligence and machine learning. This is defining the strategies of organizations that are seeking ways to compete against threats as well as taking advantage of developing new and innovative ways to serve existing and new customers. Our most progressive members are using their knowledge of external suppliers and internal markets to broker innovation, harness disruption and create greater impact from their core operational systems as well as new digital and analytical solutions.

Supplier-enabled innovation (SEI). Procurement occupies a privileged position in the business ecosystem, having external relationships with key stakeholders as well as thousands of external suppliers. But in many organizations, this opportunity is untapped. There are strong and positive correlations found in organizations with advanced collaboration capabilities and their ability to significantly increase their earnings growth rate. We launched the SEI Centre to address this need and provide the frameworks and practical experience to systemize, accelerate and profit from SEI.

Tips for understanding procurement and adopting a value-based price position

The following thoughts summarize this chapter:

1 Always remember that procurement and buying are different. As a KAMgr, you need to be speaking with those most strategic leaders dealing with suppliers within the customer operation. They can be thought of as procurement, with

buyers executing their instructions at a local level. These exact definitions may not always be applicable to your customer's business but the idea that there are a few strategic players is a robust one. Focus on building relationships with 'the strategic few'.

2 Selling, KAM and value-based negotiation are intimately connected. Do a good job selling and KAM becomes easier. Do a good job with KAM and you will have an easier job securing a value-based price.

3 Always focus on value, even if procurement is pushing you towards a price-based conversation.

4 Be clear about cost, price, value and risk. These phrases can be interchanged and misunderstood. Be clear with your KAM team and your customer about the differences.

5 Dropping your price is not adding value.

6 As you increase the complexity of your offer you need to consider the contract options of how you structure your price and how you will be rewarded. If you are delivering high levels of value, why not be rewarded based on outcome? KAM is a more complex way of working; your contract structure may need to be more accommodating to align with the increased complexity, value and risk levels.

7 You need your KAM team to help construct a value-based negotiation strategy and plan. They have a perspective and knowledge that you will not have on your own.

8 KAM is a relationship activity. You need to know who is in procurement, buying and the decision-making/users of your product and service. Spend time building relationships and developing your network (across the customer business and your own).

9 Role playing is a great way to 'test' your negotiation framework before you enter the live negotiation. There are plenty of retired buyers around (look on LinkedIn). Try to find a buyer from the same industry as your customer and hire them to put you through your paces.

10 Study negotiation principles and use them alongside the ideas presented in this chapter. This is a value-based/KAM chapter, and is only effective when it 'stands on the shoulders of negotiation giants' such as the book *Getting to Yes* [2].

References

[1] Kraljic, P (1983) Purchasing must become supply management, *Harvard Business Review*, September.

[2] Fisher, R and Ury, W (1982) *Getting to Yes: How to negotiate agreement without giving in*, Random House Business Books.

International key account management

11

'Culture makes people understand each other better. And if they understand each other better in their soul, it is easier to overcome the economic and political barriers. But first they have to understand that their neighbour is, in the end, just like them, with the same problems, the same questions.'

PAULO COELHO

What are the added complexities of managing international accounts and how do we decide whether this is the right approach for us?

Overview

This chapter looks at the key issue of managing international and pan-geographic key accounts where the customer and/or the supplier may be operating in a number of different countries. International key account management has become an increasingly significant topic for many organizations as a result of progressive globalization and industry consolidation. International key accounts may also be, for example, multinational customers who wish to buy in a centralized or coordinated way across a number of geographies or even globally. They may also have an expectation of being supplied and serviced by a single supplier worldwide in a consistent and coordinated way.

On one level, international KAM can be seen as a more complex form of KAM, and indeed, much of the academic literature puts it in this context, especially in relation to global account management (GAM). However, the international dimension of KAM adds a number of fundamentally different aspects that are not so evident in local KAM. These include cross-cultural issues (to do with, for example, people, systems, processes), the management of globally dispersed and cross-cultural teams, the management of global versus local issues and conflict, managing global logistics competences, the location of global account managers and the management of global (and cross-cultural) communications.

So, implementing international KAM brings some further complexities to the management of already large and complex customers and this chapter provides some insights into how organizations can structure, resource and manage these types of customer.

Managing international key accounts

In this section we look at some of the issues and challenges in managing international key accounts as opposed to local key accounts.

Different types of international key account

There are four different types of key account management, as shown in Figure 11.1. This chapter is not going to focus on local key account management (LKAM) but on the other three types of international KAM (IKAM), namely multinational KAM (MKAM), regional KAM (RKAM) and global KAM (GKAM), which is also often referred to as GAM.

Multinational key account management (MKAM)

Multinational key account management (MKAM) can be a constructive approach where the customer is in a few international countries and it makes sense to manage

Figure 11.1   Four different types of key account management

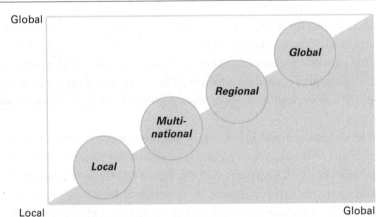

Figure 11.2 Example of a multinational key account management (MKAM) Structure

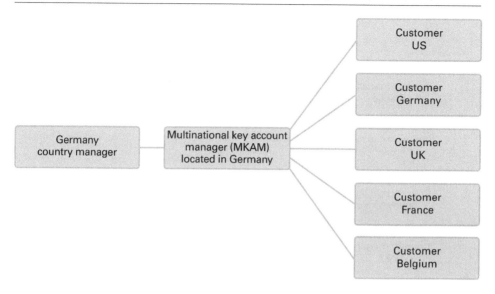

them across those countries. Figure 11.2 shows an example of an MKAM structure. The MKAM account manager is often situated in the most appropriate country, either because the customer's headquarters is there or because it makes sense from a geography and travel perspective. The MKAM account manager may be the main contact for the customer in each country or there may also be a local key account manager in each country. Generally, in most cases, the local key account managers will be reporting into the local management with a dotted-line relationship with the MKAM account manager who will be facilitating the strategic relationship with the customer at the pan-geographic level.

Regional key account management (RKAM)

Regional key account management (RKAM) can be a good way of organizing if the customer is regionally based, for example largely in Europe or largely in Asia Pacific or North and South America. It is also used if a GKAM approach proves too complex and difficult and the supplier, therefore, finds it easier to structure on a regional basis. Equally, customers may also prefer to be managed on a regional basis rather than on a global basis. A typical RKAM structure can be found in Figure 11.3. RKAM tends to work well if the whole company is structured on a regional basis and the customer is as well. As with MKAM, the RKAM account manager will often be situated in the most appropriate country for managing that region, either because the customer's headquarters is there or again because it makes sense from a geography and travel perspective. The RKAM

Figure 11.3 Example of a regional account management (RKAM) Structure

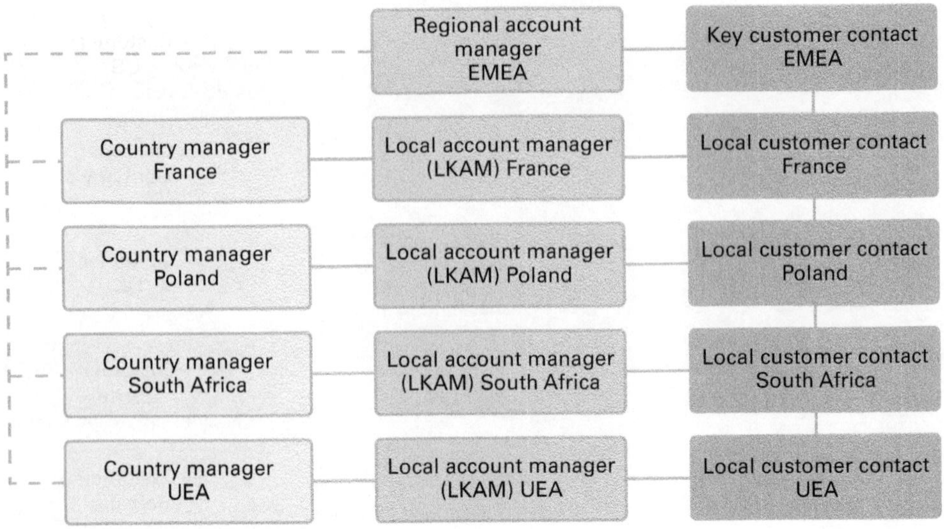

account manager will generally be responsible for the customer relationship at the regional strategic level and then there will usually be an LKAM or a salesperson at local level in each country reporting in to local management as with the MKAM model.

Global key account management (GKAM)

The most complex form of international KAM is global key account management (GKAM), where the relationship with the customer is a fully global model. Both the customer and the supplier have the capability to operate on a global basis and there is generally a centrally negotiated agreement between the parties at a global level, which is then rolled out at regional and/or local level on both sides. Sometimes there is a structure that involves a central global-level relationship managed by the GKAM account manager, with both RKAM and LKAM account managers involved; sometimes there will be just GKAM centrally, which is cascaded directly to the LKAM account managers or salespeople in each country. A real example of a GKAM structure and how it interfaces with the customer is shown in Figure 11.4. In many cases the GKAM account manager will be located near the customer's headquarters and, for some global customers, even in the customer's headquarters. At this level of international KAM, the GKAM account manager is very much a global coordinating role and as with the other international KAM structures, the LKAM and/or RKAM account managers will report into local management with the GKAM account manager reporting in centrally and, in some organizations, directly to the board.

Figure 11.4 Real example of a global account management (GKAM) structure
from a courier company

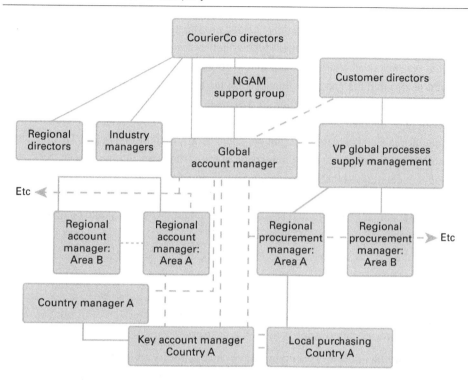

In reality, some organizations are executing all four types of KAM across their key
account portfolio. They may have, for example, a couple of GKAM accounts, a few
RKAM accounts and a number of MKAM accounts as well as LKAM accounts. This
is because, as with KAM generally, each key account is different and therefore the
approach will not always be the same.

How do I choose the right international KAM approach for my customers?

Is implementing an IKAM approach the right thing to do for a customer and if so,
which approach would be best? What might some of the decision factors be for
deciding whether to implement international KAM with a key customer? Here are
some factors to consider:

1 *The customer is requesting it*: customers sometimes demand that the supplier
should be able to supply them on an international, regional or global basis. If the
supplier is able to meet this request then it makes sense for the supplier to implement an international KAM approach with that customer.

Voice of the practitioner

One practitioner describes how they decided on who their global accounts should be.
'We got the senior management team together and we spent some time defining what we saw as an international or global corporate account. One of the main criteria was that the customer themselves was organized for purchasing on a centralized as opposed to a decentralized basis. We also looked at their own desire to be handled on a global basis. The fact that they had asked us to bid on a global basis and also the fact that we could clearly identify champions for us within their business were major decision factors. The main difference with the global accounts was that we made a strategic decision to put specific resources in place to manage them on a global basis. So, we ended up initially picking five global accounts.' (International key account manager (IKAMgr), global components company.)

---

2 *Economies of scale*: it is actually more efficient and cost-effective to take an internationally coordinated approach to the customer.

3 *Our capability*: does my company have the capability to manage pan-geographic customers?

   – Do I have processes and structures that can function on a pan-geographic basis?

   – Do I have the systems and particularly the information systems infrastructure to support pan-geographic customer management?

   – Do I have the people capabilities? Will I need to recruit and develop different people than I have now?

4 *Costs and ROI*: is it likely that the costs of implementing this approach are ultimately unlikely to deliver the ROI that we would need?

5 *Customer capability*: does the customer have the capabilities and structure to be a pan-geographic customer? This might sound flippant, but there are examples of organizations that decide to implement an international KAM approach with a customer, only to find that the customer is set up to operate on a local country level and doesn't want to be dealt with at a pan-geographic level.

6 *Sufficient traction*: unless one customer is demanding it and it is an imperative decision, then you need to ask if you have sufficient pan-geographic customers to make the implementation of the approach feasible and worthwhile.

International KAM or not?

If you can answer yes to most of the following questions then an international KAM approach may be the right way to manage your customer(s):

- I have a number of customers that are international.   ✔
- My customer(s) is asking to be supplied on an international basis.   ✔
- I have systems and process that can operate on a pan-geographic basis.   ✔
- I have key account managers who have international capability.   ✔
- My customer is capable of being managed at a pan-geographic level.   ✔
- I will gain business efficiencies and better ROI with international KAM.   ✔
- The customer(s) will get more value from international KAM.   ✔

Managerial issues around implementing international key accounts

There are a number of managerial issues and challenges that may need to be considered when implementing IKAM; we will now look at some of these.

Do we have highly competent IKAMgrs?

The first issue is recruiting and developing IKAMgrs who have the right competences and skills to carry out the role. IKAMgrs will need to undertake the full role set of the key account manager as described in Chapter 7. However, in addition to these, there are two further areas of competence that IKAMgrs need to develop: intercultural competence and virtual team leadership.

Intercultural competence An ability to manage across and within different cultures is a major part of the role and is dealt with in more detail later in this chapter. Successful IKAMgrs enjoy and feel comfortable with operating in an environment that is truly multinational.

Virtual team leadership While key account managers have to lead virtual teams where they have no direct responsibility for people on the team, there are added complexities once the key account becomes pan-geographic:

Geography: due to the nature of global relationships, many members of both the supplier's and the customer's teams can be located in different countries around the world. This means that they rarely get together face to face, so developing and motivating the team are key challenges. An IKAMgr will often be managing two virtual teams, as discussed in Chapter 7:

- a pan-geographic delivery team;
- a pan-geographic customer-facing team.

As one global account manager points out: 'I need to build a team internally that can respond to our needs quickly and flexibly. I want to know that wherever I am in the world, the people at local level know and understand our requirements.'

Reporting structure: as already outlined above, local key account managers in each country generally report in to the local country structure, with a dotted-line responsibility to the IKAMgr. However, there are instances of global accounts in some companies where there is a team reporting directly to the GKAMgr. This is the case with a global courier company who have a team comprising an operations manager for the customer, dedicated customer service and technical support, a finance manager and a logistics expert.

Temporal: many members of the team may operate in different time zones, making it difficult for them to operate as a team at a given moment in time. One way in which some companies manage this situation is to change the times of weekly team telephone conference calls, for example, so that the team members take it in turns to be the one to get up at 2 am for the call!

Different types of IKAMgr role: some research insights

Research carried out on the role of the IKAMgr [1] produced some interesting findings. The overall finding was that the IKAMgr's role may be subject to change, depending on the degree of sophistication both of the customer in global or international account relationships, and of the IKAMgr in the role.

Four roles were identified, presented in Figure 11.5. Where the customer and IKAMgr both have high levels of sophistication, then the IKAMgr is likely to be able to adopt the role of the *IKAM strategist*. They would be operating at a very strategic level internally and externally, having a fully effective account team, seeking business opportunities for both organizations, and involved at senior management level with the customer and internally.

Where the sophistication level of the IKAMgr is high, but that of the customer organization is low, then the role of the IKAMgr is more likely to be that of the *IKAM relationship builder*. The role here would be to build the relationship with the customer to a more strategic level. Activities might include developing some new

Figure 11.5   Different types of international key account manager role

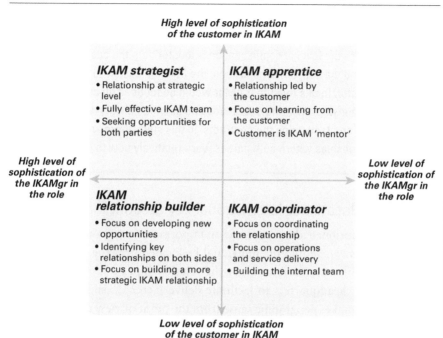

**High level of sophistication
of the customer in IKAM**

IKAM strategist
- Relationship at strategic level
- Fully effective IKAM team
- Seeking opportunities for both parties

IKAM apprentice
- Relationship led by the customer
- Focus on learning from the customer
- Customer is IKAM 'mentor'

**High level of
sophistication of
the IKAMgr in
the role**

**Low level of
sophistication of
the IKAMgr in
the role**

**IKAM
relationship builder**
- Focus on developing new opportunities
- Identifying key relationships on both sides
- Focus on building a more strategic IKAM relationship

IKAM coordinator
- Focus on coordinating the relationship
- Focus on operations and service delivery
- Building the internal team

**Low level of sophistication
of the customer in IKAM**

opportunities to move the customer forward, building up some key relationships, helping to set up their teams, doing some consultancy, and facilitating meetings between the organizations at senior level. An example of this would be one global relationship where the global account manager was very experienced in GAM but the customer had only been involved in it for a year.

Where the sophistication level of the customer in IKAM is high, but that of the IKAMgr is low, then the role of the IKAMgr is more likely to be that of the *IKAM apprentice*. Given that it is suggested that many customers are driving global IKAM, then this type of situation is likely to exist. In this research study, one IKAMgr, who worked for a global IT company, expressed the view that she was new to IKAM but was being groomed to take over from the current IKAMgr in two years' time, to ensure continuity for the global customer. She also mentioned that the customer had been actively encouraging her in the role and was making sure she attended meetings with their senior team including the European board. Her key customer contact also mentioned that he was acting as a *mentor* to the supplier's IKAMgr and saw it as an opportunity to shape the nature of the relationship in the future. There was also evidence of this in another relationship between the IKAMgr of a components company and his customer, a global electronics company that had been involved in IKAM for a lot longer than the components company. The customer expressed that he had been a catalyst for the supplier to adopt an IKAM approach. He also said that while the supplier's IKAMgr was a *natural* in the role, he thought that he could help him to develop his strategic IKAM skills further.

Finally, where the level of sophistication is low for both the customer organization and the supplier organization, the IKAMgr is likely to be more of an *IKAM coordinator*. In this role the IKAMgr would be focused on coordinating the customer relationship, ensuring operations and service delivery, building the internal teams and facilitating the contracts. In this study there were two examples of global relationships where both parties were relatively new to IKAM.

Where do we locate our international key account managers?

This has been mentioned above, but it is an important managerial issue and one that is not easy to answer. Should the individual be located near the headquarters of the customer to enable easy facilitation of the relationship, or should they be located near the supplier headquarters to facilitate delivery etc? Or should they be located somewhere that makes geographic sense from the point of view of travel? This really needs to be decided on a case-by-case basis as it may be dependent on, for example, the complexity of the customer solution where it would make sense for the individual to be near the supplier. If the customer is very demanding then it would make sense to locate near the customer.

Expatriates or local employees?

Twenty years ago many IKAMgrs working for multinational and global companies were expatriates from the Western-oriented parts of the organization who were then working in other countries. However, this model has been changing and many companies now recruit local people at all levels of key account management from local to global. A recent study of advertisements for key account manager jobs across the globe found that most were seeking local people who could speak the indigenous language as well as English. Companies also reported that they had more success with this model than the expatriate model.

What support systems do we need in place for IKAM?

IKAM could not have existed before the advent of the internet and successful IKAM is heavily reliant on having robust and supportive systems, in particular IT systems and strategic key account plans.

IT systems Successful key account management relies on having good information systems in place; for IKAM it is even more imperative. This is in part because

Figure 11.6 Nested approach to key account planning in an international context

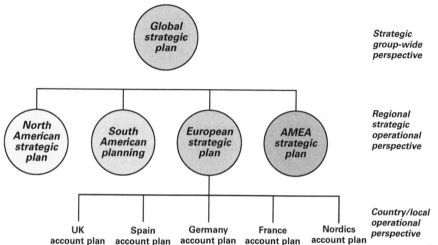

the more global the customer, the more complex the information we need in order to manage the relationship. The international account team all need to be able to access customer information on a 24/7 basis in order to serve the customer. Real-time information allowing the tracking of the relationship around the world is important, as is the ability to communicate easily as a team across the geographies.

Strategic key account plans We have already discussed the importance of key account planning in Chapter 3. Again, for international accounts the plan is part of building the pan-geographic team as it acts as a vehicle for exchanging information. However, building a global account plan can be a complex business as plans for a global customer will probably need to be formed on a number of levels; they may be aggregated from a local level, through a regional level and up to a global level. Figure 11.6 shows such a *nested* approach for account planning. This allows the local teams to *own* their plan at local level in order to ensure buy-in and empowerment in the different countries, while at the same time having an overall global plan for the central strategic relationship with the customer.

The voice of the practitioner: strategic account planning for international accounts

'There is an international account plan for all the global customers. We had a global account planning session a few weeks ago in which I was involved. We flew in 15 people from around the world for two-and-a-half days because it was so important. We have a formal global account plan document that the global account manager uses to make sure that everyone understands what is going on.' (Global account team member, global oil and gas company.)

'We have a formal plan that we do at the beginning of the year and actually we're doing it now... I do it with the team... We have put a template in from each of the countries so that we get an understanding of what their initiatives are at local level with the customer and what are their key issues and opportunities, so that we can then aggregate and incorporate these to create the global account plan.' (Global account manager, global logistics company.)

Global vs local: some common pitfalls of IKAM

As well as some of the implementation issues already discussed, in IKAM there are some specific and often common challenges around managing the global versus the local interfaces that many organizations report having to tackle. Many of these issues are caused by the tensions between what people at the local country level need to achieve in terms of local goals and KPIs and what needs to be achieved for the overall international relationship at MKAM, RKAM or GKAM level. Some surprisingly common key factors contributing to this are:

1 Misalignment of goals and KPIs between the global and local levels, eg short-term at local level versus long-term at regional or global level.

2 Misalignment of rewards and compensation, eg sales commission-type rewards at local level versus more long-term compensation at regional or global level based on a more *balanced scorecard* approach.

3 The questions of *'who takes the sale?'* or *'who made the sale?'* can cause a lot of grief internally. Was this achieved, for example, by the global account manager or should it be attributed to the local level?

4 The global level being seen as interfering by the local level, leading to country managers ignoring the global level and encouraging their staff to do so too.

5 While the customer may be an important account in some countries, in others it is not even on the radar as a key customer.

6 Different levels of service, including pricing, can lead to customer dissatisfaction and complaints.

7 Customers also do not adhere to the global or regional contract or agreement and continue to act locally as they please.

Let's look at how some companies have tackled these issues of global vs local.

Figure 11.7 Example of a nested balanced scorecard

Strategic group wide perspective balanced scorecard

GLOBAL TARGETS		75% Threshold	100% TARGET	125% Stretch
Strategy targets	Lead Indicators	Develop a 5-year strategy… research and understand the customer.	Develop a 5-year strategy and agree with global business team.	Agree strategy with the global network. Gain a global team. Gain approval from the customer.
Commercial targets	Lag Indicators	Grow sales by 5% in 2 years.	Grow sales by 15%. Increase GROUP share of wallet by 20%.	Grow sales by 40% in 2 years. Increase GROUP share of wallet by 20%. Elevate customer to… [eg top 5 position in portfolio].

Regional/local strategic and operational perspective balanced scorecard

REGIONAL TARGETS		75% Threshold	100% TARGET	125% Stretch
Strategy targets	Lead Indicators	Support the development of a 5-year strategy… provide customer insights.	Support the 5-year strategy and attend regular Webex/ team sessions. Invest resources to grow country by country.	Seek to gain support of the 5-year strategy with customers across your region.
Commercial targets	Lag Indicators	Grow sales by 5% in 2 years.	Grow sales by 15%. Increase LOCAL share of wallet by 20%.	Grow sales by 40% in 2 years. Increase LOCAL share of wallet by 20%. Help to elevate customer to… [eg top 5 position in global portfolio].

1 Misalignment of goals and KPIs

This is a common factor in IKAM, largely as a result of goals and KPIs for key accounts being set at country level and not connected to or cascaded from the MKAM, RKAM or GKAM levels. One way to get more coherence is to take the *nested* approach (outlined earlier for key account plans) to the KPIs and produce a *balanced scorecard* for each level of the account, as shown in Figure 11.7. This approach can also take account of local differences if these exist, so at local level there may be some common KPIs for each country plus a few specific ones. The specific ones may also be needed if the customer has different things they are measuring in terms of KPIs at local level. Nesting also allows for the development of team KPIs and overall KPIs for the account at the strategic level.

2 Misalignment of rewards and compensation

This is another common pitfall which is also closely tied in with the first issue above. Some organizations have developed rewards and compensation systems for international accounts that reward people on a number of levels as part of their overall compensation. For example, a KAMgr at country level may have a compensation package that is made up of individual KPIs, team KPIs and overall KPIs for the global account. The nesting approach can once again be useful here.

3 Who takes the sale?

This particular issue is a major one for many companies practising IKAM. It is often the result of the information systems being insufficiently capable or transparent at aggregating data on international customers from what are often disparate systems, or is a further output of issues 1 and 2 above. In reality, provided that you don't double-count sales, revenue or profit figures, most organizations can get round this problem by simply cutting and analysing the data in different ways. So, it should be possible to identify the individual or local contribution on the one hand and the overall contribution on the other. Many companies have instigated such an approach in order to avoid the constant internal conflicts and arguments that take place on this issue.

4 Global 'interference' at local level

This is another thorny issue and is often the result of the local management team feeling that they are losing power as a result of the MKAM, RKAM or GKAM structure. The country managers, in particular, often report feeling threatened by, for example, the global account manager. They see this as both interference in *their territory*, and as being told what to do by someone who may, in the hierarchy, be less senior than them.

This is a tricky situation to manage and will generally continue to be a problem if the leaders of the company do not position the international accounts as an overall organizational strategic approach that is above country level and which is designed to benefit the company as a whole. The international account managers need to be sympathetic to this situation. As one GAMgr from a global components company said:

> I don't just need to be a diplomat, I need to have a Master's in Diplomacy. I laugh, but in all seriousness, on this account there are a lot of skills I need to have to help influence developments internally, particularly with the local leadership in the countries.

Another issue is local teams ignoring or bypassing the global contract or agreement and *doing their own thing* locally. Many organizations have said that the key thing here is vigorous internal marketing of the contract or agreement at local level, highlighting the benefits both at local and strategic level of adhering to, for example, the global agreement. Again, companies have used KPIs and other incentives to encourage the uptake at local level of the global or regional agreement with the customer. As one IKAMgr said:

> Even though you have these global agreements you still have to sell the agreement at the street level day to day. I can make all the agreements in the world if you like, but if nobody tells the troops then we have a problem and the contract will die. It is my job to make sure they are keeping all these people engaged on the contract. This is in terms of the customer's organization as well as our own.

So it is also about adaptability, as this regional account manager pointed out:

> I think the main role, as each region wants to go off and do its own thing, is you have to pull them all together. You have to understand the requirements that are different within that region and therefore be flexible and develop with them solutions that can be adapted to each region.

5 *Relative importance of the customer*

This is a common problem where, for example, the global account might be a key account in some countries but is way down the list in other countries who then do not want to invest time and resources in that account as they will see no return on investment and no rewards from managing that account. From the global perspective, however, it is imperative that the customer feels they are treated as a key account in every country and that the service is consistent. A global logistics company had to implement a system of incentivizing those countries where the customer wasn't important, including recognizing that they were over-resourcing a customer at local level that otherwise would not have deserved that investment. The IKAMgr also needs to be able to use powerful arguments at the local level to persuade them of the importance of the global customer to the overall organization.

6 Different levels of service and pricing

This is another difficult area to manage and one with no easy answers. There will be customers who demand the same level of pricing and service across all the countries involved in the relationship. Others will recognize that there will be differences depending on, for example, the country infrastructure, eg transport, the nature of the service or product in that country, or the level of the relationship at local level. Overcoming the global pricing issue can be problematic. One company addressed this by having an open-book conversation with the customer that showed the different costs to serve in each country; they subsequently agreed with the customer a price that reflected the overall costs across the world into a single unit price that applied in each country.

7 Customers not adhering to the global contract or agreement

Many suppliers say that one of their issues with IKAM is the customer organization ignoring the contract or agreement. As with the supplier organization, this is usually because the local countries within the customer don't see why they have to comply with the global or international agreement either. As one IKAMgr said:

> It is a big task to persuade the people at country level in the customer that there is a contract that they should be working to. I cannot do this alone. I have to rely on getting the RGAMs and LKAMs to work at all levels of the customer on this issue.

There is a real role for the IKAMgr to ensure that the agreement is taken up locally within the customer and the supplier:

> Just having a global agreement or contract does not mean that everyone in both organizations is signed up to it. At local level, you know, they could say, let us ignore it, I'm going to do it my way and forget about everything else. The contract needs to be pushed internally in both organizations if it is going to work. The global account manager is key in getting buy-in to the contract in both organizations.

The cultural dimension of managing international key accounts

If you ask IKAMgrs what their key challenges are in carrying out the role, many will identify managing different cultures, both in their organization and in the customer, as a major challenge. For example, IKAMgrs need to be *culturally aware, sensitive* to *different cultures, comfortable and adaptable in operating in different cultures* and good at *managing cross-cultural teams (customer and internal)*. Communicating across different cultures is also a major challenge for both the organizations and the IKAMgrs. International customers also recognize the important role played by intercultural competence in an international business environment.

While little has been written from an academic perspective around managing culture in an IKAM environment (with the exception of [1]), there is anecdotal evidence of its importance for successful IKAM. It is essential to integrate culture management and IKAM in order to explore the challenges so that the management can be improved, thus leading to better organizational performance and efficiency [2]. Better culture management should also lead to effective GAM leadership [3]. With the emergence of multinational companies and the importance of international sales, the global management of cross-cultural differences is likely to affect the overall performance of IKAM in many organizations.

The voice of the practitioner: the culture challenge

'Key challenges in global accounts are often cultural. There seem to be more cultural or language barriers – just the way of doing things in certain countries – that you need to overcome and understand. For example, what somebody thinks is aggressive language in one country wouldn't be thought of as at all aggressive in another country. So it's important to keep the issue of culture in the back of your mind.' (Global account manager, global logistics company.)

'Managing different cultures and communicating with different cultures is important. Different things motivate or worry different people and certain communication styles work better with some than with others. Tailored communication can work but this is hard and misinterpretation can happen. Understanding how to manage this effectively is a major part of my job.' (IKAMgr, global IT solutions company.)

'Yes, you're trying to balance the needs of the customer but then you've got the problems of slightly different cultural requirements and the different business requirements across the world. There are also the demands the parent companies are putting on individual sites which may also then be in conflict with others.' (Supply chain director, global manufacturing company.)

'Getting people to open up and talk about what the real issues are and also being able to understand the different cultures. Maybe, you know, in a certain country, you can't ask certain questions or you can't do the things that you would normally do.' (IKAMgr, global consultancy company.)

'Managing cultural issues is important. When in this global business you've got to understand the different cultures and different parts of the world, then that is key. You've got to have somebody who's comfortable in all cultural environments and all levels of management who is also aware of cultural differences and is a good listener.' (Regional account manager, global oil and gas company.)

Culture management as a construct is complex and multifaceted. Following an extensive piece of research with international customers and suppliers, four aspects of managing culture emerged as key issues in managing international relationships, as shown in Figure 11.8:

- managing different country cultures;
- managing different business cultures;
- managing different corporate cultures;
- managing different languages.

Managing different country cultures

This is about managing the different national country traits and characteristics that people may have. IKAMgrs have to build relationships with people from different countries, both within the customer and within their own organization. Every country

Figure 11.8 The four aspects of managing culture in an international context

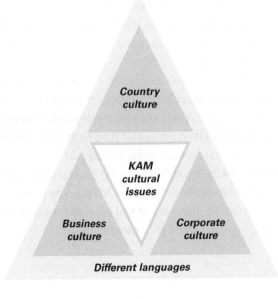

has its own characteristics and a lack of cultural knowledge can lead to misunderstanding, including, for example, losing power in negotiations. Therefore, country culture difference should be managed and the challenges recognized [2]. *National characteristics* are defined by Hofstede as those that identify people from a specific country and which highlight certain characteristics such as education and social and political behaviours [2]. According to Hofstede, the national culture is seen as being strongly rooted in the country concerned and is the most difficult aspect of culture to change.

Managing different business cultures

This aspect of culture is about understanding the different ways of doing business in different countries, or the way in which the country culture, described above, can also impact the business culture of different countries. One organization referred to this as managing the cultural business orientation of the customer and/or the internal team within their own organization. Additionally, building cooperation with different business cultures is important as different industries have their own ways of working as well as understanding the different ways of doing business in different countries. In order to better understand each other, the challenges of business culture differences should be understood by IKAMgrs. It has been stated that business cultures can be influenced by country cultures and both internal and external management should consider the culture difference between businesses.

By understanding different business cultures, IKAMgrs should be able to undertake better negotiations and build better business cooperation and relationships. It will be important to have different negotiation processes to deal with the different business cultures. On a practical level, IKAMgrs will need to be familiar with the different jurisdictions and regulatory frameworks in the countries in which they are operating.

Managing different corporate cultures

This is different from the business culture, and is about having different corporate cultures both across and within organizations. IKAMgrs may have to manage different corporate cultures internally as well as managing those of their customers. Therefore, it is necessary to understand the challenges of dealing with different corporate cultures externally as well as internally. At the same time, it is important to try to achieve a strategic fit for different corporate cultures both within the organization and within the customer.

In addition, various national cultures can have an influence on the diversity of corporate cultures. However, due to the various international corporate cultures that may be playing an important role in implementing the value and mission of the organization, the corporate culture can sometimes be more important than the country culture. Company cultures are different, as companies have their own values and strategies.

These values are reflected by, for example, dress code, timekeeping, attitudes and relationships within the organization. An organization with a positive and strong culture can increase employees' loyalty [2]. Therefore, an IKAMgr should be concerned with the different cultures of both their global accounts and their own organization.

Voice of the practitioner: managing different corporate cultures

One IKAMgr described the corporate culture in London as being different from that of the American HQ.

'It is important in global account management that global companies can talk together and this has some implications for cross-cultural issues. This is not only in terms of different national cultures but also down to understanding different corporate cultures. For example, our corporate culture in London is very different from our field offices across Europe and very different from our HQ environment in the States.' (Customer of a global component manufacturing company.)

Managing different languages

This is obviously strongly linked to the country culture and it has been suggested that one aspect of culture is the convention of how people are expected to participate in conversations. Different languages can be barriers to communication in both internal and external multinational business environments and different languages alongside different country cultures can cause misunderstandings. However, the ability to converse and understand each other in an international environment is obviously critically important. Therefore, language difference can be a challenge in both social and business settings [2]. However, a recent research study carried out at Cranfield shows that while it is clear that language is considered as a challenge in IKAM, due to the fact that English has become the universal business language and more and more people are now able to speak standard English, the language barriers are becoming fewer and fewer.

Tips from practitioners in the communications industry on managing language differences

'Talking in English in a measured way is important; being aware that for people for whom English is not their first language, to concentrate on English for a long time can be tiring, so I make sure the big issues are discussed in the first place in a conference or meeting.' (IKAMgr, global marketing agency.)

'As a native English speaker, the terminology and slang or colloquialisms can prevent people from understanding the conversation; they may understand similar things but not exactly the same, which can lead to problems further down the line. I find it important to sense-check at frequent intervals that we have a common understanding.' (Global account manager, international creative agency.)

'I am leading a war which is anti-e-mail because there is a lot of information lost in communication by e-mail when communicating with people from all over the world. As a global account manager I find it really important to not lose the tone and the body language as this is all part of understanding each other. It isn't just the words. I try my best to talk with people face to face, both internally and with the customer.' (Global account manager, global advertising company.)

How does KAM apply in different countries?

We are often asked by international and global organizations how well the concepts of KAM, which have largely developed in the Western world, translate or transfer to other countries. From some recent research we have carried out, it would appear that most of the key concepts of KAM do translate quite easily across the globe. The key processes – which include key account selection and categorization, key account planning, measures and KPIs for KAM, support systems for KAM, the roles and competences of KAMgrs and the key account team approach – are fairly homogeneous across many countries and cultures. Where the differences occur is in, for example, the softer aspects of KAM such as how relationships are built, the importance of interpersonal relationships and the impact of all aspects of culture on the relationship. For example, the understanding and respect of social networks, whether it be the *old boys' network* in the West, *wasta* in the Middle East, *blat* in Eastern Europe or *guanxi* in China, is a fundamental 'glue' to strategic customer relations. The implementation of KAM needs to be slower in some regions, often due to fragmented markets, for example in Italy, China and Spain. In other countries like France, the KAM principle, even for an advanced Western nation, has been slow to develop.

Some of the markets we studied differ significantly from the US and UK markets, where KAM is definitely more mature and prevalent. This suggests a flexible approach is needed when it comes to how KAM is implemented in other regions and countries. Practices that prove to be effective in mature markets may need to be adjusted and adapted to other contexts.

Hofstede [2] offers a highly researched and well-constructed set of criteria for those looking to understand the cultural dimensions of countries in which a company may operate which, in turn, should make it easier to translate the concept of KAM into other cultures. For example, KAMgrs looking after accounts that span different countries need to understand how the account organization might behave in each country. Also, organizations may design the way that they recruit and position KAMgrs (and the teams that work with them), based on the Hofstede cultural best fit, which again should make it easier to embed KAM concepts in less mature markets. Finally, organizations need to be very aware that each country may behave differently and the way that they might accept or reject KAM principles will be influenced by these core behaviours. For example, a country with a tendency towards long-term business strategies will have more empathy towards strategic KAM planning than those with short-term business approaches.

Implementation of KAM in a developing region: the Arab world

The Arab world is a vital part of the developing/emerging countries and is an interesting case study for looking at the application of KAM in an emerging economy context, including forming an understanding of the way in which Western companies implement and use KAM in a non-Western context.

A case study [4] in the domain of KAM in this emerging context was carried out based on a telecommunications company in the Middle East. This Arab company adopted Western KAM principles and segmented their customers based on 'future potential, strategic market position and reference value; the strategic account process has not been dominated by the sales revenue criterion alone.' The uniqueness of this study relates to the three important culture-related factors that are behind the success of KAM implementation in an Arab country. First, top-level management had to be involved (as Arab cultures are characterized by high power distance). Second, personal relationship development/personal contacts were substantially more important than had been reported in the Western literature. Third, trust was of vital importance, as it would have to be developed between the parties before engaging in business negotiations. The study concludes that the time spent on these factors may seem excessive for western KAM, but it is considered normal in an Arab country [4].

A Cranfield PhD [5] also identified how KAM relationship management is applied in an Arab context and the factors that influence these relationships. The research found that companies in the region (Western or Arab-owned) are increasingly adopting KAM principles to gain a competitive advantage. These principles are adapted to an Arab context but with some changes that take the Arab culture into consideration. The principles were divided into formal and informal. The formal aspects differ from western KAM in the selection criteria for account managers, as 'age' and 'established networks of contacts' are more important and prioritized. Another difference relates to heavy senior management involvement, which reflects a rather 'hands-on' approach while the Western approach is labelled as more 'hands-off'. Customization and special activities are offered to key accounts but they differ in intensity according to the industry.

The informal aspects differ in three ways. First, gaining and building close and long-term personal relationships is valued more than 'product delivery, cost and efficiency'. Second, using *wasta* networks, eg friends and family, to build close relationships based on trust is heavily important. Finally, business discussions can only be made after building strong relationships through utilizing these connections.

Conclusion

This chapter has specifically focused on the issues and challenges around managing international key accounts. IKAM inevitably involves more complexity and difficulties than managing local key accounts. In particular, there are challenges around the global versus local approaches to key accounts and the issue of intercultural competence. It is clear that managing different cultures is a key defining aspect of IKAM and a major difference from LKAM.

The main message for companies is that it is critical to decide whether or not an IKAM approach is right for you and your customers. In many cases, an LKAM approach will still be the most appropriate way to manage the customer.

Questions for managers

- Is IKAM the right way to manage some of your pan-geographic accounts?
- Do you have the infrastructure in place to manage international accounts?
- Does the customer have the right structure to be managed as an international account?
- Do you really have global accounts or are they more multinational or regional?

- Do you have key account managers that are culturally sensitive and competent?
- Do you have the right KPIs and reward systems in place to facilitate the success of IKAM?
- Have you identified the potential global vs local issues for your organization and planned for them accordingly?
- Have you made sure that the ROI from implementing this approach for international customers is positive?

References

[1] Holt, S (2003) *The Role of the Global Account Manager: A boundary role theory perspective*, PhD Thesis, Cranfield School of Management, Cranfield University, Bedford.

[2] Hofstede, G (2001) *Culture's Consequences: Comparing values, behaviours, institutions, and organisations across nations*, Sage Publications, London.

[3] McDonald, M and Ryals, L (2008) *Key Account Plans: The practitioners' guide to profitable planning*, Butterworth-Heinemann, Oxford.

[4] Al-Husan, F and Brennan, R (2009) Strategic account management in an emerging economy: a case study approach, *Journal of Business & Industrial Marketing*, 24 (8), pp. 611–20.

[5] Al-Husan, F (2011) *Key Account Management in an Arab Context*, PhD Thesis, Cranfield University, Bedford.

PART FOUR
Assessing your KAM programme: a framework

The KAM Framework

12

'No matter how great the talent or effort, some things just take time. You can't produce a baby in one month by getting nine women pregnant.'

WARREN BUFFETT

Question: How do organizations build KAM programmes that deliver an exceptional and sustainable competitive advantage?

A different way of doing business

Becoming effective at key account management is a notoriously challenging activity for many organizations. The Sales Executive Council researched its members in 2005 and found that some 80 per cent of companies have to restart their KAM initiatives within a three-year period. This suggests that a number of things are not being executed correctly and the desired results are not being delivered. Within the Cranfield KAM Best Practice Club, this phenomenon is something that members recognize and seek to address. No one wants to be a member of the 'tried and failed' club, but it is useful to understand some of the reasons why organizations struggle.

This final chapter provides insights into how organizations should develop to become really effective with KAM. An organization that addresses the challenges (and opportunities) that come with managing large complex customers and successfully navigates through the pitfalls and obstacles (that almost everyone faces) will be on a launch pad to a successful programme, rather than one that has shaky foundations. There are ways to approach building a strong KAM organization and lessons that can be learned to make the task less daunting. Here are some thoughts regarding how KAM should be considered and positioned by senior leaders.

A different business model

There is no need to repeat the descriptions and dialogue covered elsewhere in this book. KAM is different from traditional selling and account management. It requires a ramping-up and leveraging of resources around a smaller portfolio of higher-value, more complex customers. Managing this set of customers needs a different approach to that required for planning, managing relationships, developing and delivering value, and measuring performance. Everything changes and can make an organization creak if systems are not built around these challenges. KAM is a different business model with a different way of working.

You can't train your way out of this

As a consultant and trainer, it can be frustrating when working with cohorts of managers who need 'training' on KAM. Ask the question, 'How many key account managers (KAMgrs) does your organization have?' There should be a response of '10', '20', '30' or maybe '50'. When delegates say '500', the organization has a total portfolio of 2,000 customers and, as an individual, he/she is responsible for 100 key accounts, you know that the fundamental KAM due diligence has not been conducted by senior management. As one senior manager once advised: 'We have struggled with KAM and are now thinking that we simply cannot train our way out of this problem...'.

Part of the solution to building a KAM programme is, of course, training and development. It also requires a number of other critical organizational factors.

Salespeople may not be your best key account managers

The profile of a salesperson is very different to the profile of a KAMgr. Salespeople generally do not strategize, manage teams, manage P&L accounts and develop value propositions. They are also typically not strong project managers. All these skills are critical for the effective KAMgr. Salespeople can make exceptional KAMgrs, but they typically cannot make the transition after a three-day training course. The transition may take years of investment, but in the long run is better for the salesperson, the customer's business and your bottom line.

Take your time and invest

As Warren Buffett says, 'you cannot produce a baby in one month by making nine women pregnant'. The organizations that are very good at KAM have spent a significant number of years investing, reviewing, adapting and focusing on their KAM initiatives. If you have a large, complex organization then your KAM initiative, like any other transformation, will need time, effort and investment.

Stick to the plan

Organizations such as Siemens, Oracle, Fujitsu, P&G and Unilever are regarded as strong and capable KAM organizations. They did not get there straight away; they made errors and had to repeat stages. These companies all have one thing in common: they had an intention to make KAM a competitive advantage and they had a plan. Great KAM organizations keep going and keep the faith.

Fix the problem with talented people

If 80 per cent of your profit is potentially coming from just 20 customers, developing a strategy and an actionable plan should be high on your agenda. For something so critical, you need your best talent analysing, reviewing and developing a KAM programme that will enable your company to prosper and advance against your competitors. And yet, many organizations that are not customer-centric do not recognize the importance of building a strong KAM-focused business. KAM needs time and effort from talented people and leadership. Get it established as one of the top three-to-five strategic initiatives and it will attract talent.

Follow a system

The Cranfield KAM Best Practice Club recognized that there was a need to build a model to help organizations start addressing the complexities of building and implementing a high-performance KAM programme. The KAM Framework has been developed and is described here as a robust and proven model, which can be utilized by organizations looking to develop by managing and growing large, complex, strategically important customers.

Organizational capability and individual competence

'Key account management is more than just the KAMgr' is a great phrase, often resonating with many practitioners seeking to implement KAM programmes. It captures a critical component of any KAM initiative: there is a difference between focusing on selecting and developing KAMgrs and creating an environment in which they can operate effectively.

A useful way to pin this concept down is to define the two related, but different, characteristics of capability and competence. This is a small but very important point; too often organizations talk about their KAM initiatives and send out confusing communications regarding what they are trying to achieve. Having clarity regarding capability and competence is highly beneficial:

Capability: describes the wider organizational environment within which the KAMgr operates. Factors such as structure, processes, planning tools, methods of measuring performance, IT systems, and practical aspects such as equipment all contribute towards capability.

Competence: describes aspects of an individual and, specifically in relation to the KAMgr, this describes the 'people' aspects of the individual: their personal skills and abilities, attitudes, development, motivation and approach to business.

Making this distinction is important for managers as they start to plan and detail the blueprint in order to build an effective organization. Problems arise when there is solely a focus on the KAMgr, alongside the attitude of 'Get those salespeople trained in KAM and we will be able to back to business quickly.' This approach lacks critical understanding and does not explore all the aspects of a strong KAM business model.

The KAM Framework provides a set of standards that help to define the difference between capability and competence. Practitioners have found it useful in order to understand the complexity and breadth of KAM, as well as to enable clearer discussions across their organizations. At the heart of the Framework sits the requirement to think of KAM as an organization-wide issue. It is important to keep in mind, of course, that as well as this 'wider' notion of organizational capability, having a large pool of highly skilled KAMgrs is also critical, as pointed out by one learning and development director.

The voice of the practitioner

Overheard by a guest at a Cranfield KAM Best Practice Club event coffee break.
    'Yes I agree, key account management is more than just the key account manager – BUT the key account manager is really BLOODY important!' (Global learning and development director, technology company.)

Strategy–capability–change

A common question asked by many practitioners leading KAM programmes is 'How should we think about getting started with a KAM initiative?' It can be overwhelming and pressure can be loaded on those accountable. The challenge is to introduce KAM, but where to start? Figure 12.1 shows a good way to structure the thinking process by splitting the challenge into three main parts: strategy, capability and change.

These three stages work in a loop, starting with an external analysis that sparks the need for a new response/strategy, followed by an internal review of capabilities to deliver against this new strategy, with the final stage being execution of the new

Figure 12.1 Three phases of an effective KAM programme

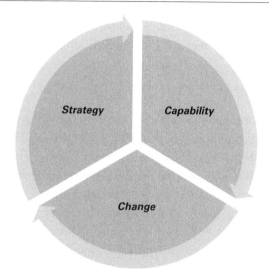

KAM standards (inevitably requiring organizational change). These are joined in a loop, since external markets keep changing and a new response is always required. The first journey around the loop is always the toughest to action (but potentially has the greatest impact).

Strategy

Conduct an external analysis of the environment and market within which your organization operates. Consider how your competitors are behaving and what your customers need and value. When applied, models suggested elsewhere in this book (such as the 9-box SWOT) work really well to establish your own strategy. One essential action that should start this stage is to form a KAM strategy/steering group. If your organization has a dedicated 'Centre of Excellence' group tasked with owning and developing KAM capability, they should see this as a priority. The strategy steering group should comprise members from across the business, providing expertise and insights from sales groups, regional/country leadership, functional heads and key account directors/leaders of KAM teams. It is also essential to have a board-level director who can act as a sponsor and advisor to this group.

The KAM strategy group should meet on a regular basis. Face-to-face meetings, whilst expensive, are very productive. Meetings on a quarterly basis can be complemented by webinar sessions. What is important is that the team members all see value in a KAM initiative, are able to contribute time and have a passion for organic growth/customer management. This team will form the strategy for the organization, overseeing the external review, formation of a vision and then identifying strategic blocks of work (with actions to make these become reality). The strategy group should have a long-term remit. Early stages will be concerned with establishing a blueprint for a new KAM business model, whilst later stages of work are concerned with overseeing adoption of new ways of working across the wider business.

Capability

If KAM is primarily a different way of doing business, then we need ways of describing and defining what the components of these new principles are. The KAM Framework has been developed to provide a language that can be used by organizations and steering groups to make sense of what these capability 'standards' might be.

As discussed previously, KAM must differentiate between capability and competence. The KAM steering group should be very mindful of these differences and start to assign resources to build new techniques. Making the right choices, in the right sequence, is an essential activity. Initial scanning of the KAM Framework can be overwhelming (there are lots of standards!). We caution that not everything has to be done at once, and for many organizations, it is not essential to complete all activities. In fact, it is urged that organizations adopting these ways of working take a model such as the KAM Framework and adapt it to their own business language. It is important that you work in this way; after all, it is your business!

Change

As KAM is a different way of working, it always requires some form of business change. Those familiar with Kotter's eight-step change model [1] will be pleased to know that it is a perfect fit with KAM programme development. Figure 12.2 shows the eight changes and advises application points in order to achieve each change for KAM.

Kotter observes that most change initiatives stumble at the first stage. There is a lack of understanding or belief that there is a need to change – there is, simply, no 'burning bridge'. This observation applies particularly well to KAM programmes. We have found that many Centre of Excellence teams (and KAM steering groups) struggle to gain traction within their organizations due to a lack of understanding about what KAM is and why there should be any sort of response. Success can start to emerge in the lower ranks of the organization (those who deal with key customers really understand the challenge), but senior levels can struggle to comprehend what is required of them. Engagement, communication and senior management buy-in are essential for your Centre of Excellence team. Use Kotter's model to overcome these hurdles:

- Build a robust case for change: what if you don't become exceptional at KAM?
- Your guiding coalition is your Centre of Excellence team and your KAM steering group.

Figure 12.2 Driving change

Change stage	KAM application
1. A sense of urgency	Conduct an external/internal audit. Why do you need KAM?
2. Form a powerful guiding coalition	Develop a cross-functional/cross-geographical KAM steering group. Have board-level sponsorship.
3. Create a vision for change	The KAM steering group develops a strategy (they utilize the KAM framework). A clear set of actions to build a KAM business model.
4. Engage and communicate the vision	Connect with the wider business. Explain the case for change, the vision and the way forward. Seek 'buy-in' from key stakeholders.
5. Empower others to implement	Look to involve talent in the organization outside the KAM steering group. Develop training and coaching programmes to develop key account managers and their teams.
6. Create quick wins	Seek to generate KAM plans that drive growth. Write these up as case studies. Gain customer endorsements to add weight to the impact of the KAM approach.
7. Build on success	Involve a wider circle of organization employees. Engage with more senior/middle managers. Use Webinar and other internal communication systems to talk about success.
8. 'Stick' – it is just the way things are done around here	Eventually... the job is done. KAM becomes 'just the way we do things around here...!' (But don't get complacent – review your strategy on a regular basis.)

Adapted from Kotter's eight-step change model

- A vision for change should come from your initial strategy meetings.

- Engagement and communication are never easy! However, in many commercial organizations we have found this to become easier with a set of success stories (showing sales growth and more profit) from your own pilot/case studies. It is hard to say no to a new way of working that grows profit with a customer by 40 per cent!

- Empower others to implement – this is where the training and coaching on a broader scale should kick in.

- Create quick wins: possibly *the* secret to any KAM programme. We urge you to develop your own case studies around carefully selected KAM plans. A strong KAM plan (endorsed by the customer and showing growth for the supplier) is a very powerful document. Build your own best practice and case studies and change will become easier!

- Build on success: keep those case studies coming and keep senior management in the loop. A great way to keep KAM plans alive and integrated into the daily working of a business/country is to have a formal process with KAMgrs presenting plans to senior leaders on a regular basis.

- Stick: we would argue that no KAM programme ever stops (there is too much external disruption requiring a response). However, there will come a point that KAM becomes accepted by leadership and is an essential part of the business model.

The voice of the practitioner

Cranfield KAM Best Practice Club event: 'Stick (just the way we do things around here). We have built our business around a KAM model. Our customers are so large and so complex that there is simply no other way of doing business. I could not imagine a business without KAM. We build all of our resources around the large global and regional mass merchandiser/retail companies, and they expect us to manage them in this way!' (Senior KAM VP, Mars Confectionery.)

The importance of a robust and shared vision

Writing is always difficult. It forces you to capture on paper concepts and ideas that you have always talked about, practised and deeply believe in as being correct. It is difficult, though, since it forces you to really describe things with intent and accuracy. Your words will be captured forever, printed on paper and are there for everybody to read. Pressure? Absolutely. You have to be confident in what you are saying, accurate in your description and precise with the words you use.

Creating (and capturing) a KAM vision is a similar challenge. Following the relative chaos of scanning the external environment and creating a strategic direction to follow in order to develop a KAM business model, a crisp vision needs to be constructed. This is the 'guiding light' that will feature at the centre of any engagement and communication initiative. Using Kotter's model, this is step three, and is often underestimated. Here are some areas that should be considered when developing a compelling vision.

Communicate the vision: 'dragging' the organization forward

It is the vision that sets the direction and future state towards which the organization strives to move. As a reference point, the vision keeps the strategy alive and provides the momentum for change. A carefully worded vision acts as a motivation for the organization through all levels, from the board to operational staff.

Reference 'the burning bridge'

A vision should reference the point that you are trying to move away from. Given that this is the reason that most organizations do not change (as they do not recognize the need to shift from their current state) it is important to capture this position.

Set organizational and personal objectives

The vision is an organizational statement. It describes how the organization will look and perform in the future. Of course, this is only useful when these organizational aspects become applicable for the leaders and managers of the business. Vision statements should ripple through the hierarchy of the business by setting personal performance objectives and goals.

Use words and numbers

The vision is described in two parts, using words and numbers. Words describe a future state about a matter that is important, for example, 'to be regarded as the leading strategic partner with the largest firms in the global medical devices sector.' Typically, these are regarded as qualitative factors and should be measured accordingly. The other construct of a vision should be expressed in numbers (the most common form of vision). For example, 'to double our share of wallet with our top 10 key account customers', or 'to grow profit by 25 per cent across our top key accounts'.

Address time

Many vision statements do not have a time allocated. With large-scale change programmes such as KAM initiatives, careful consideration should be made here. Too short a timescale and there will be pushback from the individuals looking to implement. Too long and senior management will get impatient.

Be realistic but stretching

Stating that you will triple sales and dominate your industry in the next six months may be possible but is far too stretching in that timescale. Perhaps you will achieve this vision in the next five years, but as a vision for today, it is just too stretching.

Use the language of your business and align with the wider vision

If your business is about expanding into new markets and/or introducing new products and services, align the KAM vision to complement these and to become an enabler of this bigger initiative. Also, use the language of your business. Pick up the annual company report and look at the words and phrases that are used in it. It is pointless pulling in a different direction with your KAM programme objectives when the organization has a clear strategic direction. Don't try to swim against the tide!

The KAM Framework

The KAM Framework has been developed to provide a model and a framework that describes the standards for a KAM organization. It offers a structure and a set of definitions that can be used to carry out a series of activities across a KAM initiative. It can be used to:

- *Help explain the breadth and depth of KAM.* KAM is a capability (and a set of competencies for KAMgrs). In the absence of a KAM Framework it is very difficult to explain what this means. When we look into the structure and the standards that sit within the Framework, it will become apparent just how broad and involved KAM can be. The KAM Framework overcomes this issue in a visual and condensed manner.

- *Provide a terminology for strategy.* When the KAM Centre of Excellence team starts to develop a strategy (and resulting vision) for the next two to three years, unless they have a framework to help navigate the various elements of KAM, it is tricky to be certain that all aspects have been covered. The Framework is a comprehensive model that examines and explores the full scope of KAM. It can be adopted to explain, define and describe KAM strategy.

- *Assess capability gaps.* The model really comes to life when it is used to assess a business and to start looking for gaps in the way that things are done. Later in this chapter we explore more in depth how this can be carried out. There are numerous ways that gaps can be identified; for instance, just by reading this chapter you may start looking at your KAM business model and immediately start to find performance issues. Other aspects may not be so apparent, and further discussions or research may be required to establish the gaps. Addressing these gaps will form part of your strategic planning.

- *Structure engagement and communication documents.* A simple version of the KAM Framework (such as the one shown in Figure 12.3) is often adopted by organizations as they communicate their intention to implement a new KAM strategy to the wider organization and outline areas where they are looking to make changes. The advantage of such a model is that it is simple to communicate, remember and understand. Of course, the detail and implications that sit behind the Framework can be complex, but as a way to describe and explain KAM, it is a very useful model. Again, we encourage firms to take the model, adapt and change descriptions to suit their existing business systems and ways of working – but as a basic construct the model is very robust.

Figure 12.3 describes the KAM Framework. It is split into six main sections: people aspects; structure and processes; metrics and profitability; customer planning; culture and leadership; and value-based business. Derived by a Cranfield Visiting Fellow, the model was developed with a few small workshops, and then tested and validated with KAM Best Practice Club members during conference-type events and a series on 'in-house consulting assignments'. The model has been used with large global organizations as well as smaller in-country operations. It has been used across a wide range of industrial sectors including: consumer, healthcare, pharmaceutical, engineering, technology, logistics, food, retail, professional and legal services, consulting, environmental, public services, defence, and many more. The model always provides great insight and has high impact for organizations that are struggling to advance KAM.

The main six sections of the KAM Framework can be explained further.

People aspects

KAMgrs, their leaders and the people that work for them (as KAM team members) are vital talent and need to be of the correct calibre. They should be selected, recruited, trained and developed, coached and motivated to become the driving force of your KAM business.

Figure 12.3   The KAM Framework

Structure and processes

Having great talent is futile if you do not have the right number working in the right locations, doing the right things – with the whole organization having a good understanding of how their own role assists the KAMgrs. This becomes more critical as organizations become more complex, especially if they operate on a global, cross-regional basis.

Metrics and profitability

KAM business models require an extra level of process and thinking when considering what critical parameters to measure and how. This is due to the 'bespoke' nature of KAM; a unique customer value proposition is developed and sold, therefore its performance subsequently has to be tracked (for both the supplier and the customer). With the additional investment and attention that the customer receives, there can be a problem tracking the profit/loss against the customer, since many organizations set up their systems to measure business performance by product/brand or country (but seldom by customer).

Customer planning

Planning systems are common in any organization. Planning 'customer by customer' is far less common, however, and is an absolute bedrock aspect of any KAM programme. It is the innovative and thorough generation of KAM plans (and the resulting customer value propositions that they enable) towards which KAM organizations should strive.

Culture and leadership

Given the previous discussion around how KAM initiatives fail because of reasons such as a lack of understanding or belief in the need to change, and underestimating investment requirements, it is not difficult to understand why *culture and leadership* is included in the Framework. In many ways, this is the most critical of all the standards – if your leadership team believes and wants something to happen, you have a fighting chance of it happening. If they don't – you will struggle!

Value-based business

The KAM Framework was initially developed in 2009; very few additions or changes have been made since then. This section of the Framework used to be called 'Customer management' and refers to the sales and account management activities that should be in place within an organization to enable a solid platform for KAM (activities such as negotiation and pricing, for instance). In light of the critical need for organizations to focus on 'value' and 'value co-creation', this section's title has been changed to 'Value-based business'. We think it captures the shift that organizations are making as they make traditional 'sales' more transactional (via web and third-party sales) and move direct selling towards a KAM model. These are subtle word changes but they have big impact when used to communicate the intent of a progressive organization.

Building the organization to fit customer types

One aspect of KAM that is critical (maybe the keystone activity) is to develop a customer segmentation model that is understood by leadership and which can determine your key accounts. Any segmentation model can be used – we offer several in this book and a further simple version in Figure 12.4. The purpose of this example is not to show you how to segment your customer base, but what you should do afterwards to bring it to life and have real value.

Figure 12.4 shows two stages. The first (primary customer segmentation stage) sorts customers into small/medium/large 'buckets' – probably by means of their annual turnover. The large customer bucket is your portfolio of KAM 'suspects', and these require closer examination, which can be done in the secondary stage of segmentation. This model (there are many other types) shows classification of KAM by geography (national, regional, global and strategic). Strategic may be those two or three customers who take large volumes of product from multiple divisions all over the world and who require significant investment to manage, whilst offering significant potential rewards. Of course, you should assess each 'suspect' key customer with other factors, such as buying behaviour, growth potential, history etc.

Figure 12.4 Segmenting the customer portfolio [2]

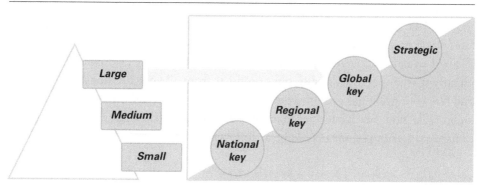

Figure 12.5   Building the organization to fit customer types [3]

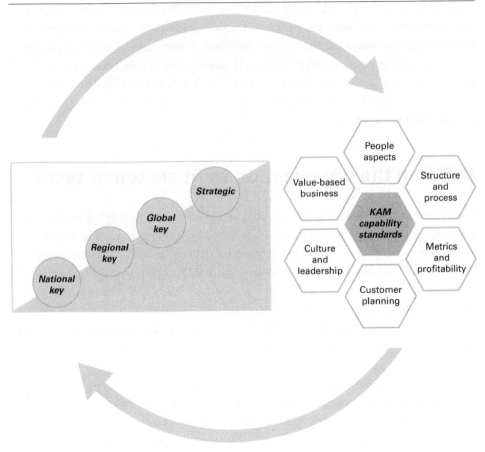

Eventually, you build a suitable segmentation model, apply it to your customer portfolio and list a number of customers (organizations) against each classification type. Excellent, bravo! But, so what?

Figure 12.5 shows how you can bring your customer segmentation model to life and start building a KAM business model around it. You do this by aligning it with the KAM Framework and by starting to design the parameters and implications for 'anointing' each customer as a particular 'type'.

So, if you anoint 'Sparkex Widget Company' as a strategic customer because you identify that it operates globally, buys products from all your divisions, behaves well and like you, AND has growth potential as if it is on steroids – then you have made a good selection. But what does that mean and what are the organizational implications? As an example, they *could* be as follows.

Strategic customers

- People aspects:
  - KAM should be general manager/VP grade;
  - high potential;
  - manager based near head office or customer head office.
- Structure and process:
  - one dedicated strategic manager per strategic customer;
  - three-four dedicated team members;
  - growth required (30 per cent pa based on investments of £1m pa);
  - minimum turnover in two years of £30m pa.
- Customer planning:
  - full customer plan required at head office level;
  - regional key account plans required at head office level;
  - local KAM plans required.

Of course, these segmentation parameters will change for any organization, which is why you should always build a method that suits your needs. However, it shows how the criteria for a strategic customer could fall outside the set parameters. Sparkex Widget Company may be a lovely customer (and the local KAMgr is desperate to have it as a strategic customer) but does it justify investment, leverage of resources and commitment as detailed above, or might these be better allocated to another customer?

Segmentation is always an emotional and challenging activity. It is a process that helps senior managers to make decisions about where and how to allocate resources. Connecting your segmentation model to the KAM Framework will provide the tools and descriptions to help make this possible.

Expanding the KAM standards

The KAM Framework is expanded below. Offered are some simple high-level descriptions to help understand what each standard is and how it might be approached.

People aspects

Personality type. Does the organization select and manage KAMgrs according to their different personality types? KAMgrs (and team members) need to be allocated by assessing personality type (Myers–Briggs MBTI can be adopted).

Figure 12.6 Expanding the standards

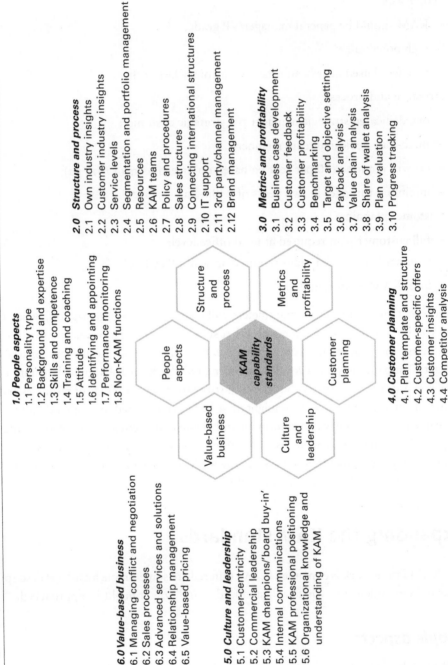

1.0 People aspects
1.1 Personality type
1.2 Background and expertise
1.3 Skills and competence
1.4 Training and coaching
1.5 Attitude
1.6 Identifying and appointing
1.7 Performance monitoring
1.8 Non-KAM functions

2.0 Structure and process
2.1 Own industry insights
2.2 Customer industry insights
2.3 Service levels
2.4 Segmentation and portfolio management
2.5 Resources
2.6 KAM teams
2.7 Policy and procedures
2.8 Sales structures
2.9 Connecting international structures
2.10 IT support
2.11 3rd party/channel management
2.12 Brand management

3.0 Metrics and profitability
3.1 Business case development
3.2 Customer feedback
3.3 Customer profitability
3.4 Benchmarking
3.5 Target and objective setting
3.6 Payback analysis
3.7 Value chain analysis
3.8 Share of wallet analysis
3.9 Plan evaluation
3.10 Progress tracking

4.0 Customer planning
4.1 Plan template and structure
4.2 Customer-specific offers
4.3 Customer insights
4.4 Competitor analysis
4.5 Route to market analysis
4.6 Action plans

5.0 Culture and leadership
5.1 Customer-centricity
5.2 Commercial leadership
5.3 KAM champions/'board buy-in'
5.4 Internal communications
5.5 KAM professional positioning
5.6 Organizational knowledge and understanding of KAM

6.0 Value-based business
6.1 Managing conflict and negotiation
6.2 Sales processes
6.3 Advanced services and solutions
6.4 Relationship management
6.5 Value-based pricing

Background and expertise. Does the organization consider the employment history of each KAMgr and the exposure they have had with all previous job roles?

Skills and competence. Does the organization identify and align different KAM roles and activities with individuals who demonstrate the skills and competences to complete these tasks?

Training and coaching. Does the organization have an adequate training, coaching and development programme for KAMgrs and all non-KAMgrs?

Attitude. Are KAMgr attitudes to working within this new business model considered and acted upon?

Identifying and appointing. Is there an appropriately developed selection, recruitment, and appointment model in place and is it widely utilized?

Performance monitoring. Are KAMgrs and team members measured appropriately? Do they have personal performance measures in their personal performance contracts, and do these measures link with the overall KAM strategy?

Non-KAM functions. Has the organization recognized that KAMgrs only succeed with support from KAM team members who may not be customer-facing? Are there suitable methods in place to manage the performance and continual support of these managers?

Structure and process

Own industry insights. Does the organization track and monitor trends and changes within the industry where it operates? Are all competitors (existing, new and potential threats) tracked and monitored? Is a KAM response considered and acted upon to address these insights?

Customer industry insights. Does the organization track and monitor trends and changes within the customer's industry (and the customer's customer's industry)? Are all competitors of the customer (existing, new and potential) tracked and monitored?

Service levels. Are customer experience standards considered and measured? Do customer service functions exist and are they built to cope with complex key customer demands?

Segmentation and portfolio management. Has the organization developed a customer segmentation model? Are different types of key account customers clearly identified? Is the model applied and understood by the business and are resources leveraged according to customer type?

Resources (access and managing). Do KAMgrs have access to resources, if required, in order to grow their customer's business?

KAM teams. Does every KAMgr have a key account team? Do these KAM teams operate effectively?

Policy and procedures. Is there a set of guidelines and procedures that map out how the KAM programme operates? Are these policies and procedures widely adopted across the business?

Sales structures. Do sales teams understand the way that they work with KAM teams? Do the sales processes and sales managers understand what they do and what the KAM teams do? Is there a tension between sales and KAM?

Connecting international structures. Where global or strategic key customers have been identified, there needs to be an alignment of objectives, plans, resources and investments. Do these exist for the international customers that you manage?

IT support. Key accounts require data to track all costs and sales by the customer (not just products and brands). Are there satisfactory IT systems in place that can provide accurate and timely data for each key account on a consolidated 'dashboard' basis?

Third-party/channel management. Just because a customer has been annointed as 'key' does not mean that all activities will be carried out on a direct basis. Third-party organizations may be used for logistics, technical, commercial and operational needs. Do you have a third-party/channel strategy developed, and does it align with your KAM programme?

Brand management. There exists a tension between brands/products and customer needs that must be managed. Do you have clear ways of working between brand teams and the KAM teams?

Metrics and profitability

Business case development. Key accounts develop unique value propositions and strategies to grow that one customer. These require additional resources and investment. Are there systems that are followed by KAMgrs in order to obtain resources? Do KAMgrs develop strong and compelling business cases, showing attractive rewards (for both you and the customer)?

Customer feedback. Do customer feedback programmes exist and are they aligned and quantified to supply performance? When there is poor customer feedback, are these issues corrected in order to improve financial performance?

Customer profitability. Do systems exist that can generate a profit and loss account for every key account customer?

Benchmarking. Is your organization part of a research group (like the Cranfield KAM Best Practice Club) so that you can benchmark your KAM performance against other industries and 'best in class' organizations?

Target and objective setting. Does each key account plan have a clear set of strategies that are split into a set of objectives? Are these targets and objectives visible and acted upon across the wider organization?

Payback analysis. When KAMgrs make business cases and gain resources to grow their customer, are they held accountable with subsequent review sessions which track actual performance versus estimated performance?

Share-of-wallet analysis. Do you calculate the opportunity for each key customer? Do you estimate and combine your historical sales, competitor sales, activities carried out by the customer and activities not carried out? Do these 'share of wallet' analysis calculations feature in regular reviews of each customer plan?

Plan evaluation. KAM stays alive and part of the overall business model when KAM plans are reviewed as part of day-to-day business. Are KAM plans reviewed by senior leaders on a regular (quarterly) basis? Do your KAMgrs present each KAM plan to cross-functional senior leaders and seek input and challenge of ideas and concepts?

Progress tracking. How often do KAMgrs meet with their team members to ensure that all strategies and actions are being completed? Do senior managers review these action-planning review sessions?

Customer planning

Plan template and structure. Have you developed a bespoke KAM plan template? Is it the model used for your KAM training efforts?

Customer-specific offers. Do your KAM plans lead towards a customer-specific value proposition/offer? Does the plan enable customer insights, supplier strategy and customer value proposition development?

Customer insights. Does your KAM plan template 'stretch' the KAMgr to really understand the customer's three- to five-year strategy (including external/internal/operational analysis)?

Competitor analysis. Are your competitor activities tracked within the plan?

Route to market analysis. Are the best methods to supply products and services to the customer tracked and planned? Does the KAM plan have a market supply diagram and analysis included?

Action plans. Does the KAM plan feature a clear set of strategies and does each strategy have a series of actions to make the strategy work?

Culture and leadership

Customer-centricity. Organizations need to focus on the customer (an outside-in approach) rather than trying to get the customer to take what they already have (an inside-out approach). KAM flourishes when senior leaders and the wider organization support the KAMgrs and look to understand the customer and develop new ways of working. Does your organization work in this way?

Commercial leadership. The make-up of the board of an organization sets the culture. If your board is made up of accountants and technical experts, they may lack commercial/KAM focus. Does your organization stipulate that every board member should have been customer facing in the past?

KAM champions/board 'buy-in'. KAM programmes need buy-in at board level. Do you have a board member acting as the sponsor of your KAM initiative?

Internal communications. KAM is a new business model – it requires change. Change depends on engagement with internal communications. Do you have a formal internal communication strategy for your KAM initiative?

KAM professional positioning. Are your KAMgrs highly regarded professionals within your organization? Are they seen as future business/board members?

Organizational knowledge and understanding of KAM. Does the whole organization understand (to a level that is pertinent to each job role) what KAM is and what they have to do as an individual to make it succeed?

Value-based business

Managing conflict and negotiation. Regardless of how well you value sell and how strong your resulting customer value proposition is, you will have to negotiate to get the best price/deal. Do you have strong conflict and negotiation models in place? Are your commercial people skilled in negotiation?

Sales processes. Sales (serving non-key customers) have to align with KAM. It is critical that the sales function focuses on value-based business and that sales is viewed as the foundation of KAM. Do your sales processes align with your KAM business model?

Advanced services and solutions. Does your organization have a means to supply bespoke offerings beyond the core product? Key account teams often develop bespoke packages that wrap services around core products. Delivering these more service-based offerings is a different business model. Is your organization capable of supplying services, advanced services and total solutions? (Tip: if it can't, don't offer them to your customer!)

Relationship management. KAM can be process- and strategy-based. KAM still relies on relationships and this aspect of selling should not be ignored. Building relationships with very senior, key decision makers is critical. Do your KAMgrs have relationship management competence?

Value-based pricing. Price and value are closely connected. KAMgrs must always discuss value and get price based on the value you supply (this will be a higher figure than cost-plus or margin-based pricing). Do you have an organizational strength in value-based pricing? Do your KAMgrs negotiate with value-based price?

What next?

The KAM Framework has been in development and use for approximately a decade. Three areas are being researched and may be added to the model. These are:

Collaboration – the ability of organizations to align with customers, suppliers and competitors in order to generate attractive value propositions and get them to market more quickly.

Account-based marketing – a means of allocating marketers to key account teams on a regular and formal basis. It is a 'forced' approach to becoming customer-centric. But why stop at just marketing? We may see ABSC (Account-Based Supply Chain), ABT (Account-Based Technology) or even ABF (Account-Based Finance). The principles of ABM work so well that these ideas could be extended to other functions.

KAM as leader? A complaint we often hear is that KAMgrs lack power within their organizations. This can render them ineffective and commercially impotent. We feel that another standard under 'people aspects' could be themed 'leadership and impact'.

Mind the gap (find the truth)

All organizations are different, and they can be thought of as having their own individual DNA. It would be crass to assume that every organization starts out with zero capability and looks at the KAM Framework with abject fear. When working with organizations we have found that there are, of course, certain areas that need robust plans to be in place (customer segmentation and a well-developed/bespoke KAM planning tool are two), but every organization will have strengths and areas that they do not need to improve – indeed, these can be areas that can be developed, often offering a source of competitive advantage that the organization had not previously considered.

> ## The voice of the practitioner
>
> 'For years we have been conducting surveys with all of our top 20 country customers. This has provided us with literally tons of data. Frankly, we have never really assessed and responded to the surveys properly... we drowned in feedback.
>
>   'Following the KAM strategy exercise, and in particular the customer segmentation session, we started to zoom in on the feedback from the really strategically important customers. Data from the last three years has given us insights that we were oblivious to. For instance, one customer recognizes that we can provide advice and information about a certain part of the global transmission industry but, for some reason, this has never come up in our routine discussions with them.
>
>   'It seems that we have an exceptional capability to conduct customer surveys and seek feedback but we are trying to do this with too many customers. Since we started focusing on the select few, we are able to take advantage of what we seem to be good at!' (Global market director, oil and gas services company.)

The standards are intended to be used in an interactive and informative way. They are usually discussed at length over a series of workshops with the KAM strategy team. This process in itself generates insights and knowledge for the customer.

A workshop session might work as follows. A topic – for example, *people aspects* – is positioned as the area of discussion and research. The facilitator presents each of the KAM standards for 'people aspects', describing what current best practice looks like. The group then discuss the subject and identify where they have gaps. To help this process, a series of question sheets are provided to allow the delegates to think about a question from the perspective of their organization. They then score out of 5 where they are at today, following a simple key:

0 = not applicable;

1 = very basic;

2 = some evidence of developed model – limited application;

3 = robust models have been developed, wider adoption evidence;

4 = robust models developed, wide use in application (methods and adoption could be improved);

5 = excellent/best in class (good systems are developed and practised everywhere).

Figure 12.7   An example of a standard for evaluating KAM dimensions

	Do you select, develop, motivate and retain the correct standard of talent?		
1.4 Training and coaching	Are you developing and coaching your KA managers and support staff to the required standards?		
Assessment statement		Score	Desired
A	**IS THERE A FORMAL TRAINING AND DEVELOPMENT PROGRAMME IN PLACE?** A fully developed training and coaching programme has been developed and all of our identified key account managers, sales managers and support staff have been through the programme. All training is reinforced with 'on the job' coaching. All departments and support staff are training appropriately.	1	5
B	**IS THE KAM PROGRAMME REGARDED AS ASPIRATIONAL FOR TALENT IN YOUR ORGANIZATION?** The KAM training and coaching programme is established and has been in place for several years. High-potential talent in our organiztion strive to become KA managers and going through the programme is recognized as an essential aspect to further a leader's growth.	2	5
C	**DO YOU HAVE FORMAL COACHING SYSTEMS TO COMPLEMENT YOUR TRAINING?** We recognize that coaching is essential to advance the impact that our KA managers have post-training. All sales managers are trained and developed to coach the KAM managers they look after. Coaching KA managers is (50–70)% of a sales manager's job role.	1.5	5
D	**ARE SALES MANAGERS TRAINED TO LEAD KEY ACCOUNT MANAGERS?** Sales managers have specific training programmes to lead KA managers and also have formal coaching development.	0	5
E	**ARE THERE TRAINING AND DEVELOPMENT PROCESSES FOR NON-KA MANAGERS?** A 'KAM for non-KA managers' training and support programme has been developed. We have identified the support functions and managers within these functions that require KAM familiarization and guidance regarding their roles to support KAM. All these managers have been trained and developed.	0	5
F	**IS THERE A CLEAR CAREER PATHWAY TO HELP SALES PEOPLE TRANSITION TO KA MANAGERS?** Our HR department has developed a detailed set of guidelines that describe how a commercial manager can progress from a basic selling role through KA manager to advanced strategic account director positions. The pathway is used during personal development discussions and to advise our managers how to progress through the organization to advance their KAM careers.	1	4
G	**DO YOU HAVE A FORMAL KAM CERTIFICATION/QUALIFICATION PROCESS?** There is a formal certification process (internal and external) that provides a level of recognized qualifications (certificate/diploma/master). The system is established and highly regarded within our organization and envied by our competitors.	0	5
	Final scores	1	5

Figure 12.7 shows an example assessment card – in this case it is from the standard *people aspects: training and coaching*. Each question has a best practice answer – so to score a 5, the organization has to show examples and evidence, which demonstrates they are operating at this level. Following the debate (it is always useful to have three or four teams scoring separately to get a mix of views), there is a discussion about where the gaps are, what are the critical ones to correct and how to fix them.

You can see that a good facilitator is critical – since they need to provide insights, manage the team, tease out where the truth lies and move the team towards a common agreed action plan.

This entire process can take several weeks/sessions and will generate a lot of output. Spider diagrams are a very effective way to capture all this data. Figure 12.8 is an example from a global supply chain and logistics organization – you can see that the big gaps (between the inner thick lines and the outer thinner lines) are for *value-based business* and *people aspects*. This organization developed new recruitment processes for non-KAM members, allocated new KAM teams, then developed

Figure 12.8 KAM assessment (all standards)

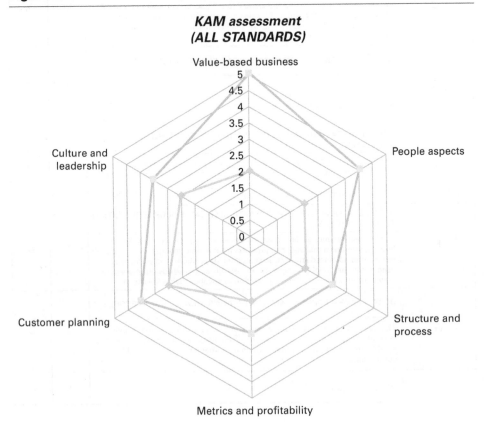

Figure 12.9   An example – 'People Aspects'

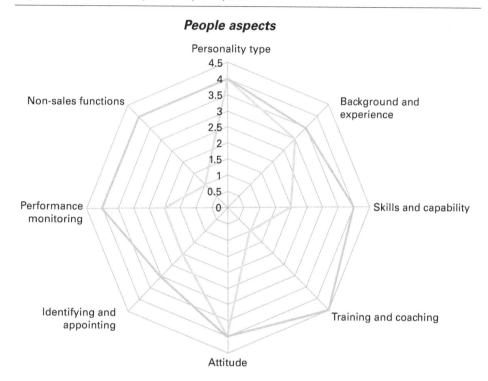

People aspects

and implemented a series of training and development courses on value-based selling, KAM and strategic account management over a period of two to three years. Later (year two/three) initiatives focused on customer sales, IT systems and business case systems. The KAMgrs were developing good value propositions and growth strategies but struggled to gain investment commitment at board level.

Figure 12.9 shows how this firm scored for the *people aspects* standards. Training and coaching was identified as a gap, along with performance monitoring. The performance-monitoring gap was addressed by providing the KAMgrs (and their team members) with clear personal performance criteria. These were used at review sessions to discuss how well they were applying the new KAM techniques and becoming effective KAM talent.

When the truth is hard to grasp

As a final note in this section, the importance of data and insight gathering must be highlighted in order to reach the truth and establish reality. So far, the process describes the KAM strategy team making judgements about their organization based on their own views – this may be somewhat jaundiced. After all, it is difficult to be honest about your own weaknesses, especially when it is your own job!

A market study provides vital information regarding the accuracy of a standard and how an organization is really performing. Ultimately, it is what the customer thinks and how they see you as a key supplier that matters. What you think is all very well, but it needs to be stress tested. Again, good facilitation and a market survey/series of interviews with your customers will lead to a more honest assessment.

The voice of the practitioner

'We were looking at standard 4.2: customer-specific offers. To get the higher scores, we were being asked about levels of innovation and constantly delivering unique sources of value to our customers. We scored ourselves as 4–5 here (we are a very innovative firm – our products renew every 12–18 months and our brand is strong).

'However, after the facilitator conducted some interviews with three of our key customers, it seems that the customers look at us as having the same performance as our competitors. In fact one customer thinks we are way behind and not innovative at all – he thinks we are a laggard! This is painful but essential information. The lesson is that we have to innovate with each customer; we can no longer rely on products and brands alone. 4–5? More like a 2!' (KAM capability lead, global technology company.)

Final thoughts and advice for adopting the KAM Framework

1 Treat KAM as an organizational capability initiative. You need to consider multiple aspects of how your systems, structures and processes fit together. Your KAMgrs are at the heart of your KAM business, however – they should be selected, developed, coached and recognized accordingly.

2 KAM is a different way of working and a different business model. Treat its implementation as a change initiative and give it time (the best organizations that practise KAM have all been through a learning curve, often taking several years).

3 Use a model (like the KAM Framework that we provide here) to define and assess your KAM capability. Remember: *You don't need to be great at everything straight away… so don't try to boil the ocean!*

4 Build your organization around a customer segmentation model (higher-opportunity/more complex key customers need more effort and investment than

smaller/lower-opportunity customers). Always get the view of the customer. Build your KAM programme based on reality, not what you think is right. Successful KAM programmes respond to the needs of the market (and build value propositions based on these needs).

A final tip: stick at it and have fun! Ultimately, KAM is about growing business and making money with carefully selected customers. What's not to like about that?

References

[1] Kotter, J (1995) Leading change: why transformation efforts fail, *Harvard Business Review*, September.
[2] Davies, M (2017) *Infinite Value: Accelerating profitable growth through value-based selling*, Bloomsbury, London.
[3] Davies, M and Ryals L (2014) The KAM Framework, a Cranfield KAM Best Practice Club Article.

EPILOGUE
Final word on implementing KAM from a global practitioner at Unilever Food Solutions

Interview with Daniel Rodriguez Martin, Chains Account Manager, Unilever Food Solutions

Unilever is a well-known consumer goods manufacturer. As they claim, on any given day, two billion people use Unilever products to look good, feel good and get more out of life. With more than 400 brands focused on health and wellbeing, Unilever touches many people's lives in many different ways. Unilever's portfolio ranges from nutritionally balanced foods to indulgent ice creams, affordable soaps, luxurious shampoos and everyday household care products. World-leading Unilever brands include Lipton, Knorr, Dove, Axe, Hellmann's and Omo, alongside trusted local names. Sustainability is integral to how Unilever does business.

We talk to Daniel Rodriguez Martin, an account manager for global customers at Unilever Food Solutions in Spain.

Q. Daniel, please tell us what your role is all about.

My overall responsibility is to ensure the integrated management of global customers with operations in the country, such as Sodexo, Aramark, McDonald's, Burger King and KFC amongst others.

My role entails creating joint annual business plans and overseeing the account P&L and the delivery of added value by coordinating the contribution of a multi-functional team. This team includes channel marketing, supply chain, technical and culinary services, finance and customer care. I also seek to help the customer business with process and product innovation and with finding new, more effective ways of working.

Q. Daniel, you have managed large complex customers for a number of years; what have you learned about key account management implementation?

Well, I have learned that even before engaging in strategic and long-term planning, you have to satisfy the customer's day-to-day requirements. Consistency of service delivery is paramount, I would say; not sufficient but indeed necessary, in the management of global accounts.

I have also learned that your job is seldom specified and detailed in any document. Customers expect that you will engage in co-creation by identifying process and product improvements, but nowhere can you find a detailed description of these tasks. Innovation and proactivity are required to continue being relevant to customers.

A key lesson learned is that you must aspire to know the customer even better than they know themself. That knowledge and understanding gives you legitimacy and significantly increases the customer's trust in you and in your organization. A thorough understanding of the customer allows you to engage in deeper conversations about its business and, as a result, to anticipate risks and identify opportunities that otherwise might not have been discovered.

Lastly, I would say, that connecting with the customer beyond the product or the core offering is part of key account management. For instance, one of my global customers, Sodexo, launched The Better Tomorrow Plan, a global initiative to promote sustainability, specifically health and wellness solutions, varied and balanced food options and food choices with reduced sugar, salt and fats. This initiative is totally aligned with Unilever's Sustainable Living Plan. Thus, we share a language and an ambition that go beyond day-to-day transactions and that inspire us to build a unique partnership between Sodexo and Unilever Food Solutions.

Q. Tell me about the internal dimension of managing global customers, your experience of working effectively within a large corporation like Unilever.

That is a crucial element of my work, yes. I would say, first, in my role, I need the full support of the senior management team. They need to endorse and back up my plans and initiatives, particularly when customers make requests that are beyond our normal practices.

For instance, I recently had to organize the process to bring into the country a product that was not in our national portfolio. The customer demanded this product which was available in Europe but that was not offered as part of our catalogue. That required a concerted effort across the supply chain, customer service, finance and information systems departments. You need senior management support to mobilize these resources and people.

The second is about 'influence without authority'. Let me explain what I mean: to deliver new ideas and propositions to my customers, I need to influence people I do not have authority over. I need to coordinate delivery from a team I do not have hierarchical control over. They are not 'my' team but in front of the customer operate like 'my' team. So, the ability to influence and persuade them is important in my role.

Reflecting on the internal dimension, I would add how crucial positive internal relationships are. I enjoy a healthy atmosphere and cordial relationships within the company. This allows, first, the sharing of knowledge and best practices about the client, that results in enhanced customer service. Second, a united team enables you to spend time focusing on your customers, not in sorting out internal disputes or misalignment. For me, the test of collaborative relationships is when you can ask someone for help and support without having to give anything in return.

I also believe mutual support within the organization somehow enables you to turn pressure from the market and customers into enjoyment and fun. When you know you can count on your colleagues' support, you feel more encouraged to face challenging episodes that often occur in global account management positions.

Q. Building on the topic of value creation, what are the practices you deploy to add value beyond the product?

I think the technical assistance and the culinary expertise Unilever Food Solutions offers is a good example. For instance, we have a product called Phase, designed for baking and roasting applications in the professional kitchen. It is a technical product that enhances the finished results and also significantly optimizes the cooking process, delivering significant energy savings. Now, the product is sometimes seen as a premium product, and some purchasing departments are reluctant to stock it.

We ran a series of tests and carefully documented how this product helps improve the final results in roasted meals and quantified its savings and other advantages. Some of our customers, those who adopt a total cost of operation approach, got it, and ordered the product without hesitation. So I think we add value beyond the product by demonstrating outstanding results in application.

Q. Just to finish, what is your view of the future of key account management?

I think key account management is and will continue to be a people business. Irrespective of the sector and the product you sell, connecting, understanding and challenging your customer, and allowing yourself to be challenged will remain at the core of key account management.

Thank you so much Daniel.

INDEX

Note: Page numbers in *italics* indicate Figures and Tables. Numbers and acronyms in headings are filed as spelt out.